The Neolithic – Bronze Age Transition in Britain

A critical review of some archaeological and craniological concepts

Neil Brodie

BAR British Series 238

1994

Published in 2019 by
BAR Publishing, Oxford

BAR British Series 238

The Neolithic-Bronze Age Transition in Britain

© Neil Brodie and the Publisher 1994

ISBN 9780860547716 paperback
ISBN 9781407318646 e-book

DOI https://doi.org/10.30861/9780860547716

A catalogue record for this book is available from the British Library

This book is available at www.barpublishing.com

BAR Publishing is the trading name of British Archaeological Reports (Oxford) Ltd.
British Archaeological Reports was first incorporated in 1974 to publish the BAR
Series, International and British. In 1992 Hadrian Books Ltd became part of the BAR
group. This volume was originally published by Tempvs Reparatvm in conjunction
with British Archaeological Reports (Oxford) Ltd / Hadrian Books Ltd, the Series
principal publisher, in 1994. This present volume is published by BAR Publishing,
2019.

BAR
PUBLISHING

BAR titles are available from:

BAR Publishing
122 Banbury Rd, Oxford, OX2 7BP, UK
EMAIL   info@barpublishing.com
PHONE   +44 (0)1865 310431
FAX   +44 (0)1865 316916
www.barpublishing.com

CONTENTS

PREFACE

The data and arguments used in this study formed the basis of a PhD dissertation which I presented to Liverpool University in 1992. They are deliberately controversial in that they try to focus attention upon what I take to be the theoretical imprecision of many recent archaeological interpretations. I chose the case of the Beaker Culture to develop my argument but other case studies would have been equally suitable.

It is my contention that the theoretical storm which has raged for the last twenty-five years has done so around a blind eye as many interpretations have come to be accepted as "fact" without adequate critical exposure of their derivation. Often it seems that they were originally intended to be illustrative of the possibilities of a particular theoretical approach, and nothing more; but they gain unquestioning acceptance from the theoretically sympathetic and are then used to provide "solid" foundations for ever more ambitious interpretative schemata. I feel that this process is malignant and can only damage our discipline in the eyes of others and, perhaps more importantly, ourselves.

I do not intend this study to be a call for an abandonment of theory, nor even for an elaboration of further theory. I merely hope that any future archaeological interpretations will gain general acceptance on account of their content, and not their form.

This study would not have been completed without the kind help and co-operation of the following:

Dr D. Crowther, B. Sitch, Dr A. Foxon and the staff of the Hull and East Riding Museum; Dr. P. Beswick, C. Hart and the staff of the Sheffield City Museum; Dr T. Molleson, Dr. R. Kruszynski and the staff of the Natural History Museum; Dr. R. Foley and C. Duhig of the Department of Biological Anthropology, Cambridge; Dr. P. Robinson and the staff of Devizes Museum; C. Coneybeare and the staff of the Salisbury Museum.

The advice of the following individuals was also indispensable:

Dr L. Barfield, D. Brothwell, J. Dawes, Dr J. A. Gowlett, T. Manby, Dr J. J. Taylor and Dr I. K. Whitbread.

For their constant support and encouragement I would also like to thank Tony Barnes, Iris Hazlehurst, Jennifer Mirdamadi, Stella Morrey, Dorothy and John Steel and Louise Steel.

The work presented in this study was originally supported by a Major State Award from the British Academy. It is dedicated to my parents: James and Winifred Brodie.

Chapter One

INTRODUCTION.
THE BEAKER CULTURE: CHANGING INTERPRETATIONS

Introduction

This volume presents a study of the Neolithic-Bronze Age transition in Britain. It attempts a solution to the "Beaker Problem" in that it sets out to ascertain the method by which the Beaker culture was introduced into Britain, whether it was by migration or diffusion. Originally, it was envisaged that two, separate, studies of two, independent, bodies of data - archaeological and craniological - might converge upon a common conclusion. In the event, this did not occur. Different stories emerged, with largely unrelated themes. As a result the presentation falls logically into two parts. Each part can be approached as an independent piece of work, each includes its own introduction and conclusion. An overall conclusion is also presented, however, which attempts to draw together some common threads. It also enlarges the scope of the discussion, briefly and dramatically, by considering the different contexts within which explanations of the Beaker culture proceed: archaeological, philosophical and sociological. In so doing it tries to create a better defined environment for any further studies of the Beaker culture that might take place in the future.

Part One (Chapters 1-5) reviews the different theoretical depictions of an archaeological culture which appear in the literature, and considers their impact upon interpretations of the Beaker culture. The case for Beaker culture diffusion - the method of cultural expansion currently favoured by most British prehistorians - is critically examined, and possible arguments for preferring an alternative, migrationist, explanation are developed.

In Part Two (Chapters 6-9), an original study of English Neolithic and Bronze Age crania is presented. It considers possible aetiologies of morphological change, and suggests how they might have effected, or contributed to, the transition from the dolichocephalic form of the Neolithic skull to the brachycephalic form of the Bronze Age one. For the first time, an accurate account of the provenance of each cranium is provided, thereby avoiding the archaeological imprecision of previous studies.

This study is problem oriented and it is aimed at an archaeological audience. Extraneous scientific discussion has been kept to a minimum and sometimes, to maintain narrative flow, relegated to appendices. The resultant, hoped for, clarity of presentation has not been achieved at the expense of scientific accuracy, however, the issues involved are clear.

The Beaker Culture in Europe: Origins

The existence of a pan-European archaeological culture was recognised by scholars in several countries at about the turn of the century (Mercer 1977, Harrison 1980). Ultimately christened the "Beaker Culture", it was characterised by a number of artefact-types including small copper daggers, barbed and tanged flint arrowheads, stone wristguards, v-bored conical buttons and, of course, the eponymous Bell Beaker pottery. These artefact-types were given cohesion as an assemblage by their frequent association with each other in funerary contexts, and the assemblage was held to represent the material signature of a distinct race, or folk: the "Beaker Folk". For a large part of this century there was much scholarly debate over the identity, and likely origins, of this putative "folk". The extensive European distribution of Beaker assemblages suggested them to be the archaeological residue of a nomadic people, metal prospectors perhaps, mounted warriors or wandering tinkers; the emphasis of description resting always upon mobility, a mobility which would explain the, apparently rapid, spread of the Beaker culture, and which would also explain the widespread discoveries of Beaker graves but seeming scarcity of settlements. In the absence of an absolute chronology however attempts to pinpoint the origin of the Beaker culture, and thus the homeland of the "Beaker Folk", were severely hampered. As a result complicated schemes evolved which called for a continent wide series of crosscutting migratory movements which would include all possible originating foci.

The first synthesis was attempted by the Spanish archaeologist Castle in 1927 who suggested an Iberian origin for the Beaker Folk. This made some sense of the ceramic sequence. Thus, the most widely distributed Beaker type - the comb impressed and zone decorated Maritime Beaker - was thought to stand at the head of several, diverging, regional sequences of ceramic development. It was thought to represent the earliest Beaker ceramic type, probably evolving from out of the general milieu of impressed wares present in Neolithic Iberia. While an Iberian origin for the Beaker Folk made some sense of the ceramic sequence, it made much less sense of other features of the culture. It was difficult to reconcile an Iberian origin with what seemed to be the central European antecedents of other components of the culture: the metalwork types, the wristguards and the buttons. It was also difficult to see why such large numbers of "Beaker Folk" should have decamped northwards from the Iberian peninsula to find new homes in Britain and the Low Countries, the areas of maximum Beaker density (Harrison 1980: 12). The general feeling, perhaps, was summarised by Childe who wrote in 1950:

"I find this view quite incredible but having nothing better to offer I shall accept it."
(Childe 1969: 76)

Something better was offered in 1963 by the German archaeologist Sangmeister who attempted to resolve the apparent dichotomy of origins by suggesting a migratory scheme of flow and counterflow, of "flux" and "reflux". According to this scheme an initial "flux" of "Beaker Folk" had emigrated from Iberia to central Europe, carrying with them their distinctive zoned pottery and possibly travelling via the Atlantic seaboards and the rivers Rhine and Rhone. Once in central Europe they adopted the practice of single grave burial from their Corded Ware neighbours, as well as their metal technology. Central Europe was also the location for the creation of a hybrid form of pottery which combined the shape of the Bell Beaker with the local practice of cord decoration, the resultant style being known as All-Over-Corded, or AOC. Equipped with the, now classic, Bell Beaker assemblage there was a second movement, or reflux, of "Beaker Folk" back through western Europe and on to Iberia. The colonisation of the British Isles took place with their passing.

While the "flux/reflux" theory of Sangmeister provided a more satisfactory explanation of the data then available than did the "Iberian origins" theory of Castillo, it was in itself not without problems, as enumerated by Clarke (1970: 45ff). The Beaker culture of the reflux did not, in itself, present as a coherent entity. It seemed, instead, to be an artificial construct of at least three separate archaeological entities and failed to explain the full range of spatial and temporal variation in a satisfactory manner. There was also no evidence to be derived from either stratigraphy or C14 dates which might confirm that the Maritime Beakers of the "flux" predated the AOC Beakers of the "reflux". Indeed, what evidence there was seemed instead to suggest the contrary.

Clarke's mention of C14 dating was significant. The difficulties encountered by early attempts to assign an origin to the Beaker culture were, in no small part, due to the absence of any independent mechanism of absolute dating. This archaeological lacuna has since been filled, in part at least, by the development of C14 dating. Dutch scholars were the first to take advantage of this dating technique when they demonstrated that the early stages of Beaker ceramic development had taken place in the lower Rhine basin (Lanting & van der Waals 1976). AOC Beakers were shown, by C14 dating, to be consistently earlier in date than either Maritime Beakers or their Veluwe derivatives. Furthermore, AOC Beakers shared some associations with the pottery of the local Corded Ware variant, the Standvoetbeker culture. Upon occasion AOC Beakers had been found within the same grave as a Corded Ware pot. Lanting and van der Waals stressed, however, that although a sequence of ceramic succession was apparent, it was not until during the currency of the more developed Veluwe Beakers that other artefacts typical of the Beaker culture appeared: the wristguards, v-bored buttons and objects of metal manufacture. It has since been suggested that it might prove possible to extend the Corded Ware-Beaker ceramic sequence to other areas of western Corded Ware presence, particularly around the middle Rhine and the Saale (Neustupný 1984).

The Beaker Culture in Europe: Variability

The current watchword of Beaker scholars appears to be variability, a variability that finds expression in both the spatial patterning of the Beaker culture and also in its development through time. There is also some realisation that the processes underlying this variability must be complex.

The spatial variability of the Beaker culture has been described by Clarke (1976: 472), who identified two levels of expression:

Type 1 regional presence: a high density of Beaker findspots, many domestic sites, considerable local Beaker continuity and time depth (300-500 C14 years).

Type 2 regional presence: a low density of Beaker findspots, few domestic sites, considerable local, non-Beaker, continuity and little Beaker time depth (100-300 C14 years).

Type A domestic presence: a high proportion of decorated Beakers in domestic assemblages, accompanied by recognisably Beaker domestic wares.

Type B domestic presence: a low proportion of decorated Beakers in domestic assemblages, accompanied by domestic wares of local, non-Beaker, tradition.

Clarke suggested that there were correlations between his Types 1 and A, and Types 2 and B. Although these correlations might be interpreted as being indicative of a Beaker "core" area with a more dispersed periphery, he emphasised that, in reality, the situation would have been more complicated, with an "interfingering" of the different types (Clarke 1976: 474). This variability of types within a region has been well illustrated by Barfield's excavations in northern Italy (1987). Case (1987) retained Clarke's notion of differential presence, albeit with a rather looser definition of core, which he considered to include all areas which betrayed any presence of the Beaker culture proper - that is Beakers found in association with copper knives, wristguards and buttons, regardless of whether the domestic ware was

Beaker in form or not. However, Case presented a more resolved description of the periphery, suggesting that it was possible to differentiate between:

Beaker presence: elements of the Beaker culture found in association with material which is fully characteristic of local, non-Beaker cultures.

Beaker influence: non-Beaker cultural assemblages showing evidence of Beaker culture influence.

Clarke's use of chronological depth as a criterion of spatial differentiation is symptomatic of the increased chronological resolution now available for Beaker studies. It is thought that the Beaker culture spread over a large area of central and western Europe around 2600 calBC and persisted in most areas until 2000 calBC, although it had largely disappeared from central Europe by 2300 calBC and lingered on in Britain until about 1800 calBC. The composition, or nature, of the Beaker culture also appeared to have changed through time (Harrison 1980: 10; Lewthwaite 1987: 36). Thus, in its initial, expansionary, phase it seems to have been largely a ceramic phenomenon, with the spread of AOC and Maritime Beakers. It was only in its later stages that the fully integrated and characteristic artefact "package" of the Beaker culture emerged as a material entity.

Many scholars have chosen to explain this variability of expression as reflecting the operation of multiple causes, thus moving beyond the deployment of simple, unitary, migrationist explanation. Thus it is envisaged that trade and the diffusionary movement of technologies, or ideologies, may have joined migration in providing vectors for cultural spread. Clarke specifically warned that:

"A universal, Pan-European, single factor explanation is unlikely to be a realistic hypothesis to account for the variability in local densities, settlement and domestic contexts, association and distribution patterns and varied time depths."

(Clarke 1976: 461).

The Beaker Culture in Britain: Migration or Diffusion?

Towards the end of the 19th century Darwin's new theory of biological evolution was used to provide scientific respectability for emerging theories which proposed the existence of genetically based differences between classes and between races. The alleged superior intellectual endowment of Europeans, particularly that of the middle and upper classes, was claimed to be the outcome of thousands of years of natural selection. In contrast, the "noble savage" was portrayed as having the mentality of a child and being in need of paternal protection - a justification for the tightening grip upon the world of European colonialism.

These theories of intellectual inequality necessitated the denial of humankind's universal capacity for innovation. It was argued instead that complex technologies or sophisticated forms of social organisation would only be invented or developed by the mentally more evolved races

and would then need to be passed on to "inferior" races by processes of migration or diffusion. For a while it was fashionable to suggest that all innovations had been carried from a central civilising hearth to the four corners of the earth by a migrating super-race, whether it be Aryan, Egyptian or Atlantean. Outside of Nazi Germany however these theories were discarded as the archaeological record became better known. It was proposed instead that cultural novelties would have been disseminated from an innovatory centre by a series of localised migrations and secondary diffusion processes.

During the first half of the 20th century, the classical or historical education of British archaeologists gave them no reason to doubt such a view - the early texts were replete with references to migration. It was a view which also accorded well with the narrative of the Old Testament. (Adams et al 1978: 497ff; Trigger 1989: 161). The poor state of knowledge of the archaeological record reinforced this theoretical disposition to interpret cultural discontinuities as being indicative of immigration. As a result of varying intensities of fieldwork, the evidence of archaeology was often spatially or chronologically intermittent and emphasised cultural discontinuity at the expense of continuity. Furthermore, in the absence of any absolute dating technique, an unrealistically short chronology was adopted whereby whole periods of cultural change were compressed into small intervals, too short for any possible process of internally generated change or evolution to have taken place. The models of migration used varied. Sometimes they envisaged the movement of entire peoples but often had more of a diffusionist nature whereby a small number of people would transmit a superior culture to more backward, but grateful, recipients. Megalithic missionaries and Mycenaean traders joined putative Beaker metal prospectors in such an endeavour. Early syntheses of British prehistory made much use of migration models, to the almost total exclusion of any other models in fact, but such an approach was essentially negative. It credited indigenous peoples with neither the wit nor the vision to better their lot and came to be considered as academically sterile, archaeology was written as history in the simplest possible sense.

In 1966, Clark called attention to the increasing sense of unease being felt by a "younger school" of archaeologists when asked to contemplate the invasion ridden interpretations of British prehistory. He emphasised instead that there were many aspects of continuity to be found expressed in insular traditions, and suggested that cultural developments could be adequately explained without recourse to hypothetical invaders or immigrants. The "Beaker Folk" were a notable exception to his general theme however, not surprising perhaps as, in their case, there seemed to be an overwhelming amount of evidence in favour of immigration. This evidence has recently been summarised by Burl as including:

"...to the Beaker itself, a form of pottery and decoration unknown previously in the British Isles, and fired by an unprecedently skilful technique, has to be added the novel barbed and tanged arrowheads, the bracers, copper knives and small articles of gold, the emergence of a round headed people, a preference for single burial in flat graves or under very low round barrows, the deposition of grave goods, the brewing of beer, a knowledge of metalworking, the domestication of the horse and the herding of a smaller breed of cattle, Bos longifrons, unlike the bigger indigenous Bos frontosus of the British Neolithic."

(Burl 1987: 110)

The foreign origins of many of these cultural and economic innovations are disputed, but it is not intended to become embroiled in such disputes here. Similarly, the existence of Beaker domestic sites would appear, on the face of it, to present irrefutable proof of an immigrant "Beaker Folk". These sites are small households or farmsteads from which not only was the distinctive Beaker fineware recovered but also a complementary range of Beaker-type domestic wares - including rusticated or plain Beaker shaped vessels with sometimes also larger, possibly storage, vessels similar to the Dutch potbekers. Again, however, the true significance of these sites is disputed.

Recent interpretations of Beaker immigration vary and are often based on historical analogy. Thus Case (1977) suggested that the "Beaker Folk" may have been comprised of small groups of mixed farmers who, once established, would have established relations (both peaceable and warlike) with the indigenes by engaging in feuding and seasonal raiding, and trade and marriage. The analogy of Viking society as described in the Icelandic sagas was invoked to add colour to his outline sketch. Taylor (1983) on the other hand thought that, in absolute terms, the number of immigrants would have been small, but with a disproportionately large cultural influence because of their economic domination of native societies and their continuing links with the continent, much as would be the case with the later spread of the La Tène Celts. Ashbee (1978: 137) looked to the arrival of the Saxons in late Roman Britain for his analogy and suggested that, on account of their martial qualities, the "Beaker Folk" may have been invited into Britain to act as mercenaries for the insular late Neolithic societies.

The structuring of the immigration process is also a subject that has attracted some attention. It is thought likely that any large scale movement of people would have been preceded by a period of intensified contact between the indigenous communities of late Neolithic Britain and their Beaker counterparts across the North Sea. This "contact phase" would have seen the establishment of exchange links, or alliances, across the sea and an increase in the frequency of seasonal visits (Clarke 1976: 474, Case 1977: 74). Lewthwaite has suggested that this might have been a period of "familiarisation" (1987: 48) during which time the incipient "Beaker Folk" would have availed themselves of the technologies and skills of maritime travel and transport. It would also have been a period of exploration as the opportunities for settlement were discovered and their possible benefits evaluated.

Although some scholars still choose to view the introduction of Beakers into Britain as an event, or series of events, with a human, migratory, vector it is probably true to say that this is no longer the mainstream, or orthodox, view. More recent treatments of the Neolithic-Bronze Age transition in Britain have emphasised the role played by

indigenous development and have chosen instead to characterise the Beaker introduction as a process of diffusion (Burgess 1980, Gibson 1982, Bradley 1984, Clarke et al 1985, Thomas 1991). These works take their lead from the keynote papers of Burgess & Shennan (1976) and Whittle (1981). In these two, closely argued, papers it was proposed that the Beaker culture did not constitute a culture in the original, Childean, sense - it was instead an artefact assemblage without any uniform or consistent associations of housetype, subsistence economy or burial ritual. To further weaken the characterisation of the Beaker culture as a representation of an immigrant folk the supposed continental origins of what had traditionally been considered to be the non-artefact components of the culture were closely scrutinised. Thus the novelty of the Beaker single grave tradition was questioned and the straightforward interpretation of the settlement evidence was also challenged.

Burgess (Burgess & Shennan 1976: 311) pointed out that in Britain single grave inhumation under a round barrow is not necessarily a Beaker introduction. In southern England for instance there were, apparently, Neolithic round barrows at Linch Hill and Handley Down 26 while a larger series of such barrows were known from eastern Yorkshire. Burgess expanded upon this by pointing out that large numbers of round barrows are known which cover unaccompanied burials, they are generally assigned a Bronze Age date solely by virtue of their round mound. It is perhaps possible that a substantial number of such monuments may in fact have been constructed during the Neolithic and thus pre-date the arrival of Beaker pottery.

It remains an unfortunate fact that few Beaker domestic sites have been excavated and it is often the case on those sites that have that the affinities of the coarse ware component of the ceramic assemblage are indistinct. It is often classified as Beaker because of the presence at the site of better characterised and hence archaeologically visible Beaker fineware. Burgess (Burgess & Shennan 1976: 320) argued that in some cases the associated domestic wares were recognisably Beaker but that often they were not. In these latter cases the vessels are of either uncertain form or of a type which is not Beaker, they are more likely to be representative of indigenous traditions. Whittle (1981: 314) developed this theme and pointed to an apparent temporal ordering in the composition of the ceramic assemblages recovered from Beaker settlements. There are very few "pure" Beaker settlement sites known from before 2150 calBC, early Beaker fineware forms are generally found in association with indigenous late Neolithic types - Grooved or Peterborough ware. The majority of settlement sites with domestic pottery that is recognisably Beaker in form are associated with late styles of Beaker fineware and probably date to after 2150 calBC. Whittle concluded (1981: 320) that prior to 2150 calBC Beaker fineware was possibly ritual or mortuary in nature and is found on sites of otherwise indigenous tradition. After 2150 calBC, however, domestic pottery increasingly took on the form and style of the previously ritual Beaker fineware while new types were introduced to replace Beakers as ritual ware: Food Vessels and Collared Urns. Thus Beaker settlements are not viewed as being the dwelling places of a distinct "Beaker Folk", instead they form a coherent sequence which demonstrates, in a settlement context, the gradual adoption of Beaker pottery by an otherwise autocthonous population.

When attacking the concept of a migrating "Beaker Folk", therefore, Whittle, Burgess and Shennan have made two basic points:

1) That the Beaker culture is not a culture as originally defined by Childe. It could not, therefore, be indicative of a distinct people, or folk.

2) That many of the non-material cultural novelties of the British early Bronze Age cultures did in fact have insular antecedents. They need not have been introduced by an immigration from the continent.

To replace a migrationist interpretation of the Beaker culture it was argued instead that Beakers and their associated artefacts constituted a diffusionary artefact package. A diffusionary vector would have been provided by elite-group interaction, Beaker assemblages would have been adopted by indigenous communities and accommodated within pre-existing social formations, acting either as markers or as instruments of social change.

Conclusion

For the greater part of this century the pan-European Beaker culture was considered to be the archaeological signifier of a migrating people. However, in Britain, this hypothesis has come under sustained attack in recent years. A new orthodoxy has emerged which depicts a diffusion of the Beaker culture taking place as either a cause or an effect of late Neolithic social restructuring. Although Clarke (1976: 460) took pains to emphasise, in a Beaker context, that theory formulation should be accompanied by stringent testing, to date a stringent testing of the diffusion hypothesis has not materialised. The first part of this study sets out to rectify this omission.

In Chapter Two it is described how the change in fortunes of the Beaker culture is best regarded as being one symptom of a more general theoretical shift that has taken place amongst prehistorians. It is also argued that the denial of any equivalence between a Beaker culture and a "Beaker Folk" is not altogether warranted.

The various diffusionist models which have been proposed to account for the Beaker penetration of British late Neolithic society are described in Chapter Three, and criticised as being inadequate for the task.

The claim that Neolithic and Bronze age burial customs show an essential continuity is rejected in Chapter Four after an analysis of the late Neolithic and early Bronze Age tombs of eastern Yorkshire. It is further argued that proposed schemes of ceramic and settlement continuity are logically inconsistent.

Finally, in Chapter Five, the possibilities of a "Beaker Folk" for explaining the archaeological changes seen to occur in Britain at the time of transition from the Neolithic to the Bronze Age are reconsidered.

Chapter Two

CULTURE AND ETHNICITY

Introduction

For a large part of the 20th century the dominant mode of archaeological interpretation has been culture-historical. Prehistorians, as their name suggests, have laboured to construct quasi-history from out of the material remains of a pre-literate antiquity. To aid them in this task the static concept of a unitary, archaeological, culture was adopted as a means of spatial categorisation, of entity formation. For the explanation of temporal change in the constitution of these entities, these archaeological cultures, recourse was made to the dynamic processes of migration and diffusion. Prehistory was:

"...... aimed at distilling from archaeological remains a preliterate substitute for the conventional politico-military history with cultures, instead of statesmen, as actors, and migrations in place of battles."
(Childe 1958: 70).

The "Beaker Folk" held a pre-eminent place in many of these prehistories, but as the theoretical underpinnings of the culture-history approach were critically scrutinised, and found to be wanting, so too was the reality of a "Beaker Folk" questioned, and doubted. These doubts, outlined in the previous chapter, are thus best regarded as a specific symptom of a more general malaise - the diminishing credibility of the archaeological culture as a classificatory heuristic and the consequent abandonment of the culture-historical mode of archaeological interpretation. The background to these changing patterns of explanation, and issues arising, are explored further during the course of this chapter.

The Archaeological Culture

The culture-historical mode of archaeological interpretation has been well described, and discussed, by several authors. The following synthesis is taken, in part, from Trigger (1989) and Daniel & Renfrew (1988).

The concept of an archaeological culture owed its initial inspiration to the nationalist movements which had emerged in the wake of the Napoleonic occupation of Europe. As it became politically desirable for them to lay claim to a tract of land, romantically inclined intellectuals seized upon the evidence of archaeology to legitimise their claims by posturing as the descendants of prehistoric inhabitants, and as their rightful heirs. This practice was particularly pronounced in central Europe where the authority of Tacitus' *Germania* was on hand to assist with the mapping out of Iron Age tribes. The German archaeologist Kossinna systematised the concept of a discrete archaeological culture, delineated in time and space. He argued that geographically coherent assemblages of archaeological artefacts, termed cultures, were in fact the remnant traces of ancient tribes and were therefore available for the construction of a surrogate history. Kossinna believed that if cultural and ethnic groups were equivalent entities then it would be possible to trace the movements of historically attested groups back through time into prehistory. He termed his approach to the archaeological record Siedlungsarchäologie (settlement archaeology).

Childe, and the New Archaeology

During the early 20th century implicit use was made of the culture concept by several British archaeologists when organising their data, but it is Childe who is generally credited with both the popularisation of the method and its detailed exposition. As his thinking matured Childe gradually weakened his definition of an archaeological culture and became less sure of its interpretation. It is possible to discriminate in his work between an early, confident, use of the concept during the 1920s and 1930s, and a later, more cautious, appraisal during the 1950s.

Childe's earliest definition of culture is well known and often quoted:

"We find certain types of remains - pots, implements, ornaments, burial rites, house forms - constantly recurring together. Such a complex of regularly associated traits we shall term a 'cultural group' or just a 'culture'."
(Childe 1929: vi).

He went on to explain how to differentiate between episodes of migration or diffusion that might present in the archaeological record. A transfer of a culture, in its entirety, from one location to another would be a firm indication of a

6

migration but the transfer of only one or two cultural traits would be more difficult to interpret. Whilst not excluding migration it might also result from trade or imitation (ibid: vi-vii). Cultures were considered to be self evident in the archaeological record, to be observed facts (Childe 1935: 3), and thought to be the material remnants of a people. Childe was careful to explain that he used the term "people" to describe a social grouping united by common language and customs, that there was no necessary correspondence between an archaeological culture and a racial group, which was a biological, not a social, entity (Childe 1933). Although human societies could be viewed as functioning organisms (Childe 1935: 3), with culture an integrated epiphenomenon, culture in itself was not homogeneous. At least two different, albeit interacting, cultural spheres could be discerned. Whilst tools and other utilitarian artefacts might be described as material culture, and possess adaptive significance, other archaeological remains, such as burials, would be indicative of spiritual culture. For the materialist spiritual culture appeared to possess no function, although Childe admitted that it might play a role in the maintenance of group solidarity (ibid: 14).

This early description of an archaeological culture, and explanation of its significance, seems to have been influenced by the developing anthropological school of structural-functionalism, which portrayed pre-industrial societies as isolated organic entities, relatively autonomous in both structure and function. This portrayal was in good accord with the spatially discrete nature of an archaeological culture (Trigger 1989: 245, Childe 1933: 3). This prototypic theory of an archaeological culture has been called by Clarke the "cultural brick theory" which:

"....necessarily assumes that cultural assemblages are monothetic sets of types, that all the components occur at all the sites, and that they all share identical distribution boundaries."

(Clarke 1968: 247).

It must certainly have been the theory in the minds of scholars who were:

"....worried that Beakers in no sense satisfy the criteria that denote a culture in Childe's *original* sense."
(Burgess, in Burgess & Shennan 1976: 309).

Similarly, the definition of migration in mind seems to have been that of Childe in his early days:

"The break which the Bell Beakers represent in the various local sequences has been much over- emphasised, and close examination of particular contexts shows that we are not dealing with the *wholesale transference* of a material assemblage from one area to another, the view implicit in the literature which has favoured migration hypotheses."
(Shennan, in Burgess & Shennan 1976: 324).

The italics in both of these quotes have been added for emphasis.

Familiarity with the culture concept ultimately bred contempt. As early as 1941, in Germany, Wahle had demonstrated, using archaeological assemblages of early historical date, that there was no direct relationship between an ethnic group and a culture, or that a change in one necessarily indicated a change in the other. This theme was developed by Childe who found it increasingly difficult to maintain a precise and useable definition of culture, or even to assign meaning to the definition. He ceased to regard cultures as facts, as concrete entities with an existence independent of the observer. Instead he suggested that the delineation of a culture was a subjective exercise, which required the archaeologist to decide what was, or was not, a socially distinctive cultural type (Childe 1963: 50). He abandoned the position that a culture was, to use Clarke's terminology, a monothetic set of types, suggesting instead that it was necessary for only two or three diagnostic types to be found in association, but that they need not recur together on every site assigned to a culture (Childe 1956: 33). Childe had come, in fact, to view an archaeological culture as a polythetic set of artefact types (after Clarke 1968: 231).

The problems associated with an archaeological identification of a migration also came to be better appreciated. Environmentally adapted cultural types might change in character as a people moved from one environment to another (Childe 1956: 136) and the retention or expression of types might depend upon the relative levels of technological prowess enjoyed by the immigrant and host communities.

Most damage was inflicted upon the culture/people axiom however by Childe's retreat from any substantive definition of the term people. In his early years, a people had been defined as a social grouping united by custom and language, but this definition was dropped:

"So for the archaeologist the unit or society must remain the group enjoying the same culture - ie, giving concrete expression to common traditions. Such a group may comprise a number of settlements or local communities. Perhaps we might call its members a people, but we have no right to assume that this people as a whole spoke a single language or acted as a political unit, still less that all its members were related physiologically or belonged to one zoological race."
(Childe 1963: 49).

"Cultures are assemblages of types that are associated because they are made by the same people."
(Childe 1956: 111).

"To a prehistorian a people are just what they did."
(Ibid: 111).

These definitions reduced the culture/people equivalence to a meaningless circularity. Beakers would satisfy the criteria that denoted a culture in Childe's ultimate sense, but little understanding would be derived from the satisfaction.

From amidst the wreckage of his culture concept Childe seemed to advocate its abandonment. He emphasised instead the unique time depth of the archaeological record and drew attention to the correspondingly large amount of information encapsulated therein which related to past patterns of behaviour. He suggested that the temporal span of this record, and its material constitution, could most usefully be used to reconstruct the course of technological evolution as an indicator of the progressive growth of human knowledge (1956: 160-162).

Childe was advocating an evolutionist, or processual, archaeology. It is not surprising to find then that with the advent of the New Archaeology the dismantling of the archaeological concept of a culture continued further. Renfrew (1977) argued that cultures, even as subjective constructs, were in fact illusions. That, in spatial terms, the archaeological record was better considered to be a continuum, with any discontinuities arising out of topographical, but not social, barriers to human interaction (1977: 94). He followed Childe in proposing that the realistic goal of prehistory was the reconstruction of long term process and suggested that diachronic change in settlement patterning might be indicative of developing strategies of resource allocation, of social evolution.

The possibility of an archaeological theory of social evolution was a central concern of the New Archaeology that grew up during the 1960s. Major changes which had occurred in the structure of human societies were known only from archaeological testimony - they had preceded the keeping of historical records and they were therefore amenable to archaeological, but not historical, investigation. By concentrating their research effort onto these processes of long term change the "New" or "processual" archaeologists hoped to secure for the study of prehistory a respectable and an independent status within academe. Major projects were identified - the origins of agriculture and the rise of the state - but their identification had an unfortunate consequence for British, and other north European, prehistorians. As neither process of change had been of primary occurrence in Britain there was little that a study of British prehistory could contribute to their understanding (Renfrew 1982: 2). Processual archaeologists in Britain had come perilously close to arguing themselves out of a job. They managed to rescue themselves from this ignomious fate by suggesting that the emergence of ranked societies in prehistoric Europe was a social process suitable for, and in need of, clarification.

When describing this process of emergence it was pointed out that in the early Neolithic there was little to suggest anything other than an egalitarian society, but that by the end of the Neolithic it seemed that social hierarchies had begun to develop, and had continued to do so through into the Iron Age (Shennan 1982: 10). This concept of a progressive hierarchisation of prehistoric society has not yet received the degree of critical analysis accorded to the culture/people concept and it is not yet clear just how real it is. It might be argued, for instance, that processes of technological elaboration and population increase contributed to an increasing archaeological visibility of ranked societies through time, that they had been in existence since the early Neolithic and that, in fact, there was no emergence to explain. Nevertheless, it was within this theoretical context of evolving social hierarchies that interpretations of the Beaker culture

began to change. Instead of being indicative of a people, or folk, the culture was now considered to be either an instrument or a marker of social change.

Specific hypotheses which seek to explain the role of the Beaker culture in social evolution will be considered in the next chapter, it is intended here to further explore the, not yet abandoned, relationship between an archaeological culture and a social, or ethnic, group.

Primordial and Circumstantial Ethnicity

Within anthropology impatience with functionalist concepts of closed, homeostatic, societies has encouraged the emergence of alternative schemata in which the interactions between societies are seen to be of more importance than the internal functioning of individual societies (Barth 1969, Wolf 1980). This has, in turn, helped to focus attention upon social processes of group formation and demarcation so that a more fuller understanding of ethnogenesis has followed. It comes as no surprise to find that ethnicity is a complex phenomenon and that its expression is variable, two different aspects have been explored and are termed primordial and circumstantial (Scott 1990: 148; Rex 1986: 80). The term primordial ethnicity describes a group's sense of self-identity and its persistence through time. In contrast, circumstantial ethnicity describes the active manipulation of ethnic difference by a group in an attempt to achieve or to maintain unequal access to productive resources. Ethnic groups should not be considered as possessing a coherent political organization, they are conceptual rather than political entities (Cornell 1988).

Members of an ethnic group conform to, and judge others by, a degree of adherence to a socially agreed set of behavioural conventions, which renders the members mutually intelligible and engenders a sense of familiarity, or togetherness. This is primordial ethnicity and it is reinforced by the sharing of a cultural idiom which might include a common history or mythology of ethnogenesis, the possession of a common name by means of which group members can categorise themselves, and a common language (Smith 1986: 22; Barth 1969). This shared cultural idiom might also find expression through the media of artefacts, clothing and architecture although there may be variation within the overall material cultural repertoire of an ethnic group, if its members occupy more than one ecological zone for instance.

Where ethnic groups co-exist their autonomies are the product of a discriminatory boundary. This boundary need not be sharp or two-dimensional, after the fashion of a modern frontier, but might be fuzzy and cultural, with a material aspect, although not all items of material culture are equally suffused with ethnic significance. The crucial function of the cultural traits chosen to act as ethnic signalling devices is to maintain a boundary around a group so that, internally, the culture of a group does not need to be homogeneous, it just needs to be recognisably different from that of adjacent groups (Rex 1986: 85; Barth 1969: 15). Ethnic boundaries then are cultural but are not always biological. Individuals or groups are often able to change their ethnic allegiance by adopting the material symbols and the behavioural norms of a target membership group. Although this might result in some residual tension or ambiguity for converts this dissipates for their descendants who can expect to become fully integrated within the host society (Barth 1969). The constitution of an ethnic boundary is malleable however and it is its opportunistic manipulation which underpins the concept of circumstantial ethnicity.

It has been proposed that ethnic groups function as an expression of communal support. By outward identification with a particular group, and hence implied acceptance of its behavioural norms, a member is entitled to receive the help of fellow members of the group in preference to outsiders. Thus ethnic membership functions as a means of achieving a certain level of security. Ethnic distinctions become more marked, or exaggerated, during times of between group stress when the question might be asked: "Whose side are you on?". Individuals intermediate or ambiguous in their membership categorisation will find themselves abandoned by both sides (Barth 1969: 36; Hodder 1982: 26). The increased importance of the ethnic boundary in such circumstances causes its cultural definition to be rendered more precise, and more visible. Cultural differences are emphasised. This opportunistic emphasis of ethnic identity is termed circumstantial ethnicity. Conversely however, the distinctiveness of ethnic boundaries may lapse during periods of peaceful coexistence. It is a corollary of this latter fact that in areas of population stasis and in the absence of competition for resources circumstantial ethnic demarcation remains undeveloped and thus it is not necessarily a permanent feature of social interaction. Primordial ethnicity may, in effect, lie dormant, available for activation when circumstances demand.

Whether circumstantial emphasis of ethnicity is a universal phenomenon is not known. Recourse to ethnic demarcation is certainly not the only strategy available to social groups engaged in competition over access to limited resources. It suggests, however, that, although primordial ethnicity may be a product of human psychology, a response to the cognitive necessity of categorisation, the expression of this ethnicity should not be considered as deterministic but as situational; as such it removes the theoretical underpinnings of Siedlungarchäeologie as developed by Kossinna. It emphasises the social and opportunistic nature of expressed ethnic sentiment whilst denying what is biological or permanent - it is unlikely that an ethnic group will possess an unbroken and unsullied history. However, at certain times and places, in certain contexts, ethnicity will develop as an important mediator of social discourse. By extension, ethnicity should, from time to time, find expression within the archaeological record, although the character of this expression might not be straightforward.

Passive Networks and Active Boundaries

Despite problems of subjectivity, definition and interpretation the axiomatic relationship between an archaeological culture and a people, or ethnic group, was never fully relinquished by prehistorians as a potential principle of data organisation, and of explanation. The complexity of the relationship has become increasingly clear however (Clarke 1968: 231). Progress has been made in disentangling the skein of relations that exist between social formations and their deployed material culture by the realisation that artefacts may, in fact, act as material intersections for two interacting, and partly coalesced, modes of behavioural expression: actively and passively produced style (Sackett 1986,1990).

The term active style is used to define the deliberate and conscious manipulation of symbols to transmit information about status or identity. It is an intentional statement. Items of material culture may be manufactured, or utilised, as symbols or else used in a symbolic manner. For maximum effect the stylistic message needs to be understood by its target and may be context specific. Passive style is a learned, but unconscious, way of doing. It is a conventional pattern of behaviour acquired by observation and imitation of an individual's proximate social environment during childhood and adolescence. Passive style may be expressed through an artefactual medium as techniques of fabrication and decoration are learned by example. Although artefacts so produced are not deliberately imbued with any kind of information or signal they might be perceived to be so by an outside observer. These two modes of stylistic expression are bound up with alternative, but complementary, methods of conceptualizing human societies - as either passively produced communication networks (Clarke 1968), or else as actively maintained bounded entities (Hodder 1982).

If human settlements are considered as nodes in a two dimensional communication network it might be expected that, in a topographically neutral environment, the levels of social interaction between these nodes would equilibrate at a uniform steady-state. If, furthermore, methods of artefact production were learned passively within a social matrix then it would follow that artefact design would vary continuously, and thus surviving material culture would show a pattern of continuous, and not discontinuous, variation. Distinct areas of cultural similarity - cultures - would not exist. This seems to be the position of Renfrew (1977: 94), as already described. This steady-state model of human interaction is ahistorical, however. It assumes homeostasis and it takes no account of dynamic processes (demographic, social, ecological or whatever) that may be acting to keep the network in a state of disequilibrium, with disconformities giving rise to areas of greater or lesser interaction. In reality, of course, the areas of greater interaction would take the stage as discrete social groups.

This characterisation of a social group as a network of dense interaction forms the basis of Clarke's analysis of the culture/people conundrum (Clarke 1968: 252, 362-3). If techniques of artefact manufacture are born out of social tradition, and if their style is a passive production of this tradition, then the degree of artefact similarity would be expected to correlate positively with the degree of human interaction. It follows that the material culture assemblages of separate social networks should be marked by high within group similarity and low between group similarity. As these similarity groups, or cultures, are socially produced there should be a rough chorological concordance between the social group and the archaeological culture:

"The social network precipitates and maintains the culture area and the boundaries of the two should be broadly concurrent. A series of adjoining but largely discrete socio-cultural networks can therefore be compared with a series of adjacent saucers each holding a specific artefact type pool, linked only with difficulty across the watersheds between the network areas. This is the basis by means of which the long evaporated web of social patterning may be traced in the precipitated pattern of pooled artefact-types."

(Clarke 1968: 252)

As an interactive social group is, almost by definition, united by behavioural expression and language, it might be considered to be an ethnic group. There might not be a precise agreement between ethnicity, language and material culture but there must at least be an approximate one (Clarke 1968: 291,364).

This view of ethnic groups, and of cultures, as "saucers of interaction" has been criticised as its attendant characterisation of individuals, or communities - as passive nodes in an interaction network - denies them their very essence, it denies them their ability to actively participate in social life (Hodder 1982: 185). Human society provides an arena for the playing out of cross-cutting strategies of inter-group competition; the groups being defined by multiple criteria including age, gender, ethnicity, status and religion. As material artefacts will be selectively manipulated in these competitions and used symbolically to demarcate group boundaries the diffusion of their style will not be passive, it will be hedged in by a number of restrictions or taboos. This active, but restricted, use of material culture as an aid to boundary demarcation suggests that the distribution of some artefacts will indeed be limited both in time and in space, but it does not necessarily follow that the distributions will be indicative of ethnicity.

The active and passive modes of cultural production are neither contradictory nor are they mutually exclusive - they are complementary. Whilst the symbolic use of artefact design to signify ethnic identity may create a barrier to inter-societal interaction it may be used simultaneously within a society to provide a common medium for transmitting information about personal or group identity, a medium which would facilitate intra-societal interaction. Material culture will be active, therefore, in preventing the stabilisation of social interaction to a uniform steady-state as envisaged by Renfrew; it will be active in providing the social context for passively produced stylistic expression, in forming the "saucers" of Clarke within which interaction might take place. A relationship might also be discerned between the two modes of stylistic expression and the two aspects of ethnicity discussed previously. Circumstantial emphasis of ethnic identity would certainly be reinforced by active strategies of symbolic display, but it seems also that primordial ethnicity might find unconscious expression through the passive reproduction of cultural forms.

It follows from this discussion of the various roles that material culture might play in society that ethnic groups, upon occasion at least, should be clearly reflected in the archaeological record. This might either be by ethnically specific symbols or, perhaps more likely, by the material residue of ethnically correlated passive interaction. This seems not to be the case however, they often appear indistinct, or not at all. This is for four reasons:

1) There is no absolute necessity for an ethnic group to be in exclusive occupation of a geographical area. Different groups might occupy different niches within a single area, valley dwellers and hill dwellers, for instance. However, archaeological cultures are used for purposes of chronological, as well as spatial, description. Thus, it is often a problem to determine the correct nature of the relationship between two, geographically co-terminous, cultures which may present archaeologically as a palimpsest. This problem has continually bedeviled studies of the Beaker culture and will be returned to in succeeding chapters. It is to be hoped that the increasing availability of C14 dates will alleviate this problem by allowing the construction of an independent time scale against which spatially assessed cultural variation might be measured.

2) Archaeological cultures are not generally regarded as being short lived entities. In European prehistory, at any rate, they are usually thought to persist for periods of time that are several centuries or more long. It is unrealistic to assume that stable spatial boundaries would be maintained over such a span of time, but fluctuating boundaries would blur the spatial expression of a culture and do anything but facilitate its archaeological interpretation. This cultural blurring would be exacerbated by the differential response of actively and passively produced artefact style to changes in ethnic group composition. Alterations in the size or composition of ethnic groups caused by boundary crossing or by fission or fusion might find expression in altered distributions of ethnically specific symbols while being simultaneously obscurred by the survival of pre-existent "passive style zones" as ancestral ways-of-doing were maintained within a changed ethnic milieu.

3) There is a, still salient, tendency to view cultures as "cultural bricks", with a well defined boundary in time, as well as in space. There is little justification for such a view. The constituent artefact types of a culture are unlikely to be changed, or abandoned, en masse. There will be a process of gradual change, or development, of the various artefact types through time so that what might be clear from a synchronic perspective might be much less so from a diachronic one.

4) Ethnically significant patterning in material culture might be crosscut by alternative patterns arising out of pan-societal or pan-ethnic stylistic unity. Environmental effects would obviously be important here, but so might social considerations. The exclusive use of certain artefacts by interacting elites would certainly act to muddy the water, and indeed it is one of the phenomena used to explain the pan-European occurrence of the Beaker culture. This suggests that it is the more everyday artefacts that may be used for ethnic symbolling, not artefacts produced for exchange or status-linked display. Ethnically correlated passive style will also be found in products of household manufacture, not those of demand-driven specialist manufacture.

These obstacles to definition do not justify the abandonment of the archaeological culture, however, instead they call for a sharpening of analytical tools (Clarke 1968: 232). Nor yet do they render the concept of an archaeological culture meaningless, even in the context of a New or of a post-processual archaeology.

Ethnic Groups and a Processual Prehistory

In an important paper Shennan (1989) has argued that ethnicity is a product of the disintegration of pre-urban modes of social organisation, that it might be considered to be an epiphenomenon of the appearance of states (ibid: 15). Although this argument is well made it is not open to refutation. It implies that absence of ethnic sentiment lies outside of history and is therefore unknowable. It might just as well be assumed that some form of ethnic sentiment, some form of us and them recognition, has deep evolutionary roots. Ehret (1988: 570), on the other hand, has claimed that large scale inter-regional diffusion networks would themselves not operate in the absence of class-based urban communities; although this claim is open to refutation perhaps with the Beaker culture providing a test case. Nevertheless, appeals to post-urban social reconfigurations favour neither the migrationist nor the diffusionist but, in any event, to a processual archaeologist the debate is sterile, or at least unnecessary.

Shennan is careful to state that his argument is directed against an emic conception of ethnicity - ethnicity as a subjective category of self-recognition:

"Ethnicity must be distinguished from mere spatial variation and should refer to self-conscious identification with a particular social group at least partly based on a specific locality or origin. If we accept this definition, then it appears that prehistoric archaeology is in a difficult position as far as investigating it is concerned, since it does not have access to people's self-conscious identifications."

(ibid: 14)

A contrary viewpoint might be adopted, however, one that considers ethnicity to be an etic category - a subjective construct of an outside observer (Sackett 1990: 35). What is familiar, conventional and unremarkable for a native is alien and esoteric to the perception of a foreigner. When viewed from the outside an ethnic group might appear in more than one guise. It might appear to lack conscious ethnic symbolising, the passive correlates of ethnicity alone would suffice to provide a group with an homogeneity and a cohesion recognisable to outsiders. Alternatively, an etic ascription of ethnicity may be founded on the premise of "not us", or "other". Thus, to the Romano-British observer it mattered little that the Jutes were not ethnically homogeneous, they were recognisably not British and were awarded an identity on that basis.

Now it might be thought that such etic definitions of ethnicity undermine the relevance of the concept, and this is one of the points that Shennan makes (1989: 11). However, it is crucial here to emphasise that the nature of ethnic categorisation, whether it be emic or etic, is irrelevant to a processual prehistory; but that the identification of ethnic groups is of fundamental importance. If it is accepted that the true goal of prehistory is the explanation of long term change, which it must surely be, then it is of prime importance to identify, and isolate, materially advertised "ethnic" irruptions into evolutionary sequences of change. The nature of ethnic categorisation is unimportant, even if it is only a subjective construct of the archaeologist. If the Beaker culture was indeed disseminated by a migrating people it matters little whether the societies involved constituted a self-cognisant "Beaker Folk", or else if "Beaker Folk" is merely a label attached to the phenomenon by the archaeologist for descriptive convenience. The migration would still be substantive and its effects upon regional sequences of cultural development would need to be fully defined before any explanation of social evolution could be realistically attempted.

Conclusion

In this chapter several topics have been broached, and themes developed. It has been described how the definition of an archaeological culture changed through time, how its ethnic relations have been visualised, and how the social mechanisms of its formation might have operated. But it has also been recounted how disillusionment with the very concept of an archaeological culture led to its abandonment by many scholars, and how this abandonment fatally undermined the culture-historical mode of archaeological explanation. The consequent rise to predominance of the New Archaeology, which advocated processual explanations of social evolution, was also noted.

It is against this background that the change in interpretation of the Beaker culture, from a migrating folk to a diffusing artefact package, must be considered. Specific arguments brought to bear against the idea of a migratory "Beaker Folk" hinged upon observations that the regional variation exhibited by the Beaker culture prevented it from satisfying Childe's original criteria for either a culture or a migration. Although more developed definitions were available they were never utilised. In view of this, then, it seems that the underlying reason for the change in interpretation was the shift in the dominant mode of archaeological thought, from culture-historical to processual. Thus, although the case of the Beaker culture is a specific one it is a member of a more general class. The significance of this will be discussed further in the conclusion of this volume, but for the time being it is intended to avoid generalities and keep to specifics. In the next chapter, therefore, three proposed models of Beaker diffusion will be critically examined, and their heuristic potential assessed.

Chapter Three

THE DIFFUSION OF THE BEAKER CULTURE INTO BRITAIN

Introduction

During the course of the previous chapters it has been described how dissatisfaction with both the static explanation of the archaeological culture and the dynamic explanation of migration resulted in their discard. Thereafter the entire genus of culture-historical explanation was abandoned by the processualist prehistorians of the New Archaeology. Included in this abandonment was the specific case of a migratory "Beaker Folk". In a British context, however, the intrusive nature of the Beaker culture was an archaeological fact that could not easily be ignored. It precluded any characterisation of the Beaker assemblages that was purely evolutionist in content although they were, and still are, sometimes seen as being in some way linked to the evolution of ranked societies. Nevertheless, a diffusionist hypothesis was required to explain the Beaker presence in Britain, and several were forthcoming. Unfortunately, they have often suffered from incomplete formulation or an imprecise definition which has produced a rather vague explanatory framework. In this chapter, therefore, an attempt will be made to clarify the various hypotheses which have been suggested. Their theoretical bases will then be open to critical examination.

Diffusion Model One: Beakers as Prestige Items

One theory of Beaker diffusionary spread suggests that the various components of the cultural assemblage under question acted as prestige items within societies whose political systems can be considered to have been articulated by means of a prestige goods economy. The economy of such a society is composed of several autonomous spheres of exchange, within each of these spheres transactions can only be enacted with certain socially agreed classes of goods (Ekholm 1977; Bohannon 1955). Trading of articles between disparate spheres is either not sanctioned or considered to be so unequal economically as not to be countenanced except as a policy of last resort. The segregation of such an economy may be complex but two generic levels of exchange can be recognised. At a basic level, goods of a household or agricultural nature circulate and are exchanged in socially neutral barter transactions. Of more importance, however, is the existence of higher level, prestige spheres of exchange. At this level, certain socially or ritually important transactions

require the transfer of specifically recognised types of valuable articles, termed here prestige items. As such transactions typically include bride or slave purchase, they form the basis of strategies aimed at productive and reproductive success. The acquisition and maintenance of power, therefore, requires a successful balancing act to be performed between the accumulation of prestige items and their judicious employment, either directly, or indirectly as payment to retainers or kin. Thus, in a prestige goods economy, the prestige items do not only symbolise power, they actively confer it; the source of power lies in monopolising control over the supply of prestige items into the exchange sphere. Such a monopoly can stifle social change if it is used to maintain an ordered structure of status relationships (Douglas 1967:132), but it is the dynamic aspect of a prestige goods economy that has interested archaeologists, when a hierarchical ranking of lineages emerges after their relative access to a supply of prestige items, for whatever reasons, becomes unequal. It is then possible for a single lineage to benefit from their preferential access by exchanging prestige items with associated lineages for wives or slaves, thus increasing their own productive and reproductive potential at the expense of their neighbours.

Thorpe and Richards (1984) have considered the incorporation of Beaker components into the political systems of societies extant during the late Neolithic of two distinct areas of Britain - Wessex and Yorkshire - as being indicative of an extending network of continental prestige goods exchange. They suggest that, already by the end of the earlier Neolithic in Yorkshire, there was an incipient prestige goods exchange system in operation, as evidenced by the large numbers of polished stone axes imported into the area from Cornwall and the Lake District. If faced by successful competition for control over the importation of stone axes into the area already established elites could follow one of two strategies, or both. They could intensify pre-existing practices, in effect an inflationary strategy whereby increasing numbers of items, in this case axes, would be needed to satisfy the requirements of prestige transactions. Alternatively, a policy of diversification might be adopted, so that novel types of prestige items would be introduced into the exchange sphere. Evidence for the latter process is adduced from the range of specialised flintwork that became current during the later Neolithic. Given a policy of diversification operating to maintain exclusiveness there would be a predisposition to link into the continental Beaker network in order to gain access to a wider range of exotic materials.

In contrast to Yorkshire, Thorpe and Richards suggest that social relations during the late Neolithic of Wessex may have been articulated by means of a "ritual authority structure". Positions of political power within such an "authority structure" are hierarchically tiered in a dendritic fashion and are a function of genealogical distance from an apical chief, whose right to power is ultimately sanctioned by descent from territorial gods or ancestors. A chief may demand tribute or corvee from his subjects in return for which they will expect protection from the supernatural, and perhaps also material or military assistance in times of need. The existence of late Neolithic "ritual authority structures" in Wessex is predicated upon the large amount of communal labour thought to have been necessary for the construction of large henges such as Durrington Walls or Avebury, and also on their possible ceremonial functions. Thorpe and Richards (1984: 77) point out that after 2800/2700 calBC there is an apparent spatial separation of elements of late Neolithic culture with Grooved Ware and associated artefacts found concentrated in the localities of the large henges while in more peripheral areas the predominant ceramic is that of the Peterborough tradition. They propose that this chorological divergence of material culture reflects a corresponding geographical divergence in the relations of power. Peripheral, commoner, groups were being denied access to the material paraphernalia of ritual authority monopolised by a Grooved Ware "aristocracy"; and perhaps as a result enjoyed a moderate amount of autonomy, with a looser political organisation permitting the emergence of "big man" type strategies of status acquisition. It is in these peripheral areas that Beakers first appear, elements of a continental prestige goods system adopted by alienated, and perhaps semi-autonomous "big men". Ultimately the individualising prestige goods system would have undermined the communal basis of the "ritual authority's" political structure leading to its ultimate collapse and general replacement by a more anarchic prestige goods economy.

This minimal summary of the prestige goods model omits more than it includes but presents a basic outline of the processes envisaged as being contributory to its operation and spread. There remain faults in the exposition, however. The exact social mechanisms responsible for the ultimate acceptance of Beaker ceramics and their associated artefacts remain largely conjectural. In Yorkshire for example it is proposed that:

".... there was a natural tendency to link into the continental Beaker exchange network with its access to exotic materials."
(Thorpe and Richards 1984:73).

Maybe, but maybe not. The prior existence of a political system articulated by means of prestige goods exchange is no guarantee of the automatic acceptance into that system of alien prestige items. Similarly it does not follow that artefacts considered by one society to be imbued with the symbolic quality of prestige would of necessity retain that nebulous quality upon their adoption in material form by a different society. The reverse would be more probable if foreign prestige items were considered to be a threat to already established relations of patronage.

A second assumption in need of some clarification concerns the putative interaction between a "ritual authority structure" and a prestige goods economy, an interaction thought to be of critical importance for explaining the introduction of Beakers into Wessex. Thus it is stated that:

"..... ritual authority structures are essentially static and prestige goods economies are essentially active. This also implies that where the two systems come into contact it is the prestige goods economy which will dominate."
(Thorpe and Richards 1984: 68)

This is all far from clear. It is true that a prestige goods economy is essentially active but it is also essentially unstable. The flow of prestige items through a hierarchical lineage system proceeds from the top down but is balanced by an upwardly moving counterflow of wives or slaves. As a result, in a patrilineal society, the dominant lineage undergoes a dramatic increase in population which might reach such a scale as to overburden the resource base, thus causing the collapse of the system (Ekholm 1977: 120-124). This centralising tendency of patrilineal societies is avoided in societies which practise matrilineal descent with avunculocal residence of offspring. Although brides still move up the hierarchy, children are returned downwards to prevent central congestion. This configuration is still far from stable, however, as men from the lowest ranking lineages are forced to find wives outside of the political area articulated by the prestige goods economy (Ekholm 1977: 125). If a lineage is unsuccessful in this task, it will fail to reproduce itself biologically and thus cease to exist, exposing in the process the next highest lineage to a similar fate.

It is open to the lower ranked lineages in a prestige goods system to obtain wives either by raiding or kidnap from a terrorised hinterland or by adopting a policy of military conquest to impose themselves as a military aristocracy on a subject population (Friedman & Rowlands 1977: 226-227). This cannot be the scenario envisaged by Thorpe and Richards as depicting the extension of the Beaker culture into Britain as it would, in effect, posit the spread of an actual "Beaker Folk" with a society organised around a prestige goods economy, and whose incursions could be characterised as the layering of an aristocratic elite over a subjected, indigenous population; thus explaining the mixed nature of the archaeological remains. It is an alternative, diffusionist, model that is implied:

"It is proposed that the Beaker/Peterborough association represents the penetration of the ritual authority system by a prestige goods economy operated by high ranking continental groups working through lower status "big men" in Wessex and lower ranking elite lineages."
(Thorpe and Richards 1984: 77).

13

For this penetration to occur the lower ranking Wessex lineages and "big men" would have had to establish links with the continental groups but the nature of these links are not specified. It is not likely that peripheral groups in Wessex would become directly incorporated into a continental prestige goods economy. They themselves would require a dependent periphery to prevent their immediate collapse and the distances involved are, in any case, too great. A more realistic scenario would envisage the establishment of a straightforward trading partnership with a continental group, the foreign artefacts so acquired being used to infiltrate and re-orient any pre-existing, embryonic, prestige network in their favour, thus undermining and causing the collapse of the established "ritual authority structure". Although more likely this scenario remains open to the same set of objections put forward for the Yorkshire explanation, it also implies that Beakers and their associated artefacts should be of foreign manufacture, which is not the case.

Thus a prestige goods economy may be characterised as active insofar as it requires a constant input of excess females for its continuing existence - it must expand or collapse (Ekholm 1977: 128). However, the model contains no prescriptive mechanism for prestige goods economy dominance over an "authority structure", it would depend upon the solidarity and perhaps the military muscle of the "ritual authority structure" and would be historically contingent. Of the strategies proposed for prestige goods economy expansion, whether raiding or trading, or migration or diffusion, no single one is a necessary concomitant of prestige goods economy/"ritual authority structure" interaction. There is little in the archaeology to distinguish between them. It seems likely on theoretical grounds, however, that, assuming Beaker society was organised around a prestige goods economy; a migrationist explanation of its spread, as an aristocratic elite, might present fewer problems of interpretation than one of diffusion.

Diffusion Model Two: Beakers as Status Symbols

A different explanation for the appearance of single burials with accompanying Beaker paraphernalia across Europe has been provided by Thomas (1987). He argues that the basic productive and reproductive unit of the earliest agriculturalists in temperate areas of Europe would have been the tribal segment, or lineage, a corporate group with rights in land inherited from a real or imagined founding ancestor. Settlement tended to be static and relatively nucleated as early arable agriculture would have been dependent upon a simple technology, and thus labour intensive; it may have been left largely in the hands of women while the men tended livestock away from home. Women were therefore important for both agricultural production and biological reproduction. They were necessary for both the short and long term survival of the lineage and their exchange between lineages was likely to be strictly controlled through the medium of brideprice. However, following Sherratt (1981) and Goody (1977), Thomas suggests that the adoption of plough agriculture would have necessitated a re-ordering of these relations of production. The ox-drawn plough enabled a larger area of land to be brought under cultivation by a smaller number of people, thus encouraging the development of a more dispersed

settlement pattern and the break up of centralised lineage residence groups. At the same time the plough would usurp the central role of the female in crop cultivation and her status as a food producer would be downgraded. The break up of the lineage residence groups and of their close control over social reproduction would have resulted in a greater emphasis on individual prowess which, combined with the female loss of status, would have encouraged the emergence of a warrior ethos, advertised in death by the single burials of the Corded Ware and Beaker cultures with their accompaniments of drinking vessels, weapons and ornaments.

An important feature of this model is that Beakers and their associated artefacts are no longer regarded as prestige items. That is, they are no longer regarded as material objects which, in themselves, possess the facility to confer status by means of their possession or distribution; they are no longer considered to have an active role to play in the generation or maintenance of social inequality. Instead they are seen to be emblematic of status, their use is restricted to an elite whose position of authority rests upon direct appropriation of the productive output of their dependent, or subject, community. The use of Beakers would be restricted by social sanction or public ridicule and they would be symbols - status symbols.

Although the general thesis of Thomas' argument is persuasive it fails to provide a coherent account of why the emergence of a male warrior elite in a variety of areas should necessarily be marked by the adoption of Beaker assemblages. It was evidently not the case in some regions. As will be described in the next chapter the practice of weapon-accompanied male inhumation had been employed in the Yorkshire Wolds for centuries before the appearance of the first Beaker. It also fails to explain just exactly why it is that Beaker pots should be chosen to act as status symbols. With the socially passive role of status symbol, however, it at least seems that the diffusionary spread of Beakers would not be as problematical as it would be if they were acting as prestige items; their adoption by a community would not directly threaten the exchange relations underpinning the established social order. Local elites may well have wished to ape their continental peers and to impress their neighbours. This diffusionist model of Beaker culture spread is, therefore, predicated upon the notion that its constituent artefacts would have been considered as fitting accoutrements for high status individuals, the artefacts themselves being considered exotic or in some way of value.

Beakers as Primitive Valuables

It is a central assertion of both the "prestige item" and "status symbol" models of Beaker diffusion that the constituent artefacts of Beaker assemblages were considered to be valuable by late Neolithic societies across Europe. The idea that Beaker assemblages may have been so considered was originally proposed by Shennan (1976, 1977) following his study of central European material. In this area the bulk of the so-called "Beaker" pottery which was recovered from settlement and burial contexts consisted in fact of undecorated cups, jugs and bowls, known collectively as Begleitkeramik, a range of vessels whose origins could be traced back to preceding Corded Ware assemblages and which ultimately developed into proto-Únetice forms. It was against this backcloth of ceramic and cultural continuity that true Bell Beaker assemblages appeared, usually in funerary contexts and often seeming to act as a marker of high status male burials. Furthermore, the various elements of the Beaker assemblage did not appear to share a coherent genesis in either a cultural or geographical sense; instead the different artefact types were acquired from a variety of backgrounds. The fine Bell Beaker pottery itself had originated in more westerly Corded Ware areas while the rudiments of copper metallurgy would have been imported from the Carpathian basin. This led Shennan to suggest that the various elements of the Beaker assemblage had been adopted from their different sources by local elites who were pursuing a strategy of status demarcation and that therefore the Beaker assemblages must be seen to represent a "status kit", not a complete archaeological culture.

Whatever the ultimate merits of this hypothesis, it was derived from a study of the central European material and so, not surprisingly, presents an original and parsimonious explanation of this material. To recap, in central Europe, the various constituent artefacts of the Beaker assemblage share a synchronous appearance, that is the decorated Beaker fineware, together with associated weaponry and ornaments, seem to have passed into usage at a single point in time. Furthermore, the Beaker pottery was of a fine decorated type from the outset and would have contrasted noticeably with the plain, locally made, Begleitkeramik. It is perhaps not unreasonable therefore to argue that the artefacts were functioning as primitive valuables. There are, however, crucial differences between those conditions attending the appearance of Beaker assemblages in central Europe and those further west, differences of such a type as to seriously weaken the credibility of the status kit model. In western Europe, not only is there more evidence of Beaker settlements with associated Beaker-type domestic wares, but also the initial Beaker expansion was not accompanied by the more exotic components of the assemblage (Case 1977: 77). If the spread of the Beaker culture into Britain is to be considered to result from a process of diffusion then it was a diffusion that in its early stages was purely a ceramic phenomenon. Moreover, the earliest pottery in many areas, AOC, was not as well finished and as remarkable as later Beaker products were to be. Thus, before any decision can be reached concerning the acceptance or otherwise of the "status symbols" or "prestige items" models of Beaker culture diffusion, it needs to determined whether pottery alone, and in particular AOC and Maritime pottery, could function within a society in such a way as to bestow prestige, or to be emblematic of status. If, in fact, it would have been considered to have possessed the quality of "value".

Following Marx, it is possible to assess the value of an artefact in terms of its labour value; labour value being a measure of the amount of labour, or energy, invested in its manufacture (Elster 1986: 64). That the value of a prestige item may be related to its labour value has been illustrated in the case of the Raffia cloths of the Lele (Douglas 1967:131). These cloths are handwoven by the male members of the tribe and are required by the same for a variety of status related transactions. In theory, any man should be able to weave enough cloth to satisfy his personal requirements but in practice the quantity of cloth needed is such that it is impossible for a single individual to produce sufficient, he therefore becomes dependent upon his lineage elders to meet his needs. Clarke (1976) invoked the concept of labour value when suggesting that the fineware Beaker might have functioned as a primitive valuable, and he made several assumptions about the conditions of prehistoric ceramic manufacture, backing up his argument with ethnographic analogies. Thus, the decorated fineware Beaker was not a simple household product, it represented a significant input of time and energy that, from a utilitarian point of view, would have been better spent in direct subsistence related pursuits. Ethnographic data from the Goodenough Islands showed that the manufacturing time for a comparable pot might be 5.3 hours (Table 3.1) which Clarke characterised as representing:

Table 3.1.
Time spent in the manufacture of a single pot. (after Clarke 1976: 469).

Processes	Time
Quarrying clay; selective digging, transport, storage.	1.3 hours
Preparation of clay; wetting the clay, kneading and cleaning.	0.5 hours
Building the vessel; forming rolls, rolling strips, ring building the vessel.	1.0 hours
Initial drying, smoothing the exterior. Decorating the vessel, lifting, beating, trimming, preparing rim, decorating, scraping and burnishing the interior.	1.5 hours plus
Drying the vessel; firing the vessel; gathering fuel, preparing the fire, setting the vessels, lighting the fire, tending and removing vessels.	1.0 hours

Total time = 5.3 hours per vessel.

"an expensive chunk of congealed time and energy."
(1976: 470).

He went on to suggest that fineware Beakers would not be generally available as their production would require a favourable locus with regard to good potting clay, abundant and suitable fuel, water and good agricultural land. Thus centres of production might emerge in which it would be expected that the high standard of finish of such a Beaker would be achieved by semi-specialised craftsmen and it would be regarded as a valuable object, to be utilised in exchange networks. Clarke suggested that such Beakers may have travelled considerable distances by means of such networks, which were undoubtedly in prior existence throughout Europe transporting, amongst other things, stone axes, obsidian, amber and shells. Again ethnographic analogy was invoked to show how, from the Amphlett Islands, finished pots were transported by canoe and traded in exchange for a variety of commodities, both agricultural and material.

There are a number of preliminary observations that can be made concerning this hypothesis. The time taken to produce a pot in the ethnographic example given is a maximum and does not take into account possible economies of scale. For instance, to produce two pots together, the time expended in obtaining and preparing the clay and in firing would not increase appreciably, only the time taken to build the vessels would be doubled. The time taken in manufacture would therefore be, say, eight hours, that is four hours per pot. Furthermore, activities such as obtaining clay or firewood might be performed secondary to other, subsistence related, activities such as herding or plant gathering, thereby reducing even further the absolute amount of time spent on pot manufacture. Children might also be employed for unskilled tasks such as fetching water or firewood. Thus Clarke's estimate (1976: 470) of 4 to 6 hours work for a fineware Beaker is too high, 4 hours or less seems a more realistic estimate. On top of this, it must be remembered that ceramic manufacture is ideally suited to being a household craft and it can be carried out in an interrupted fashion, that is at some stages work on pot construction can be left off in order to attend to other chores, and be resumed at a later time (Arnold 1985: 101). Thus it is entirely feasible that pot manufacture may have been a household activity, as such it is also likely to have been included within the realm of female productive activity (Arnold 1985: 102).

In his analysis, Clarke chose to compare the apparent cost of prehistoric Beaker production with that of modern western ceramics. A better comparison, however, would be with the manufacturing time of prehistoric artefacts which are thought to have had a high probability of having functioned as valuable objects due to their exotic nature. Nearer in time to Beakers, it has been estimated that a single, spherical, jet bead would have taken about 3 hours to manufacture, exclusive of the time taken in obtaining raw material (Shepherd 1985: 212). On occasion large numbers of jet beads have been recovered from burials, which it is assumed were strung together with spacer plates and end terminals into complex necklaces. Such necklaces would require a labour input orders of magnitude greater than proposed for a fineware Beaker.

In any case, any concept which implies a universal equivalence between labour input and value is likely to be oversimplified and wrong. It is probable that there would have existed in prehistoric societies a "value gap" between the labour of male and female, objects of male manufacture being considered of value while those of female manufacture were not. Hodder's (1986: 105ff) discussion of the Ilchamus females' decoration of milk containing calabashes is illuminating in this respect. Seen as unimportant, or trivial, by the males, the decoration is manipulated by the females to draw attention to their reproductive contribution to the domestic economy. Alternatively, female labour might indeed be predicated upon the expectation of an ultimate economic benefit, but a benefit which need not be archaeologically tangible. Her labour might be considered to be a form of social investment. To enlarge, consider a hypothetical society in which, for whatever reasons, it is important for a man to be seen to be married to an industrious wife, as advertised by her standard of potting. The wife's expenditure of time contributes to the social standing of her husband which, ultimately, might be turned to economic advantage. Thus the woman's labour would be rewarded, but the immediate object of her labour, the pot, would retain no intrinsic value. Thus there can be no necessary simple or direct relationship between the time invested in the manufacture of an artefact and its intra-societal value as a status symbol or its inter-societal value as an exchange item, particularly if the article is of female manufacture, which seems probable at least in the case of the Beaker. The provision at burial of a female produced, high quality, Beaker may even have been an action which achieved significance by virtue of the material role played by the Beaker in the everyday discourse of female society, a role which acted to exclude it from any male considerations of appropriate status display. This remains, of course, unknowable.

It can be argued, then, that the value status of primitive prestige items, or status symbols, cannot be totally or adequately described by reference to objective manufacturing criteria. Instead, value ascription will partly be by social consensus. Such social assignation of value is to some extent arbitrary, although some defining characteristics of value, or prestige, constantly recur. Valuable items tend to be exotic in appearance and pleasing to the senses, they are rare, may be durable or else be suitable for conspicuous consumption (Renfrew 1985: 160). Examples of primitive valuables include precious metals, semi-precious stones, a variety of different seashells, feathers, cloth, furs, livestock and human beings. It might be countered, however, that the ascription of value by reference to a defining criterion of rarity is merely a transformation of the defining criterion of labour - that it is open to anyone to obtain a jade axe, if she or he are willing to spend the time and effort in searching out the jade and fashioning the axe. The time of course would not be available, it is a situation similar to that already described for the Raffia cloths of the Lele. In any event, ceramic articles are rarely found to function as primitive valuables. Pottery may often be exotic in appearance but it is neither durable, suitable for conspicuous consumption nor is it particularly rare. An exception to the latter observation might be made in cases where there is a pronounced technology gap existing between contacting societies so that high quality pots might become desirable items in communities whose native potters are unable to reproduce an acceptable equivalent. It is highly unlikely that a technological gap of such magnitude existed between the ceramic production capabilities of the societies extant in late Neolithic Europe. Experimental work has shown that the fabrication of a Beaker is, in fact, a relatively straightforward task (Gibson 1982: 72).

Where it has been demonstrated archaeologically that a qualitatively distinct ceramic assemblage has prestige connotations (that is, it is found associated with other, more orthodox, prestige items) the distinction might be due more to the superior standard of finish than to any difference in vessel form or type (Steponaitis 1984: 291). Again, it has been shown in experimental work (Gibson 1982: 72) that the most labour intensive part of the Beaker production process would have been the refinement of the fabric and the decoration of the formed pot. Within the known corpus of Beaker pottery, both funerary and domestic, standards of finish vary greatly suggesting that levels of labour investment also varied in a parallel fashion. Why some Beakers were finished to a higher standard than others, and also to a higher standard than previous types of Neolithic pottery, remains unknown, but it is conceivable that considerations of display or status signalling were at least partly responsible. Pierpoint (1980: 59), for instance, has claimed that in Yorkshire there was a tendency for males to be buried with Beakers of a higher quality than those which accompanied females or children. But if vessel quality was being manipulated in such a way within a society, it does not seem likely that there would be a simultaneous usage of the distinct Bell Beaker form itself for similar reasons of display without envisaging a situation whereby a complex set of nested status gradations were being expressed through the medium of a ceramic repertoire highly heterogeneous in both form and finish. This seems most unlikely.

An important prediction of Clarke's model (1976: 467) is that fineware Beakers would be found in locations far removed from their place of manufacture and would therefore be valuable on account of their rarity. This overcomes some of the objections outlined previously, and it is also a prediction open to empirical verification or refutation by means of ceramic characterisation studies. However, to date, there have been few studies of provenance carried out which are able to test this prediction, although a petrological study of Beakers in south-western England has shown them to have been of local manufacture (Pearson 1990). This study is particularly significant as pots made from the gabbroic clay of the Lizard peninsula are found throughout Cornwall in contexts dating from Neolithic to Roman. The Beakers are an exception however, they seem to mark a distinct break in the regional tradition of ceramic production and movement (Harris 1990: 4). Similarly, petrological studies of Beaker material from three separate locations in Ireland: Lough Gur, Dalkey Island and the Boyne Valley; in all cases pointed to local manufacture (Cleary 1983: 113, Brindley 1984). There is therefore at the moment little evidence of large scale exchange of Beaker fineware although a more extensive research programme might alter current perceptions, particularly if the programme was designed to include areas without adequate resources for successful potting.

It must also be remembered that the large scale movement of Beaker fineware may have been a problem. There have been large quantities of such pottery recovered from locations throughout Britain and Europe, quantities much in excess of stone axes, for instance. Although it might be argued that pottery is more fragile than stone axes and that, therefore, a higher rate of breakage and discard is a prior expectation, it would nevertheless imply the existence of a well developed system of communication and transport to maintain supplies. The difficulty of this in inland areas away from major river routes should not be underestimated, Clarke's suggested analogy of the Amphlett Islanders is not altogether apposite as they are able to transport all their pots in canoes.

Beakers as Primitive Valuables - A Test

If Beaker pottery was indeed functioning as a primitive valuable, it might be expected that it would share with other, more conventional valuables, an isomorphic distribution within society; a distribution restricted by convention to certain sectors, or members, of a community and which might find expression within the mortuary domain. To test this hypothesis, the allocation of probable prestige items or status symbols to the early Bronze Age burials of eastern Yorkshire was examined, and compared to that of the ceramic Beakers and, for practical reasons, Food Vessels. Items chosen as being the most likely to have functioned as valuables were those made of jet, amber and metal. No attempt was made to differentially score burials on a quantitative basis, so that for instance a single jet button was considered to be of equal significance to a jet necklace. The reasons for this are many, but the decision may be justified by the observation that whereas coarse distinctions within a society may be expressed, and survive, within the mortuary domain, investigations of more subtle distinctions are host to a whole range of problems, both depositional and post-depositional (Bradley 1988). The study was restricted to inhumation burials as they were better described from a demographic point of view by 19th century archaeologists and it seems in any case unlikely that the cremated burial population differed significantly in its composition.

Information for the study was derived from Greenwell (1877, 1890), Mortimer (1905), Brewster (1980), Dent (1983), Powelsland (1986) and Stead (1959). The distribution of artefacts was initially, and as it turned out, fruitfully, compared against burials using the criterion of age as being the factor most likely to affect the provision of valuables. There were in total 747 inhumation burials for which reasonably accurate age data was available. The burials were divided into three groups: child, adolescent and adult. As the socially recognised onset of adulthood would have occurred sometime during the teenage years, the adolescent group was arbitrarily deemed to include anyone between the ages of thirteen to eighteen inclusive, but was in fact a non-category. It includes members of both the child and the adult categories and acts to remove the fuzziness of the boundary. It thereby constitutes a grey area between distinct categories. Thus the child group was compared directly with the adult group, with the results for adolescents being expected to fall somewhere in-between. Burials associated with either a Beaker, Food Vessel, worked jet, worked amber, a metal artefact, or any combination thereof, were scored (Table 3.2). The occasional Collared Vessel or Accessory Cup accompanying a burial were included in the Food Vessel group, all other artefact associations were ignored. In Table 3.3, the jet and metal associated burials are collapsed into a single class of prestige burials and the relative percentages are presented. Using a Chi-squared test, the only significant difference between adult and child burials was found to be in the provision of metal and jewellery, which was largely restricted to adults. There is little evidence to suggest that ceramics at burial, whether Food Vessel or Beaker, were as restricted in their inclusion as were the more conventional valuables. Children were as likely to be provided with pots as were adults.

These results might be challenged, and explained away, as the effects of emulatory devaluation. It is worth, therefore, considering them in more depth. The emulation model would predict that, initially, fine Beakers would have been restricted to adult burials, but as time passed and metal and jet objects became more widely available, pottery would become devalued and thus be considered as a fitting accompaniment for a child. From this it would follow that the proportion of children within the class of burials receiving a Food Vessel should be larger than the proportion within the Beaker class, (assuming the chronological precedence of Beakers in these burials). This turns out not to be the case, however, as 29% of all Beakers were with children as opposed to 30% of Food Vessels - not a significant increase. It is also a corollary of the emulation model that the children

allocated metal or jet should be late in the burial sequence whereas, in fact, two of them were Beaker burials, one a Food Vessel and one had no ceramic accompaniment.

This brief survey of a single aspect of the material surviving in the archaeological record from a burial tradition which lasted the best part of a millennium can be nothing other than superficial, but, as with all such studies, while negative evidence might be inconclusive positive conclusions cannot be ignored. Whatever sumptuary convolutions were affecting the depository practices at death of the adult population on the Yorkshire Wolds during the 3rd and 2nd millennia BC, children, by and large, were not considered fit recipients for valuable or prestigious artefacts - they were fit only for pots.

The "status kit" and "prestige items" model of Beaker diffusion seem then to be fatally flawed. In order to explain the particular circumstances attending the introduction of the Beaker culture into Britain it would require that the ceramic fineware alone be regarded by the late Neolithic societies as being valuable in some way. This is a role for which pottery is ill-suited. Suggestions that fineware Beakers may have functioned in such a manner by virtue of the labour invested in their manufacture and by their participation in exchange networks have been shown to be unfounded. Alternative suggestions seem worse. After 15 years of processual sturm, and 10 years of post-processual drang, it is depressing to learn that Beakers proved desirable to the Neolithic inhabitants of Britain

".....in consequence of their novelty, their association with distant places, or even an appearance which might be judged attractive."

(Thomas 1991: 101)

Table 3.2.   Burial Associations

ASSOCIATIONS	CHILD	ADOLESCENT	ADULT
Beaker only	16	5	33
Beaker & jet	1		2
Beaker & bronze	1		3
Beaker, jet & bronze			1
Food Vessel	41	9	79
FV & jet			2
FV & bronze			7
FV, jet & bronze	1		2
jet	1	3	12
bronze		4	20
jet & bronze			6
Total number of burials studied	205	48	494

18

Table 3.3.   Percentage of burials with "valuable" or ceramic associations

	CHILD		ADULT	
Total no. of burials	205		494	
	no. burials	% burials	no. burials	% burials
with Beakers	18	8.8	39	7.9
with Food Vessels	42	20.5	90	18.2
total ceramic burials	60	29.3	129	26.1
with prestige items	4	2.0	55	11.1

Diffusion Model Three: The Cult Package

While the ceramic Bell Beaker itself may lack the necessary attributes to qualify as a status symbol or as a prestige item, it might perhaps have been assigned an important role in society by virtue of its contents or usage. Attention has focused on the role Beaker pottery may have played in male drinking rituals which could have accompanied the introduction of alcohol into Neolithic societies. It might be expected that, because of its potentially anti-social consequences, the performance and manner of alcohol consumption would be liable to strict societal control or sanction. The occasion of alcohol drinking would thus be marked out both by ritual practices and by the utilisation of distinctive items of material culture, in this case the Bell Beaker and associated artifacts. It is proposed that such a combination of behaviour and material, a "cult package", might spread through societies with very different forms of internal organisation; the rapid spread of the peyote cult through the diverse Indian tribes of north America during the late nineteenth and early twentieth centuries is invoked as an appropriate analogy (Burgess and Shennan 1976: 311). The analogy, however, is not a good one. The peyote cult was but one symptom of a general reconstruction of Indian society as it strove to adjust to the norms and realities of European domination. It was regarded by its participants as being an Indian equivalent of Christianity and offered a more progressive alternative to archaic tribal religions, while at the same time maintaining a distance from the "white man's religion". Although a pan-Indian phenomenon, its acceptance was often by the younger, or more educated, members of Indian society, often in the face of opposition from tribal conservatives or elders (Hertzberg 1971: 248). It is doubtful if the cult would have been so readily accepted by unstressed societies. It is also worth remembering that the rapid spread of the peyote cult was undoubtedly facilitated by the developing communication infrastructure within the United States, peyote buttons themselves were often obtained through the good offices of the U.S. Mail! (Hertzberg 1971: 281).

The peyote cult aside, Dietler (1990) has reviewed the ethnographic evidence of alcohol consumption and drawn attention to several distinctions that must be made when considering the diffusionary spread of alcoholic drinks. The adoption by a society of alien drinking customs, or of a novel alcoholic beverage, may have many causes - and many effects. These are determined by any already established role of alcohol within the adoptive society and also by its socio-

political organisation. Thus, if alcohol is unknown then the commencement of its use is likely to be socially disruptive. If the preferred alcoholic beverage of a society is not open to indigenous production, if it has to be imported, then it might function as a "prestige item" as already described. When foreign drinking customs are adopted for their symbolic potential however, it is usually by an hierarchical society with an already established syntax of status demarcation. The drinking customs and accoutrements then act as status symbols, again as already described. On the face of it, this latter situation seems to provide a good underlying rationale for the diffusion of Beakers as status symbols as it overcomes the problem created by their apparent lack of intrinsic value.

Several other objections remain, however. In the first place, it presupposes that societies throughout late Neolithic western Europe possessed a roughly comparable form of social organisation, and one which was predisposed to penetration by a novel drinking ritual. This seems unlikely, to say the least. It is certainly possible to point to the different forms of society implied by the fortified settlements and metal using communities of Iberia when compared to the scattered homesteads of north-west Europe. Thorpe and Richards have claimed, as already recorded, that forms of social organisation in Britain differed radically. Secondly, the faithful reproduction of a coherent body of custom and material represented by a drinking cult is not a simple exercise. It is dependent upon the nature of the relations that exist between donor and recipient societies, and is only likely to occur in conditions of close contact (Dietler 1990: 378). Finally, Case (1987: 119) has pointed out that, although the range of Beaker ceramics does include some types which will have been used as drinking vessels, not all were suitable for such usage, nor does it mean that they were manufactured for this purpose. It is also often the case that Beakers were deposited in graves on their sides or inverted, evidently not containing a liquid. The Beaker recovered from Ashgrove, Fife, contained a residue which, when examined, was found to contain predominantly lime pollen with smaller amounts of meadowsweet, heather and ribwort. Although such a residue might remain had the Beaker originally contained a honey-based mead, it could equally well indicate that it had originally contained honey. It is quite possible, in fact, that unfermented honey may have been more of a prized commodity than alcohol, which, if available in cereal-based form, may have been relatively abundant. Domestic bees were probably not hived in temperate Europe until late antiquity or the early middle ages (Sherratt 1987: 95), during the Neolithic and

Bronze Age, honey would most probably have been collected from wild populations of bees and would have been a scarce resource; its sugary impact upon Neolithic taste buds cannot now be imagined but should not be underestimated. The horn spoon recovered from the Beaker at Broomend, Aberdeen, would seem to have been of more use in extracting viscous honey from a pot than the more liquid mead or beer from what is, after all, supposed to be a drinking vessel. The amount of honey available to late Neolithic societies would have been extremely limited, however. quantities would not have been large enough to have driven a putative elite honey-slurping cult.

Thus, although the "cult package" model of Beaker diffusion seems to be the best of a bad bunch, it does not deserve to be uncritically accepted. While it might be the case that ritual alcohol consumption played a central, or at least important, role in Beaker society it is more likely that the primary diffusion of the custom through Europe would have been by means of a migratory folk, at least in the first instance. Local processes of diffusion, or acculturation, may have followed as a secondary occurrence.

Conclusion

It has been argued in this chapter that the various models which have been proposed to explain a Beaker culture diffusion into Britain are unsatisfactory. Perhaps the most convincing is that of the "cult package", although this too is beset by problems. Can it be, perhaps, that prehistorians were over hasty in their abandonment of the traditional, migrationist, explanations of the Beaker Culture? In the next chapter the evidence of settlements and of burials will be reviewed, and arguments in favour of their continuity criticised.

Chapter Four

SETTLEMENT AND BURIAL DURING THE NEOLITHIC AND EARLY BRONZE AGE

Introduction

During the course of Chapter Three it was argued that the theoretical bases of the diffusionist explanations put forward to explain Beaker Culture spread are insecure. In this chapter attention is focused upon more substantial issues as the diffusionist claims of continuity in settlement and in mortuary ritual are critically examined.

Death and Burial in Neolithic and Early Bronze Age Yorkshire

Traditionally the most convincing evidence of a Beaker immigration was considered to be the change in funerary rite occurring at the Neolithic/Beaker interface. Neolithic burials had been collective in character and interred in communal long barrows or chamber tombs. There were few grave goods included in such burials and the skeletons were mixed. To some scholars this suggested an egalitarian society. In contrast, the Beaker immigrants brought with them the continental practice of individual inhumation under a round mound with inclusion of grave goods to denote individual status. Beaker society was ranked. In recent years, however, this view has been challenged and the new orthodoxy denies the significance, or even the actuality, of this change in burial practice.

With the excavation of sites such as Hambledon Hill (Mercer 1980) and Offham Hill (Drewett 1977), it is now apparent that earlier Neolithic burial practices were more complex than previously thought, with rites of excarnation, inhumation and cremation taking place at a variety of sites. Furthermore, the population figures suggested by the number of individuals recovered from long barrows are very low and women and children are under represented (Bradley 1984: 22) - it is evident that only a minority of the early Neolithic population were laid to rest under a long mound, perhaps the privileged element in society (Megaw and Simpson 1981: 95). During the later Neolithic, burial practices varied regionally but some areas, notably the Yorkshire Wolds, saw the indigenous development of the practice of individual inhumation under a round mound accompanied by grave goods. Burgess (1980: 53-61, 299-300) particularly has argued that it is in these later Neolithic burial practices that

the forerunners of early Bronze Age rituals are to be found, not the European mainland. Single, furnished, inhumation in a pit, shaft or cist under a round barrow were features long thought diagnostic of Beaker and early Bronze Age burial practices but all are known now to have been utilised during the Neolithic. Conversely Neolithic practices of cremation, excarnation and the reuse of a tomb for more than one burial are seen to persist into the early Bronze Age. Burgess has concluded that the appearance of the continental burial tradition affected indigenous rituals ".... only superficially." (1980:61). It has proved difficult, however, to extend this model to other parts of Britain. In the north and west, chamber tombs and passage graves seem to have continued in use until sealed off at the end of the Neolithic. In southern England, the situation is more complex and there is little evidence of single inhumation under a round barrow, although the later long barrows are smaller and tend towards being oval in shape rather than rectangular (Bradley 1984: 32). Male burials predominate and skeletons tend to maintain their integrity. Bradley (1984: 43,78) has argued that the absence of a sustained tradition of single inhumation during the southern late Neolithic may have been due to regional ideology which called for the expenditure of labour on large ritual or communal monuments which emphasised the cohesion and importance of the corporate group at the expense of the individual.

As evidence for ritual continuity in funerary custom through the period of the Neolithic - Bronze Age transition is most clearly marked in northern England, particularly Yorkshire, it is those burials that are analysed here, and the claim of ritual continuity critically scrutinised.

The classic early Neolithic funerary ritual in the Yorkshire Wolds was that of burial under an earthen long barrow. At least 18 such barrows are known to have existed and they have been discussed in detail by Manby (1970) and Ashbee (1984). Although variations do occur, the ritual and structural features associated with these northern long barrows appear to have been remarkably consistent. The standard pre-mound configuration was of a mortuary house, or structure, situated within a long, east-west aligned, mortuary enclosure with a ritual area, usually marked by a concave wooden facade, at its eastern end. The funerary ceremonies included excarnation of some, but not all, the bodies interred and the destruction of their remains by the cremation of the mortuary structure was a frequent, but not universal, practice. It was not usual to include grave goods with the burials, although sherds of Grimston Ware are sometimes found associated. Most barrows contained less than a dozen individuals, the exception being Market Weighton with 26. The erection of a covering mound acted to terminate the funerary aspect of the site while simultaneously, perhaps, marking the onset of a new period of monumental significance.

Related to these long barrows by both ritual practice and material associations are a series of round barrows. These mounds are found to cover linear cremation features, perhaps the remains of mortuary structures, and they are sometimes associated with Grimston Ware. The round cairn at Whitegrounds contained a linear burial chamber within which were 8 inhumations in various states of articulation, a C14 date of 3970-3530 calBC derived from one of the bones confirmed its early Neolithic status (Brewster 1984).

By the end of the early Neolithic the construction of long barrows had ceased but round barrows continued to be built through into the late Neolithic. Nationally, Neolithic round barrow burials have been arranged into a six stage sequence on the basis of their artefactual associations (Kinnes 1979), although in Yorkshire it is useful to accommodate later Neolithic examples within two, approximately diachronic, groups.

The first group achieves coherence by virtue of the recurrent presence of Towthorpe Ware and large leaf-shaped arrowheads as material associations, the almost complete absence of cremation, and the apparently transitional nature of the burial rite from multiple to single inhumation. The mound at Callis Wold 275 (Coombs 1976, Mortimer 1905: 161) covered a linear paved area aligned NW/SE and marked at each end by a post pit, possibly remaining from a mortuary structure. On the pavement were the bones of 10 adults and 1 child associated with 3 leaf arrowheads, there were also some burnt bones. The mortuary area was partially enclosed by a palisade trench which had originally supported a facade, there were sherds of Towthorpe ware in the fill. A similar structure was tentatively identified under the destroyed barrow at Boynton (Manby 1980), while at Aldro 88 there were the possible remains of a mortuary structure aligned east-west and containing four inhumations, a Towthorpe bowl, and a leaf arrowhead. Other barrows are distinguished by the presence of collective inhumations upon clay or paved areas, these include Towthorpe 18, Aldro 94, Sherburn 7, Sherburn 8 and Wold Newton 284. There is also an increasing frequency of graves or cists, often holding the remains of more than one individual, under the mounds at Huggate 230, Painsthorpe 99, Towthorpe 18, Aldro 94 and Wold Newton 284. Hedon Howe, with its 5 rectangular stone lined cists is probably best accommodated within this group. Cowlam 57 contained two multiple deposits of skeletons together with some individual inhumations, one with an antler macehead. The arrowheads recovered from this series of burials are notable on account of their large size, they are not representative of stray arrowheads from the Wolds area generally and Green (1980: 85) considers them to have been

prestige objects, probably manufactured specifically for funerary use. Mortimer (1905: 59,123) further observed that the arrowheads from Aldro 88 and Painsthorpe 99 were not of local flint, and that some were perhaps broken intentionally at the time of burial. The overall period of use for this barrow group remains to be determined, as does the presence of any internal phasing. The only C14 dates are from Callis Wold 275 and Boynton. They confirm the suggestion that they are early in any structural sequence - the dates cannot be distinguished from the long barrow sites. Kinnes (1979) would see some of these mounds as being multi-period in use, if not construction, and there seems little reason to contradict him.

Inhumation under a round mound survived to become the most widespread funerary rite during the late Neolithic, although the number of burials recovered is low. At Whitegrounds, a circular shaft grave was sunk into the top of the pre-existing Neolithic cairn and the body of an adult male was inserted, together with a jet slider and a Seamer type flint axe (Brewster 1984). The original cairn was enlarged and a C14 date falling within the range 3510 - 2920 calBC suggests that this burial took place early in the late Neolithic sequence. Similar secondary inhumations with accompanying monumental alteration have been recorded at the Seamer Moor, Garton Slack 37 and Kemp Howe long barrows (Manby 1988). New barrows were apparently erected at Painsthorpe 118 over an adult inhumation associated with a jet slider; and at Aldro 175 over two central inhumations associated with flint flake knives, one of which was rectangular and exceedingly fine. At Garton Slack 112, three children were individually inhumed in hollows within a ring ditch, each associated with a bone skewer pin, before a mound was raised over a central unaccompanied double inhumation of adult and child.

A more distinctive group of late Neolithic barrows has been termed the "Great Barrows" (Manby 1988) and includes Duggleby Howe, Garton Slack 79, Prior Moor, Rudston 67, Willie Howe and Wold Newton 284. All except Garton Slack 79 are located within, or adjacent, to the Great Wold valley and are notable for their large size. However, while it is evident that these barrows could well have functioned as monuments throughout the late Neolithic, the manner or timing of their construction remains uncertain. Wold Newton 284 has previously been discussed as falling within the criterial ambit of the Towthorpe group of barrows while little is known of the interiors of Prior Moor and Willie Howe, they achieve inclusion in this group by virtue of their size and position. Garton Slack 79 had been partly destroyed with the removal of about 5 or 6 skeletons by the time Mortimer (1905: 241) dug into it and found a further 8 inhumations, none of undoubted Neolithic date. There were a number of secondary insertions into the mound of Rudston 67 but the primary burial consisted of the body of a one year old child accompanied by the partial skeleton of a young woman in a woodlined cist, but without any material associations (Greenwell: 1877). The chronological status of many of these "Great Barrows", then, remains obscure but Duggleby Howe is an exception.

The southern and eastern sections of Duggleby Howe were excavated by Mortimer (1905), who discovered 13 inhumations (termed A to M) and 53 cremation deposits. The construction and utilisation of the Howe apparently spanned the later Neolithic and three or four stages of burial deposition have been proposed (Kinnes 1979, Manby 1988). The earliest mortuary activity on the site consisted of the excavation of a shaft grave and the deposition of a single male inhumation (K), accompanied by a Towthorpe Bowl and a flint core with some flakes, all within a wooden cist or chamber. Two further inhumations were placed in the fill of the shaft, an adult male (I) and a child (H), both unaccompanied except for the presence of a disembodied skull (J) with the adult. The second stage of burial deposition involved the interment of three adult males at the level of the old ground surface, two at the top of the shaft grave and one just east in a shallow grave. Each of these inhumations was furnished with grave goods. Burial (G) possessed a large flint adze, kite shaped flint arrowhead and an antler macehead; Burial (D) a finely polished rectangular flake knife comparable to the one at Aldro 175; inhumation (C) in the shallow grave had both transverse and oblique arrowheads, boars tusks blades, utilised beavers teeth and a large bone skewer pin. An inner mound was erected after this series of burials and the next stage of burial deposition involved the inhuming of 6 infants, 1 adolescent and 1 adult (A,B,E,F,L,M,N,O) within the earthen core of the mound. The inner mound also contained a cremation cemetery with at least 53 deposits, three with skewer pin associations. It is likely that this cemetery extends further to the northern (unexcavated) part of the mound and possibly to the west as well. An outer mound was erected after the deposition of the cremation deposits, but it is not clear exactly when. The large number of cremation deposits indicate a significant time interval between the two mound building episodes. It is similarly not clear if the final series of inhumations constitute a stage of burial activity distinct from the cremations or if together they form a coherent series.

Finally, it remains to consider the Beaker and early Bronze Age practice of burial under a round mound. Over 500 such round barrows are known to have existed on the Wolds with many more having been destroyed. The main descriptive corpora remain the works of Mortimer (1905) and Greenwell (1877), augmented by a series of more recent excavations, particularly the large scale projects at Garton Slack (Brewster 1980), Wetwang Slack (Dent 1979, 1983) and Heslerton (Powelsland 1986). Several synthetic studies of various aspects of burial ritual have also been published including Brewster(1973), Peterson (1969, 1972) and Tuckwell (1975). The treatment of corpse and method of interment was variable. The modal form was of crouched inhumation, either lying on the old ground surface or in a grave. Graves might be shallow pit graves or deeper shaft graves, the grave beneath Rudston 62 reached down 10.5 ft beneath the old ground surface. Cremations are also attested, however, and burials might be multiple. Peterson (1972) noted that over 100 of the Wolds graves excavated by Mortimer and Greenwell contained two or more inhumation burials, in some cases apparently interred together but sometimes sequentially. Burials might also be inserted into a barrow mound. The mounds themselves could be of one or

more constructional phases, three discrete structural episodes were identified at Tallington in Lincolnshire (Simpson 1976). The outer rim of a mound was sometimes marked by one or more post rings, a circular kerb of stones or a ditch. Such features were usually buried by subsequent mound collapse or barrow enlargement. Pit graves were often lined as wooden cists or else inhumation might take place within a monoxylous coffin or on a wooden platform (Peterson 1969). Stone cists are known from two barrows: Rudston 62 and Driffield 138. About 30% of burials were provided with an accompanying pot, usually a Beaker or a Food Vessel but sometimes a Collared Urn; less than 15% were marked out by the inclusion of jewellery manufactured from jet or of bronze weapons or tools. Often burials were unaccompanied, or attracted only a simple flint knife or some flint flakes. The frequency of provision of organic grave goods of course remains unknowable.

Mortuary Ritual: Continuity or Discontinuity?

The archaeologically recoverable evidence of the Neolithic funerary rituals practised in the Yorkshire Wolds suggests a progression from multiple, unaccompanied, burial to single inhumation with grave goods. The transition occurred during the currency of Towthorpe Ware when single inhumations accompanied by Towthorpe Bowls and/ or large leaf-shaped flint arrowheads might be found under round barrows in juxtaposition with collective, albeit fully articulated, inhumations. This change seems to have been consolidated during the later Neolithic with an increasingly fine range of goods being included in burials. However, it is evident from the small number of burials recovered that only a small part of the population received formal burial under a barrow at any stage of the Neolithic. The mode of disposal used for the majority of the population remains obscure. There is evidence, for the earlier Neolithic at any rate, that cremation might have been a more widespread practice than the limited number of crematorium barrows would suggest. The remains of funerary pyres are sometimes found under barrows, for instance Seamer Moor, while at Garton Slack 37 and Raisthorpe long barrows, deep crematorium pits were discovered. Kinnes (1979: 59) has suggested that such sites may have been relatively common, but not surviving unless fortuitously covered by a mound.

During the final Neolithic, there may have occurred a drastic change in burial practices - as witnessed by the large cremation cemetery at Duggleby Howe. It is not known how best to interpret the Duggleby Howe cremation cemetery or even what significance it warrants. It seems most likely from its stratigraphy, and from other comparable examples, that the appearance of this cremation cemetery is a constituent event of a larger chronological horizon. The appearance of cremation cemeteries during the final Neolithic seems to have been a national phenomenon and has been well described by Kinnes (1979). Associations are rare; other than the polished bone skewer pins seen at Duggleby Howe there are only the two polished ovoid maceheads recovered from Stonehenge and Dorchester II, which seem to indicate that these cemeteries are facets of the Grooved Ware culture, or complex. In Yorkshire, this appears to represent a complete inversion of the late Neolithic burial ritual, from the practice of individual inhumation with prestigious grave goods for a select portion of the population to what seems to be cremation, largely unaccompanied, for the entire community. It would of necessity disrupt any tradition of single inhumation and contribute little to succeeding early Bronze Age ritual.

It might be argued that the discovery of the few known cremation cemeteries is fortuitous, that many more similar cemeteries have gone unrecognised because of the lack of grave goods and that, in fact, they would represent the missing majority of the late Neolithic population. If this is correct, and unaccompanied cremation burial was a rite of low status disposal, contemporary with, and complementary to, a smaller number of higher status inhumations then the physical separation of these two alternatives, the preponderance of cremations and the absence of any associations with the cremations would again mark them off from early Bronze Age examples, where cremations were often furnished with grave goods and intimately mixed with inhumations, Rudston 52 for example (Greenwell 1877: 234).

In reality, there is little real continuity in burial practices. No matter how the Duggleby Howe cremation cemetery, and related examples, are interpreted; they indicate that the predominant, if not universal, mortuary rite at the end of the Neolithic was unfurnished cremation. This was in marked contrast to the furnished inhumations of the succeeding early Bronze Age. It is true that, as argued by Burgess, many features of early Bronze Age ritual were already present during the later Neolithic. These include round barrows covering pits or cists and individual inhumations with provided grave goods - which included pots, tools and weapons. This formal similarity need not necessarily indicate that early Bronze Age practices were derived from a late Neolithic substrate, however. The same range of ritual features were to be found in the Standtvoetbeker and Bell Beaker culture graves of Holland, the likely point of origin for any putative "Beaker Folk".

Beaker Settlements

Settlement remains of late Neolithic and early Bronze Age Britain are notoriously fugitive. Most settlements seem to have consisted of a few insubstantial structures of indeterminate lifespan which have been obliterated by subsequent land use to produce numerous scatters or spreads of mixed occupational debris. There are few stratified deposits. Thus, apparently "domestic" Beaker pottery has been found in a number of contexts, including pits, hearths, occupation floors and pot boiling sites; but it is often mixed with indigenous ceramics: Peterborough, Grooved Ware or Food Vessel. (Bamford 1982, Gibson 1982). Such mixed scatters of occupation debris are open to interpretation in one of two ways. First, it might be argued that they are the cumulative residue of several, discrete, episodes of settlement by people with different cultural traditions, and as such represent a mixed deposit. Alternatively, they could be seen to result from a single period of occupation by a group whose ceramic repertoire was stylistically heterogeneous, with any apparent horizontal stratigraphy resulting from use foci rather than settlement drift. (Whittle 1981: 310). It is

sometimes possible to demonstrate in fact that assemblages do derive from separate occupation events (Bamford 1982:49), but in many cases the problem is beyond resolution. Nevertheless, Whittle (1981) and Bradley (1984) have argued that the second possibility is to be preferred, and to explain the simultaneous utilisation of two different stylistic groups of pottery within one settlement they have suggested that they may represent the visible residue of emulatory cycling, using Miller's (1985) model of ceramic emulation as a heuristic. There are problems with the emulation model, however, both in its general exposition and also in the specifics of its application to late Neolithic and early Bronze Age Britain.

Miller suggests that pottery is well suited to emulation because of the ease with which new forms can be created and changed (Miller 1985: 188); but surely the very mutability which renders pottery a suitable medium for emulation would also act to exclude its use from any field of status display. As already argued, ease of manufacture and general availability are not the usual attributes of status symbols and pottery would be an unlikely candidate to act as a manipulated token in emulatory cycles. Miller's examples of emulation involving the adoption and/or abandonment of metal ornaments and utensils are more convincing than his ceramic examples. In fact, he records (1985: 187) that in contemporary India most pottery forms do not show any association with differences in caste. Where they do, it is often due to factors external to the pot - the relative costs of the foodstuffs for which the pots are used to cook, for example. In at least one case direct coercion was needed to prevent low status castes using anything other than earthenware vessels (1985:188), but it is unlikely that coercion on a scale necessary to prevent ceramic innovation would be possible in the long term. Pottery is a democratic medium, at least in the absence of centralised craft groups or fineware industries. In the case of prehistoric Britain, it is difficult to imagine how, for example, a group of high status Beaker users could prevent all and sundry making Beakers if they so desired.

Even if ceramic emulation was an acceptable strategy of social competition then archaeologically, ceramic emulation would appear as an instantaneous phenomenon, not as a series of prolonged cycles operating over periods of time several centuries long. Nevertheless, despite these objections, the emulation model has been adopted as offering a possible explanation of the complicated patterning expressed in the ceramic assemblages of late Neolithic and early Bronze age Britain.

In arguing for a process of status linked emulation, Whittle (1981) has pointed out that there is an apparent diachronic trend to be seen expressed in the compositional variability of the ceramic assemblages recovered from "Beaker" settlement sites. There are very few "pure Beaker" sites known to date from before 2150 calBC, that is, sites which possess a ceramic assemblage composed exclusively of Beaker forms, both domestic and fineware. Early Beaker fineware forms are generally found in association with indigenous Neolithic types. The majority of settlement sites which are recognisably "pure Beaker" are associated with the later styles of Beaker fineware and probably date to after 2150 calBC. Whittle concluded that prior to this date, the

Beaker fineware found on sites of indigenous tradition would have possessed a specialised function, perhaps high status or ritual, and adopted for specialised use on account of its novelty and continental background (Whittle 1981: 320, 331). After 2150 calBC, however, domestic pottery increasingly took on the form of the previously high status Beaker fineware while new ceramic types were developed to replace Beakers in this role: Food Vessels and Collared Urns. Bradley (1984: 72) has proposed a similar argument and has summarised it diagrammatically (Figure 4.1).

In this emulatory model, then, Beaker settlements are not viewed as being the dwelling places of a distinct "Beaker Folk", instead they form a coherent sequence which demonstrates, in a settlement context, the gradual adoption and assimilation of Beaker pottery by an otherwise autochthonous population, and the subsequent evolution of early Bronze Age ceramic forms. But even if, for the sake of argument, this scheme of emulation and development is admitted acceptable within the sphere of ceramic production and use then there still remain difficulties in accommodating the British material to the given model. Admittedly, in comparison to its Peterborough and Grooved Ware predecessors, Beaker pottery is a superior product, but what of Food Vessels and Collared Urns? It is difficult, in general, to accept a Collared Urn or a Food Vessel as a finer pot than a Beaker and it is equally difficult, therefore, to understand why they should be adopted as a high status ceramic. It seems unlikely that the replacement of Beakers in grave assemblages by Food Vessels and Collared Urns would have been instigated by their overt superiority over Beakers in terms of quality.

Given the equivocal nature of the settlement evidence it is not possible to refute the emulatory model by demonstrating that all Beaker domestic sites, or all Peterborough sites, were in fact culturally homogeneous and that therefore mixed deposits are the detritus of multiple settlement episodes. (It is also the case that Beaker sherds are sometimes associated with earlier Neolithic pottery, at Swarkestone, for instance, and Craike Hill (Greenfield 1960: 23, Manby 1958: 233). This is never taken to indicate contemporaneity, however, and is a timely reminder that data interpretation is indeed subjective, and one which

should give pause for thought). The emulation model is open to test, however, if, in effect, the problem of site definition is turned on its head.

As it stands, Bradley's diagram of the ceramic replacements involved in an emulation cycle might be oversimplified as it does not take into account the continuing developmental sequence of Peterborough Ware. It is now generally accepted that both vase-type Food Vessels and Collared Urns were, in the main, continuations of the Peterborough tradition; the Food Vessels developing out of the northern Meldon Bridge and Rudston sub-styles while Collared Urns were descended from the more southerly Fengate types (Smith 1973: 112; Burgess 1980: 85; Longworth 1984: 19). This suggests that Bradley's diagram should be modified to show continuity between Peterborough Ware and Collared Urns/Food Vessels. So, if all pot types were in simultaneous usage on domestic sites, it follows that subsequent to the introduction of Beakers the ceramic assemblages of all settlement sites should possess both a Beaker component and a Peterborough/Food Vessel/Urn component. It is not possible that there could be a period of time when assemblages were "pure Beaker" as it would imply the chronological severance of the Peterborough tradition and require that Food Vessels and Collared Urns be derived from a "pure Beaker" substrate. Alternatively, the demonstration of "pure Beaker" sites could be accepted if there were also "pure" sites of the Peterborough tradition providing a conduit for the continuing development of early Bronze Age ceramic types. This would in effect demonstrate the existence of two contemporary and mutually exclusive ceramic traditions. Their exclusivity would also imply that there were good reasons for visibly demarcating social or ethnic group membership, perhaps reasons of economic competition (Barth 1969, Hodder 1982). This seems particularly pertinent given the apparent similarities in the locational positioning of late Neolithic and early Bronze Age settlements.

It is, of course, generally accepted that there were "pure Beaker" settlements, if only during the late phases of the culture. (Whittle 1981, Gibson 1982). Sites such as Ross Links, Northton, Hockwold and Martlesham have been well

Figure 4.1.   Ceramic Emulation

(After Bradley 1984: 72)

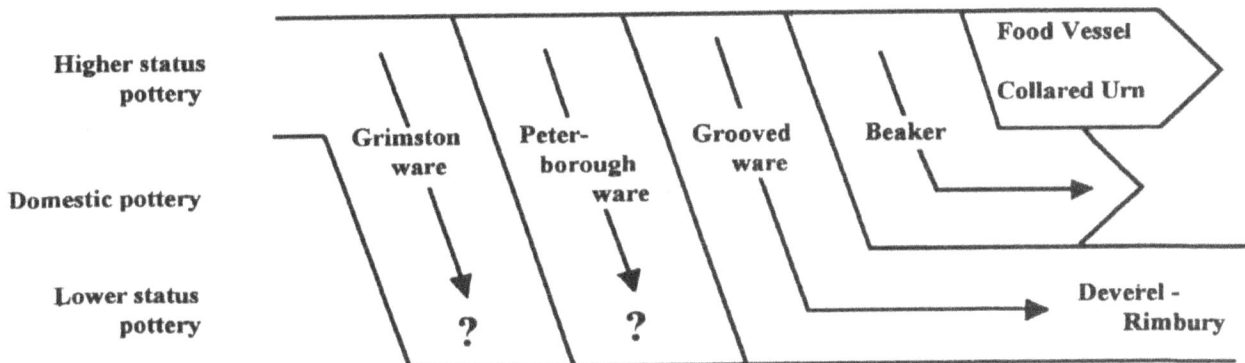

25

described and require no further elaboration here. It is significant that they are often sand-dune sites where rapid burial has successfully isolated a single settlement phase and preserved it relatively intact. It is not just Beaker settlements that have been preserved under sand-dunes, however, in recent years two Food Vessel sites have been excavated on the Isle of Islay: Kilellan Farm and Ardnave.

At Kilellan Farm midden, the bulk of the early Bronze Age pottery recovered consisted of large shouldered jars, probably round based, the majority plain but some decorated. These shouldered jars were in association with a Food Vessel assemblage which included an Irish Bowl, vase-type Food Vessels and some very large Encrusted Urns. Both the Food Vessels and shouldered jars were composed of similar fabric, but also present were some sherds of a superior fabric and decorated with cord, comb or groove ornament. The excavator claimed that these sherds were Beaker, although conceded that they were hardly typical (Burgess 1976: 200). Beaker or not, the relative proportions of material are not in accord with the emulation model. This would predict that during the currency of Food Vessels, Beakers were a lower status ware. At Kilellan Farm, therefore, the expectation would be that the midden would have contained largely Beaker domestic forms with an occasional piece of decorated Food Vessel. This was not the case. At Ardnave, a ceramic assemblage was recovered from a collapsed stone structure containing multiple occupation levels with a covering midden, it differed from that found at Kilellan Farm in that it was "pure Food Vessel". With the possible exception of a single rim sherd, the shouldered jar assemblage of Kilellan was not represented and there was not a Beaker in sight (Ritchie & Welfare 1983).

It seems, then, that any explanation of the Neolithic - early Bronze Age ceramic succession which is predicated upon a continuing process of emulation is theoretically dubious, and can derive little support from what unequivocal settlement evidence is available. The existence of "pure" Beaker and Food Vessel settlement sites indicates that the different types of late Neolithic and early Bronze Age ceramics do not constitute a cycle of style emulation; but, to some extent at least, must represent separate traditions. It seems most likely that any settlement assemblages which include sherds from different ceramic traditions should be considered as evidence for several, discrete, episodes of occupation. The diversity seen to exist within the overall ceramic repertoire of late Neolithic/early Bronze Age Britain is surely the product of several, sometimes unrelated, social processes, of which an influx of settlers from continental Europe carrying with them Beaker pottery may well have been one.

Conclusion

In this chapter it has been demonstrated that a ritual discontinuity can be seen to exist between the single inhumation burials of the late Neolithic and their early Bronze Age counterparts. They are separated by the Grooved Ware related cemeteries of unfurnished cremations, a national phenomenon exemplified in the area under study by Duggleby Howe. The interpretation of the final Neolithic cremation horizon is at present uncertain, and its significance not known. There is little evidence of continuity between Neolithic and Bronze age funerary ritual, however, and it is mistaken for Burgess to claim that the appearance of the continental, Beaker, burial tradition affected indigenous rituals "... only superficially". The question of Beaker settlements was also discussed and it was pointed out that, logically, they must have existed independently of, but have been contemporary with, indigenous settlements.

Chapter Five

THE BEAKER FOLK?

"God gave to every people a cup, a cup of clay, and from this cup they drank their life...
They all dipped in the water, but their cups were different."
(Ramon, quoted in Benedict 1935: 15).

Introduction

The theoretical basis of the Beaker diffusion hypothesis - that Beaker ceramics were desirable on account of their intrinsic value - has been refuted. Furthermore, empirically, the archaeological data do not support the case for cultural continuity through the Neolithic-Bronze Age transition. The suggested schemes of ceramic emulation, to explain the existence of Beaker settlements, and of continuous stylistic evolution of late Neolithic/Beaker pottery, to explain the ceramic diversity of the early Bronze Age, are incompatible. In eastern Yorkshire there appears to be a disjunction in burial ritual. In this chapter, therefore, the value of a migration model for explaining Beaker culture spread will be reassessed, and the possibilities of the cultural consequences of ethnic intermixing will be considered.

Migrations

The desirability of identifying archaeological indicators of prehistoric migrations was emphasised in Chapter Two, and the relative paucity of such identifications noted. Over the last two decades the consequences of random, short-distance, population movements following on from settlement fission have been considered, and the "wave of advance" model has been constructed to explain the initial spread of agricultural communities through Europe (Ammerman & Cavalli-Sforza 1979). However, the phenomenon of long-distance migration - a phenomenon of intentional, goal-directed behaviour - has been largely overlooked. Nevertheless, long distance migrations have been well described in both contemporary and historic societies, and their character, or structure, is well understood. There seems no reason to doubt that similar migrations would have occurred in prehistory (Anthony 1990: 898).

The "laws" of migration were first promulgated by Ravenstein in 1885 and provided the foundations for the construction of a generalised model of long-distance migration by Lee (1966). Structurally, Lee's model consists of three components: an area of origin, an area of destination and a variable set of intervening obstacles. The area of origin is the initial place of residence of a potential migrant or migratory group. A number of factors are operative at this location in both encouraging and discouraging migration, those which favour migration are termed "push" factors. Similarly a potential area of destination can be described by reference to a corresponding set of factors, those favouring immigration and settlement being termed "pull" factors. Separating the two areas it is envisaged that there is a set of obstacles that will act to discourage migration to a greater or lesser extent.

In industrial, and industrialising, societies with a well developed communications network information about the desirability and accessibility of potential migratory destinations is readily available. "Pull" factors are considered to play the major role in any decision making process that may take place prior to migration. It is unlikely that this would have been the case in prehistoric societies however. Knowledge of the opportunities available for settlement at distant locations would have been limited and the nature or severity of any intervening obstacles ill-defined; "push" factors present in the home environment would have been of most significance for prehistoric groups. The nature of ethnographically described "push" factors varies and they are not altogether rational - it is the potential migrants perception of the balance existing between the hazards and advantages of relocation which is realised during the decision making process, not necessarily an objective reality. Factors which influence the decision may be acute or chronic, social or personal, economic or ideological. The classic causes of migration are war and famine and need no further elaboration here. Less spectacular events may also be important in triggering migrations, however, and perhaps more frequent in occurrence (Boardman 1980: 162; Kopytoff 1987: 18ff; Mabogunje 1970: 5ff; Wolf 1982: 98). Quarrels within or between kin groups, perhaps expressed as witchcraft accusations or outright violence, can result in the ejection or departure of segments of population; as can struggles over the succession to political power. More chronic causes of emigration include impartible modes of inheritance that stress primogeniture and which encourage a constant outward movement of "younger sons" to acquire land and status of their own. This might find expression as kin-linked aristocracies spreading out and imposing themselves upon, or being accepted by, subject populations. Conversely, people might wish to escape overly repressive political regimes. Of course, migrations need not be monocausal. Anthony (1990: 898) has recently drawn attention to the Helvetic migration of 58 BC described by Julius Caesar, and which was apparently motivated by both ideological and economic "push" factors. Their territory was not large enough to adequately support their population and it was too remote for them to effectively engage in combat with their neighbours, combat which was considered necessary to enhance their martial reputation.

When, for whatever reasons, the "push" factors at an area of settlement begin to predominate there begins an attempt to explore surrounding, and more distant, regions for possible new areas of settlement. The nature, or severity, of intervening obstacles are evaluated. As is the case with "push" factors, the nature of intervening obstacles is not absolute, but is a subjective assessment. The sea may present an impassable barrier to one society while being considered an open highway by another. Obstacles also need not be physical. A strong, centralised, polity is able to offer more resistance to an unwanted stream of migrants passing through its territory than are less organised, acephalous, social groupings. Much of this exploration, or information gathering, might be secondary to other activities. Thus normal itinerant activities such as raiding or trading will intensify prior to the onset of a migration. The first Greeks to penetrate the Tyrrhenian Sea during the course of the 8th century BC were intent upon trade and their first settlements were also so concerned. It was not until the final third of the century that the productive agricultural lands of southern Italy and Sicily were permanently settled and Magna Graecia established (Coldstream 1977: 221). Migrants do not usually move into unpopulated areas; favourable destinations identified ethnographically in Africa are those of low to moderate population density which offer the physical, and perhaps more importantly, the political space for an immigrant group to establish itself and expand (Kopytoff 1987: 32).

Thus, the choice of destination area is constrained by three factors:

1) Availability of information about accessibility and suitability of potential destinations.
2) Accessibility of potential destinations.
3) Suitability of accessible destinations.

These factors act to prevent any "wave of advance" type migration, with population slowly spreading through all land available behind an expanding frontier. Instead, destinations are discrete areas and are often physically separated by a set of natural or human obstacles. Selective and directional migrations between such discrete areas are not likely to be expressed as a single event but instead will constitute a dynamic process through space and time as migrants continually reassess their opportunities. This process of long-distance, goal oriented migration between discrete locations has been termed "leapfrogging", a term which accords well with Champion's (1980: 37) description of the Celtic movement from central Europe to Asia Minor:

"What we know now as the single phenomenon of Celtic migration eastwards was more properly a spasmodic series of short migrations, each determined by opportunities of raiding or settlement as and when they chanced to occur".

Once a route between locations is established by traders or by precocious migrants then it tends both to encourage and to channel the movement of later migrants as, in effect, their knowledge of the route's existence lessens their fear of the unknown intervening obstacles. The directional or channelled movement of migrants along such a route is termed a migratory stream. There are several important consequences of migratory streams (Lee 1966). The magnitude of migrant flow in such a stream will depend upon the relative desirabilities of the home and destination areas and also upon the ease of passage. Streams might be small or alternatively they might run to completion with apparent abandonment of the area of origin. Another feature of a migration stream that is not running to completion is that there is a tendency for a counterstream of returning migrants to develop. This might be because a more direct acquaintance with an area of destination causes a re-evaluation of the relative desirability of the home location, or perhaps because of amelioration of some of the "push" factors initially operating in the area of origin. In any event, not all migrants intend permanent resettlement - some merely want to "make good" before returning home. A counterstream will carry back with it new ideas and perhaps novel innovations acquired from societies and environments outside the immediate area of contact of the home community. Migratory streams and counterstreams thus have the potential to act as vectors for the diffusion of information.

Upon arrival at a destination the immediate strategy of an immigrant group is to consolidate its position and to guarantee its security, either by increasing in numbers or by achieving political dominance over their indigenous neighbours. Relations with the home community may be exploited in an attempt to persuade more people, usually kin, to migrate by stressing the (real or imagined) advantages of the new residential location. This strategy would help to prolong the flow of a migration stream. Alternatively, or additionally, the indigenes can be incorporated into immigrant society by constructing fictitious genealogies and creating blood links through intermarriage. Political dominance might be achieved by the straightforward application of military force but more often by negotiation or manipulation. Foreigners are often perceived by preliterate societies to be in possession of extraordinary abilities or magical powers, perhaps because of a conceptual conflation of geographical with supernatural distance (Helms 1988: 4). This supernatural distance may be converted to actual political distance as incomers advertise their access to esoteric knowledge as a demonstration of their superiority and fitness to rule. It might even be that the political system introduced by the immigrants is perceived to be superior by the native inhabitants of an area who therefore acquiesce in its extension. In Russia for instance, according to later traditions the quarrelling Slav inhabitants of 9th century AD Novgorod invited a Norman prince and his followers to rule over them (Yanin 1990). In sub-Saharan Africa the Alur were often requested to furnish their neighbours with the sons of chiefs (Kopytoff 1987: 65). On the other hand, of course, immigrant enclaves might be tolerated or absorbed by a host society.

Not all migrants settle down however. Once home ties have been broken then the threshold at which "push" factors might begin to take effect is lowered, while at the same time accumulated experience allows a more informed assessment of the potential hazards and benefits of further relocation. Ethnographic studies suggest that there is an inverse correlation between the time settled in one location and the likelihood of migration. Anthony (1990: 905) has suggested that some migrant communities may develop a self-propagating dynamic of repeated migrations and that the emergence of such communities might explain the "flurries of migratory activity" which seem sometimes to be attested archaeologically.

The demographic consequences of even a moderate flow of migrants might be severe. repeated studies have demonstrated that young adults show the greatest propensity to migrate (Lewis 1982: 83), and also that migration acts as a kind of "selective filter" in that less physically fit individuals are not likely to attempt or to survive the migration process (Livi-Bacci 1992: 58). Thus, over a period of time the simple quantitative effects of a physical transfer of population are compounded by the differential fertility of the home and emigrant groups. The decrease in numbers of the home population which results from emigration might be associated with a further chronic decline if the birth rate of an ageing population falls below the death rate and thus population replacement fails to occur. In contrast, the birth rate of an initial immigrant community will exceed its death rate so that there will be a sharp population increase manifest over initial generations. In frontier societies this initial baby boom has often been sustained further by the relatively increased fertility of subsequent generations (Easterlin 1976, Livi-Bacci 1992: 59). Why this should be is not altogether clear. One suggestion is that child labour is of greater value in frontier communities where reciprocal work arrangements between kin or neighbours remain under-developed (Bogue 1976). Nevertheless, whatever the reasons, it is significant that the demographic success of an immigrant group might also be regarded as a sign of supernatural favour and, again, encourage the native inhabitants of an area to adopt the incomers' ethnicity. In subsequent generations this might serve to establish a tradition whereby the immigrant society expects to expand while its neighbours become demoralised and expect ultimately to be absorbed (Ehret 1988:570).

After surveying proto-historical migrations in temperate Europe Champion concluded that it was unlikely that they had been preceded by many earlier occurrences. He gave reasons for his conclusion:

1) Technology: the development of light, spoke-wheeled carts during the first millennium BC facilitated the large scale movement of families and belongings.

2) Economic stimulus: probably did not exist before this time as, essentially, regional populations would not have outgrown their local subsistence base.

3) Social organisation: the logistical organisation of a migration that required the movement of hundreds of thousands of people would require the intervention of a well organised central authority - on the scale of a developed chiefdom/early state.

The development of effective wheeled transport may have facilitated the kind of mass movement of peoples described in Champion's sources but in the Beaker case the riverine or maritime distribution of much of the culture might point to waterborne rather than landborne transport. The second point is arguable and in any case a subsistence shortfall is not the only stimulus for a migration, as already pointed out. The final point might again be true of the type of migrations that Champion describes, which have more the character of wholesale invasion than do many ethnographically described migrations, when only part of a community emigrates and part stays at home. Here the effective decision making unit is the household or the individual. Emigration of family members from a household is viewed as one method of ensuring the reproduction of the household through time, heads of households generally stay put and only younger males and females migrate - those with a more marginal economic role (Goldschneider 1984: 294) The decision to migrate in these circumstances might be seen as a trade-off between labour requirements and resource availability (Mazeir 1984: 219) although in reality things are probably not so simple. In the Béarn region of France, during the 20th century, many younger sons found themselves faced with the stark alternatives of celibacy at home or emigration (Bourdieu 1990: 158), thus the choice here was for the individual to make and involved more than simple economic considerations. Back in the Iron Age democracy might even take a hand, as in the 7th century BC when Therans drew lots to decide who should leave the island for Libya in order to relieve a subsistence crisis at home.

A Migratory "Beaker Folk"?

If the Beaker phenomenon were to be recast in such a modified migratory mould how would it appear?

It has been suggested that the beginning of a migration will be marked by a flurry of "scouting", an intensification of contact activities during which information about possible routes and destinations might be collected. This is precisely the pattern of activity noticed during the earliest Beaker phase in Britain by both Case (1977: 74) and Lewthwaite

(1987: 48). While Case was content in suggesting that the early scatter of AOC finds, and their coastal locations, were probably the residue of trade, Lewthwaite was more specific in suggesting that it represented a "familiarisation phase", during which time the potential of Britain for settlement was evaluated and the techniques and technologies of maritime travel perfected.

A prolonged period of Beaker migration, taking place by processes of streaming and leapfrogging as outlined earlier, would be expected to give rise to the discontinuous and nodal pattern of Beaker settlement familiar from many a distribution map. The initial expansion during the currency of AOC and early decorated forms would have been a dynamic period of population movement and countermovement but with an overall expansionary trend. Innovations would be taken up in frontier areas and rapidly disseminated throughout the expanding network of migratory groups. This would account for the apparent diffusion westward of the eastern elements of the Beaker assemblage at a time post-dating the initial ceramic spread. It would also suggest that the possible origins of the maritime Beakers should be reconsidered. Although it is evident that AOC Beakers developed within the Corded Ware matrix of north western Europe, it is by no means clear that this area was the focus of a complete unilinear sequence of typological development. There are in fact few maritime Beakers known from this area and they have not been found in association with AOC types (van der Waals 1984: 5). The technique of comb impressing which allowed the evolution of complex design structures may have been adopted anywhere in the area of initial AOC spread, perhaps southern France, and might have allowed the ceramic expression of a pattern repertoire in prior use on less permanent media.

The greater fecundity of immigrants suggests that over a century or two their numbers, and thus settlement density, should increase at a greater rate than that of the indigenous inhabitants. Again this expectation is met in Britain where Whittle (1981: 314) has argued that apparently "pure" Beaker settlements, that is settlements with both Beaker fineware and identifiable Beaker coarseware, seem to be a relatively late phenomenon, becoming common only after 2150 cal BC.

The exotic origins of Beaker immigrants, their continuing contacts with the European mainland and their fecundity may well have allowed them to overawe the indigenes, particularly after the appearance of the first copper items. Copper contained the fire of the sun and the significance of this was that both the sun and the "Beaker Folk" came from the east, a significance not likely to be overlooked. This supernatural conjunction may have been sufficient to cause the collapse of pre-existent belief systems, and thus political systems, and allowed the establishment of a new, Beaker-related, hierarchy.

At the supra-regional level, then, several features of the Beaker culture may be explained by a model of long-distance migration. It would be encouraging if more support for this model was forthcoming at the regional, or intra-regional, level. Two aspects in particular suggest themselves: the tendency of migrants to establish themselves in political interstices and the possible impact of immigration on the demographic profile of a region. The two most intensively researched areas of late Neolithic/early Bronze Age Britain - Wessex and Orkney - do seem to provide some evidence of these processes.

In the area of Stonehenge, a project of surface survey has provided a wealth of environmental and settlement data which complements the known archaeology of the monumental remains (Richards 1984). It seems that during the later Neolithic, a zone of intense, Grooved Ware related, domestic and ritual activity was bounded by the Avon Valley to the east and Stonehenge Bottom to the west, with the henge of Durrington Walls acentrically located at its eastern margin (Figure 5.1). Stonehenge itself was at this time lying abandoned, and probably overgrown; but there was some evidence of domestic activity to the west, perhaps associated with the exploitation of flint around Wilsford Down. The appearance of Beaker assemblages in the area, however, was associated with major alterations in the social organisation of the landscape. After about 2250 calBC Durrington Walls was abandoned and the entire "Durrington zone" of ritual/ domestic activity seems subsequently to have been ignored by Beaker users. Stonehenge was refurbished and work commenced upon a series of architectural elaborations. Although the area around Stonehenge itself seems to have been empty of settlement, perhaps being devoted to ritual usage, there are surface indications of Beaker activity in the western half of the study area, from Robin Hood's Ball south to Wilsford Down. This westerly zone was associated with arable farming which may have intensified during the early Bronze Age. If it is permissible to regard the late Neolithic "Durrington zone" as constituting some sort of a political centre, it is noticeable that Beaker settlement occurred outside of this area, and seems eventually to have led to its eclipse. Evidence of a similar process, albeit on a larger scale, is to be found at the northern extremity of Britain - the Orkney Islands and adjacent parts of the mainland.

Again, during the late Neolithic, the Orkney Islands were a major focus of Grooved Ware settlement and ritual (Childe 1947: 84-90, Clarke et al 1986: 92), another political centre perhaps. However, the islands are virtually devoid of Beaker finds - only three Beakers are known and there is virtually no Beaker-related metalwork (Clarke et al 1985: 92). The situation in Orkney is in marked contrast to the adjoining areas of the mainland - the northern part of the highland region - where there is a dearth of Grooved Ware but a significant Beaker presence (Mercer 1982: 259). It has been suggested that:

"Beakers caused a disjuncture in the networks on which the Orkney leaders relied. In these circumstances the power structure merely atrophied with the result that for most of the 2nd millennium there is nothing except the rich grave group from Knowes of Trotty to suggest that Orkney formed part of any wider network."

(Clarke et al 1985: 92).

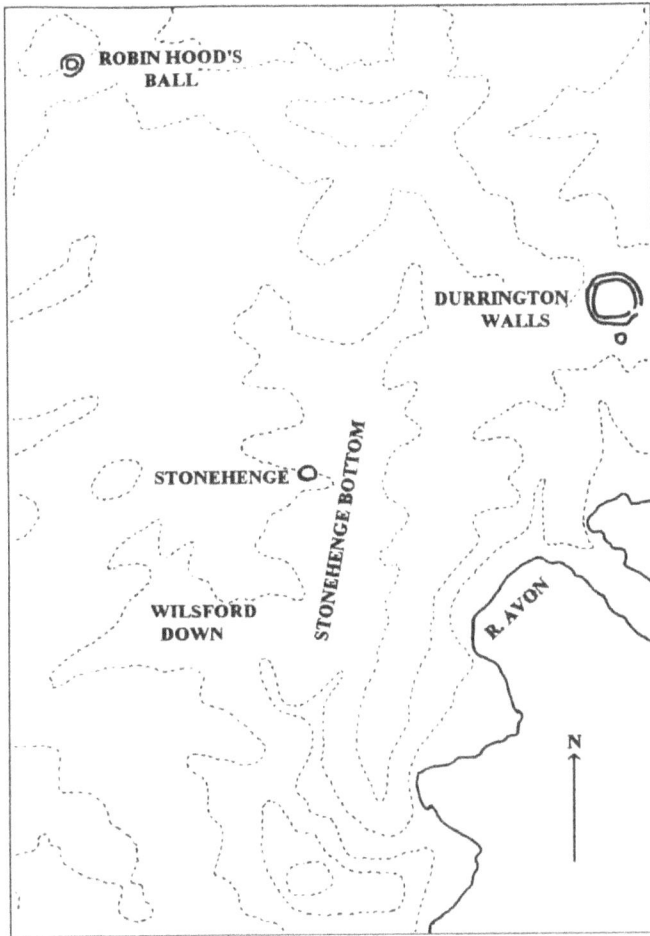

Figure 5.1. Stonehenge environs.

(After Richards 1984).

Bradley (1984: 59) has noted that most areas of Grooved Ware activity, which he termed "core areas", are linked by the sea, and suggested that the sea may have provided an avenue of contact. If this was indeed the case then the choice of the word atrophy in the above quotation may be apt, if an influx of maritime Beaker Folk was responsible for the disruption of whatever constituted the Grooved Ware network.

At the regional level, therefore, there is some suggestion of immigration into what seem to have been "politically peripheral" areas. In Wessex, furthermore, there is also some evidence, tenuous perhaps, of a Beaker-associated population increase. A significant input of high fertility migrants into a region would be expected to cause an appreciable rise in population, but the archaeological detection of such a rise remains problematical. Current methods of demographic reconstruction are not sufficiently precise for such a purpose. Intensive or extensive surface survey may suggest patterns of settlement or land-use, but can do little more. They provide no information about settlement size or duration. It is not possible therefore to arrive at comparative population estimates based upon fluctuations of settlement numbers, or density. The reconstruction of population size from burials is also a hazardous procedure. There are, however, several mutually corroborating lines of evidence currently available which point to a major change in patterns of land-use which are associated with the arrival of the Beaker culture, a change which might be suggestive of population increase.

Palynological and malacological studies of late Neolithic environments have been consistent in indicating the presence of secondary woodland, or scrub (Evans 1990; Thomas 1982; Smith 1984). Pigs, better adapted to woodland than cattle, become the predominant domestic animal on Grooved Ware sites (Grigson 1982). Similarly, woodland food plants are strongly represented in Grooved Ware contexts (Jones 1980), as are the skeletal remains of wild game (Richards & Thomas 1984: 207). Indeed, it has been suggested that the characteristic transverse arrowhead of the late Neolithic is ideally suited to hunting in wooded environments (Evans 1975: 122). This is not to suggest that the Grooved Ware users of late Neolithic Britain constituted some sort of relict population of Mesolithic hunter-gatherers - the agricultural component of their subsistence base has been well documented (Jones 1980). The diversity of food resources exploited does, however, point to an extensive, rather than intensive, system of exploitation.

This coherent picture of late Neolithic environment and subsistence does not survive the introduction of the Beaker culture, however. The percentage of wild animals in faunal assemblages falls, dramatically at Mount Pleasant where there is a stratified sequence (Richards & Thomas 1984: 207); the pig also appears to lose its place as the predominant domesticate (Grigson 1982: 307). The transverse arrowhead is not, of course, a component of Beaker flint assemblages. These different patterns of faunal exploitation and management are associated with extensive woodland clearance and an increase in importance of arable cultivation establishing a mode of subsistence that was to persist throughout the Bronze Age (Evans 1990; Thomas 1982).

The replacement of a heterogeneous and extensive system of land-use by a more homogeneous and intensive system would be a natural concomitant of rising levels of population, secondary to immigration.

As a final point, it is worth considering the maritime technology available to a nautical "Beaker Folk". For reasons of seaworthiness and limited technology it seems likely that any late Neolithic/early Bronze Age sailors who were bold enough to venture out onto the stormy waters of the Atlantic would have done so in skin boats. (Johnstone 1980: 27,112). Large boats of this type are thought to be represented by Scandinavian rock carvings of the early Bronze Age. They are depicted with quite large crews, that of the Bjornstadt example in Norway apparently consisting of 48 members. Such boats would have been capable of transporting migrants and their livestock over quite long distances, although no doubt the seasonal constraints on travel discussed by Case (1969) for early Neolithic migrants still applied. If the "Beaker Folk" were manufacturing such large boats it would perhaps explain why leatherworking was regarded as an occupation of sufficient prestige so as to warrant distinctive burial, such as that at Amesbury 51 (Ashbee: 1978b).

Ethnic Intermixing and Ceramic Style

Although the generalised model of long-distance migration successfully explains several aspects of the Beaker culture, its theory remains underdeveloped in a number of critical areas. In particular, it fails to provide a comprehensive account of the number and variety of possible accommodations that might occur between immigrant and indigenous communities when they become interspersed in a region. If they are in direct competition over resources however then a number of stable outcomes seem possible (Barth 1969: 19ff), which are enumerated below:

1) The interspersed groups might polarise into territorial entities but remain in open competition for resources. Such an outcome would be expected to result in the continuing high profile maintenance of ethnic boundaries, expressed spatially, and should be simple to detect archaeologically.

2) An accommodation might develop between the groups which would involve each in the exploitation of separate ecological niches and the development of a symbiotic relationship, such as those that exist between pastoralists and sedentary cultivators. Ethnic identities might persist but not in so marked a fashion, archaeological identification might be more problematic.

3) A stratified polyethnic, system might separate out with the individual ethnic groups accepting, willingly or unwillingly, unequal access to the resource base. The cultural differences of ethnicity would ultimately resolve themselves into a complex of status diacritica.

4) One group might displace another physically, leading to emigration of the competing group. Again this should be

simple to detect archaeologically and, indeed, is the pattern envisaged in much of the early, "migrationist", literature.

5) Most interestingly perhaps, and certainly the most complex from an archaeological point of view, would be the symbolic displacement of one group by the other. The indigenous inhabitants would remain in the region but be absorbed into the opposing ethnic group by mechanisms of boundary crossing as outlined in Chapter Two. The problem here is that, as competition is resolved, the need to clearly demarcate ethnic identity diminishes and therefore absorbed groups would be able to keep many of their ancestral customs or passive cultural traits, providing the ethnically active traits of the absorbing group were adopted. It has been shown in many apparently unified African societies, for instance, that although societal history is fabricated in order to normalise its internal relationships the histories of individual kin groups are divergent as they were incorporated into the society at different times. These groups often retain some of their ancestral practices, including burial customs, which contribute to a cultural diversity that is difficult to explain in other than historical terms (Kopytoff 1987: 5). Material culture might be likewise variegated, with similar diverse origins. Orme (1981: 203), for instance, described the material culture of the Azande as constituting a patchwork of different types acquired from conquered and assimilated, or partly assimilated, peoples.

It appears, therefore, that there are a number of cultural outcomes that may occur in response to ethnic intermixing, the third and the fifth of the alternatives outlined above seem particularly apposite for the explanation of the cultural variability exhibited by Beaker assemblages. This variability would have arisen out of the incorporation of local populations by incoming Beaker groups, initially perhaps by political coercion or accommodation with later consolidation by intermarriage. The differential contributions made by local traditions to the geographically expanding Beaker culture would account for its increasing regional diversity through time. The absolute numbers of "Beaker Folk" needed to effect a cultural transformation would not have needed to be great. Adams (1968: 210) has graphically described how a steady drip of Moslem pastoralists into Christian Nubia radically changed the culture of the region despite a large measure of population continuity. Such processes of ethnic integration would of course render questions of race unrealistic as Childe foresaw. The "Beaker Folk" ultimately would have been a biological amalgam whose origins would wait to be discovered in many corners of western and central Europe.

When it comes to considering the archaeological correlates of the above alternatives the obvious conclusion can be drawn that more attention should be paid to the full cultural assemblages of the period under question and particularly the settlement evidence. But such a conclusion is unhelpful, the present explanatory impasse is in many ways a direct result of the very lack of such evidence. It is to be hoped that this unfortunate circumstance will be progressively rectified but in the meantime other approaches are necessary. In Chapter Two it was suggested that artefacts of household manufacture might be ethnically more significant than those of specialist manufacture while in Chapter Three it was argued that Beaker pottery was probably a household, not a specialist, product. The role of ceramic style in both within and between group symbolising and the mechanisms of its stylistic transfer between populations might, then, seem to be fruitful fields for consideration. The social significance of ceramic style and its role in ethnic demarcation have been widely discussed (reviewed in Rice 1987: 244) and it seems possible to partition ceramic style into the active and passive categories (Sackett 1986,1990) discussed in Chapter Two, while bearing in mind that these categories are not fully distinct. The decoration of a pot is generally considered to be a manifestation of active style, while its technological and functional characteristics are more usually thought of as being passively produced.

Decoration may be used actively to transmit information, it may act as a medium of communication, but its interpretation is far from straightforward. It may indeed function as a device of group demarcation, and the groups might be ethnic (Ehret 1988: 571), although this need not necessarily be so (Rice 1987: 267). Decoration may also sometimes have a magico-religious aspect and be designed to communicate with ancestors, or the gods (Sterner 1989: 458); or else act as a protection against evil spirits or pollution (Donley-Reid 1990). The precise choice of message to be conveyed by ceramic decoration, or indeed by any items of material culture, is arrived at by social consensus and the underlying logic of such choices remains unknown (Lemonnier 1986: 179), if not unknowable. Decoration may also function passively, however. To an outside observer the meaning of a design might be unknown but its manner of execution may be distinctive, and recognisably ethnic.

From an archaeological perspective there are further problems with any attempt at translating, or interpreting, actively produced ceramic decoration. On account of its symbolic content, decoration is unstable through time and reflects shifting social relations. Furthermore, decoration is context dependent and its degree of elaboration may be a function of the visibility of the pot and the intensity of social interaction (Braun 1991). Decoration is also sensitive to any changes in the magico-religious beliefs of a society that may take place. The decoration of Beaker pots is assumed to have changed quite radically through time, and is indeed one of the mainstays of typologically based chronologies. The decoration of an AOC Beaker is far removed from that of a Clarke S4. The defining feature of a Beaker pot is its shape, or form, not its decoration.

Mention of vessel form moves the discussion on to a consideration of passive style. In a ceramic context passive style is thought to be more stable than active, and therefore of more use to the archaeologist as an indicator of group identity. Passive style is encapsulated by vessel form, it is a reflection of the method of its manufacture and the manner of its usage. It is manifest particularly in the more utilitarian types of pottery: cooking and storage vessels. There are three clusters of factors which together act to render the form of these vessels resistant to any processes of rapid change (Rice 1897: 460). These clusters are technological, dietary and physiological.

Potters resist changing their technology or methods of manufacture as any such changes represent a risk (Rice 1987: 462). Tried and tested manufacturing techniques are trusted, and the properties of established clays and tempering agents understood. Alterations in methods or materials may have unforeseen consequences, and experimentation be considered an unnecessary luxury. Diet also acts to stabilise vessel forms through time (Rice 1987: 462). Methods of food preparation or serving, together with flavour preferences, may be socially ingrained and again will act to discourage experimentation with new forms or fabrics.

Physiological resistance to change is engendered by motor habit patterns. These are unconscious behavioural regularities which are caused by differential muscle development, which is itself a consequence of the prolonged and habitual repetition of a set sequence of physical actions. Any change in this sequence which requires a different arrangement of muscular co-ordination is difficult, or uncomfortable (Arnold 1985: 205, 233-6; Rice 1987: 462). The stabilising influence that motor habit patterns exert on vessel form can be viewed from two perspectives: from that of the user and that of the maker. The manufacture of a pot requires a co-ordinated set of movements learned and practised over a long period of time. Any novel set which interrupted established motor habit patterns, thereby proving difficult or awkward to perform, would be resisted. From the point of view of the user, a familiar form is preferred for ease of handling. This is particularly the case with large jars which are unwieldy and difficult to manoeuvre or carry; one pattern of handling in a society is usual and the form of the jar reflects this.

Thus it seems that the form of utilitarian ceramic types, their passive style, is conservative and may therefore be a more reliable indicator of ethnicity than their decoration. This is, of course, an archaeological commonplace. It has long been known that domestic wares, are more reliable in this respect. It also seems, somewhat discouragingly, to lead back to a "pots = people" equation; although this equation may be more valid than is generally accepted provided that it can be shown that the pots are of household manufacture and that due allowance is made for the diffusion of novel technologies (Ehret 1988: 572).

In the light of these discussions of ethnic intermixing and of ceramic style more information may be derived from the settlement evidence, originally discussed in Chapter Three. There, the mixed nature of many settlement deposits was described - how Beakers are often found together with ceramics of indigenous type. Two possible explanations were proposed:

1) That the deposits might be the cumulative residue of several, discrete, episodes of settlement by people with different cultural traditions and as such represent a mixed deposit.

2) That the deposits might result from a single period of occupation by a group whose ceramic repertoire was stylistically heterogeneous, with any horizontal stratigraphy resulting from use foci rather than settlement drift.

The first of these settlement alternatives was the one preferred in Chapter Four, and is simply explained in ethnic terms as it would envisage the co-existence of indigenous and Beaker communities, each producing their own distinctive vessel forms. Eventually, ethnic integration and intermarriage would produce a fusion of ceramic types, with vessel forms of mixed ancestry emerging in the early Bronze Age. If the eventual forms of Food Vessels and Urns owed more to late Neolithic pottery than to Beakers, it might suggest a large degree of population continuity.

However, it was also noted in Chapter Four that the second of these two alternatives is the one preferred by proponents of Beaker diffusion, and that the model of ceramic emulation has been utilised for its explanation. Against this, it was pointed out that emulatory cycling failed to reconcile the existence of "pure" Beaker settlements with apparent continuity of indigenous ceramic traditions. The model of ceramic emulation is also, in this British case, in direct contradiction of an expectation generated by the above discussion of passive style - that change through time in the forms of ceramic vessels will be slow and gradual. If Beaker pottery formed a discrete stage in a unilinear sequence of ceramic development, as is envisaged in the emulation model, then the expectation of gradual stylistic change is not met. Instead, vessel forms are seen to undergo a stylistic somersault, with Peterborough forms giving way to Grooved Ware, itself supplanted by Beakers before an ultimate return to the late Neolithic related forms of Food Vessels and Urns. This is contrary to all that is known of the gradual morphological evolution of vessel form.

The second settlement alternative might also be explained differently, however, and in an ethnic fashion. The communities producing such mixed assemblages might be of indigenous ancestry but have adopted Beaker "ethnicity" some time after coming into contact with Beaker immigrants. Thus, a large part of their own cultural repertoire may have been retained, including domestic pottery, but the material diacritica of their adopted ethnic group taken up and displayed, including fineware Beakers perhaps. Beaker/indigene communities would then co-exist with "pure" Beaker communities, both recognisably Beaker in ethnic terms, and perhaps with a coherent mythology of origins, but retaining some differences of material culture, and of social customs. If the necessity for ethnic signification diminished, or the method of its symbolising change, then through time the production of discrete pottery styles would cease, and ultimately vessels of mixed ancestry would be produced. That the forms of subsequent early Bronze Age ceramics betrayed their late Neolithic ancestries, albeit with Beaker influences, is in accord with expectations generated by the above discussion of passively produced style. This process may perhaps also explain the patterning of Beaker assemblages recovered in central European contexts where distinctive Beaker vessels are usually found in association with the less fine Begleitkeramik.

Conclusion

The arguments and observations put forward during the course of this, and preceding, chapters do not "prove" that the spread of Beaker assemblages through Europe, and into Britain, was a direct concomitant of a migratory folk. They do go some way towards demonstrating that such an eventuality is one possible reading of the evidence, a more likely one, perhaps, than those which propose diffusionary spread on the lines of the cult package or status kit models. A sceptic might remain unconvinced. It is intended here, therefore, to briefly summarise the points made during the first five chapters of this study, and then to arrive at some definitive statement of conclusion.

In several regional studies it has been demonstrated that there were substantial changes in the archaeological record of the late Neolithic-early Bronze Age transition in Britain. The appearance throughout Britain of a new culture - the Beaker culture - was associated with changes in burial practices in Yorkshire; subsistence, population and political organisation in Wessex; political organisation in northern Britain. These instances are case studies only and do not pretend to provide a comprehensive picture of archaeological change at this time, but represent a "sample" - sufficient to indicate that widespread change did occur.

Whereas all these changes, and Beaker variability in general, can be explained by reference to a single model of long-distance migration this is not the case if a diffusionist explanation is attempted. Numerous individual accounts are necessary to describe changes in different parts of the country as being historically unique, but nevertheless convergent - a convergence which led to the ultimate adoption of Beaker assemblages. Not only is this inelegant, it seems unlikely. Diffusionist hypotheses are in any case further flawed, probably fatally, by the underdeveloped nature of their theoretical bases. Particularly serious is their failure to provide any satisfactory account of why ceramic Beakers should be perceived by late Neolithic societies to possess that ethereal attribute of value.

If a migrationist explanation of Beaker culture spread is more parsimonious than one of diffusion, it is also more versatile. It successfully accommodates the complex pattern of ceramic development that takes place across the late Neolithic - early Bronze Age interface, something which the various diffusionist models signally fail to do. Therefore, in consequence of its simplicity, and of its inclusive nature, a migrationist explanation of the Beaker phenomenon is preferred. A primary vector of migration would have been responsible for the initial spread of Beaker assemblages through Europe, with secondary processes of ethnic accommodation, and perhaps emulation, being responsible for its spatial variability.

In recent years there has been a tendency amongst prehistorians to view the "age of migrations" which followed the collapse of the Roman Empire as being aberrant - a unique historical happpenstance which disrupted the otherwise immobile demography of prehistoric Europe. Geographers, on the other hand, have focused attention upon more recent events, the "mobility transition" (Zelinsky 1971) or "migration transition" (Chesnais 1992: 153) of the last few centuries, when the decay of peasant social formations (and their colonial congeners) has served to unleash a second age of migrations during which time Europeans colonised a large part of the world but which continues today with population shifting from un(der)developed to developed sectors of the global economy. This raise an interesting question. Which is truly aberrant, the preceding and succeeding ages of migration or their feudal interregnum?

Feudal society was predicated upon the agricultural production of a peasant class and their dependent aristocracy were not blind to this fact. The peasantry were legally discouraged from moving unless new estates could be opened up, such as happened when the Germans moved east of the Elbe, but more usually by the internal colonisation of wastelands and forests. The 13th and 14th centuries also witnessed the onset of large scale urbanisation in Europe (Pounds 1990: 124) and thereafter rural-urban migration became an established feature of early modern societies. Thus it might be more true to say that the two "ages of migration" were in fact two "ages of inter-regional migration" separated by a period of intra-regional and rural-urban migration. Migration may be a more common response to social stress than many prehistorians are prepared to admit.

Scholars antipathetic to the idea of migrations, and particularly of a migrating "Beaker Folk", have sought to force their point home by adopting Childe's simple, but outdated, definitions of culture and migration, definitions which Childe himself had abandoned before the end of his career. However, none of the evidence adduced in this thesis to support the idea of a Beaker migration is particularly new. The basic model of long-distance migration was articulated by Lee in 1966, while ethnic boundaries were discussed by Barth in 1969. These both antedate the dissatisfaction with Childe's early definitions of culture and migration that found expression in the mid-1970s; but they were never sought out by any attempt to reconsider the possibilities of a Beaker migration in the light of more recent research. It is also the case that many of the explanatory constructs which underpin Beaker diffusion hypotheses have been uncritically, and perhaps mistakenly, accepted. Clarke's (1976) proposal of labour value for instance to explain the demand for Beaker fineware, and the emulation scheme of Bradley (1984) and Whittle (1981) used for explaining late Neolithic - early Bronze Age ceramic development. That such analytical lacunae can exist, apparently unnoticed, within the fabric of British prehistory is worrying, and possible reasons for their existence will be discussed further in the conclusion of this volume.

Chapter Six

THE STUDY OF THE CRANIA OF PREHISTORIC BRITAIN: HISTORICAL ANALYSIS

Introduction

This chapter introduces a programme of original work during which all the major collections of prehistoric crania known to be housed in English museums were visited. The crania were examined metrically and the derived data analysed statistically. In itself, the chapter reviews previous approaches to the study of British prehistoric crania and also presents a statement of aims.

Ethnology and Ethnography

The first systematic contribution to the study of British prehistoric crania appears in the first edition of D. Wilson's book: *The Archaeology and Prehistoric Annals of Scotland*, published in 1851. He provided metrical data for 15 Scottish skulls and described their archaeological contexts. After study he grouped the skulls into three broad classes: kumbecephalic, or boat-shaped; brachycephalic, or broad-headed; and a class of intermediate type. From their associated artefacts he recognised the intermediate class to be Anglo-Saxon, but was not able to ascertain, with any confidence, the correct chronological order of the remaining two classes. He did realise, however, that they were probably prehistoric and that, further, they were recovered from distinctive, and separate, sepulchral contexts. O .he basis of their apparently "primitive" morphology, Wilson suggested that the kumbecephalic skulls were of greater antiquity than the brachycephalic types (1851: 169), no doubt influenced in this conclusion by craniological data being collected at that time from contemporary "primitive" societies in Australia and North America which had shown them to be of a dolichocephalic cranial type.

Wilson was an evolutionist. He saw himself as heir to a "British School" of ethnology. This was a declaration of commitment to the theory of monogenism, championed in Britain by J. C. Prichard, and which held that all humans were members of a single species. The distinguishing features of the various "racial" groups, including head shape, were thought to be acquired, their acquisition being determined by their relative level of civilisation. Thus it was thought that the physiognomy of a people would alter in association with their intellectual faculties and their social customs (ibid: 164).

This was a biological statement of the "psychic unity" of mankind. Nevertheless, despite his evolutionist tendencies, Wilson considered that the difference in cranial form that existed between his kumbecephalic and brachycephalic classes was of such a magnitude that it was justifiable to propose that they had originally belonged to two separate races.

This conclusion was partly in accord with the work of the Scandinavians, Nilsson and Retzius, who had suggested that the prehistoric crania of Scandinavia were the surviving markers of three successive races which they had been able to place in chronological order on the basis of their archaeological associations. The earliest race were characterised by a brachycephalic skull form and had been hunter-gatherers; the second were dolichocephalic, or long-headed, farmers; while the final skull was of intermediate type and belonged to a Bronze Age race, tentatively identified as "Celts" (ibid: 163). This concern with identifying a "Celtic" race was to be taken up in Britain and was a consequence of the discovery of the Indo-European group of languages, thought to have descended from a single ancestral form, proto-Indo-European. The putative lexicon of the proto-Indo-European speakers suggested a homeland in northern Europe or central Asia (Renfrew 1987: 14); it was assumed, therefore, that the Indo-European languages had been carried west by an invading race , or races, foremost amongst which would have been the "Celts". The westerly distribution of the non-Indo-European languages known to have survived, at least into classical times, strengthened this conviction. Wilson himself argued that both his kumbecephalic and his brachycephalic classes of crania must have pre-dated the "Celts" as the true "Celtic" skull, known from the early historical period, was intermediate in form.

The tentative diachronic succession proposed by Wilson for his Scottish crania was confirmed by Bateman in England (1852). Bateman noted that the chambered tombs he excavated only ever contained flint artefacts, never bronze, and must therefore predate the smaller round barrows which sometimes did contain burials accompanied by bronze. He further observed that the chamber tomb interments possessed boat-shaped skulls, which he preferred to call dolichocephalic, whereas those of the round barrows were of a short round form, quite different in morphology from those of the

Romano-British period. Bateman thought that the earliest round barrows would have been built at the end of the Neolithic and that therefore the introduction of bronze working post-dated the arrival of a new people.

In the second edition of his book, Wilson confirmed Bateman's suggestions but maintained that the "Celts" must have arrived at a time subsequent to that of the brachycephalic race (Wilson 1863: 320). He was aware that in taking this stance he was in contradiction of the proposed Scandinavian sequence but he argued that the racial history of Britain was more complex than that of Scandinavia, the position of the latter being more peripheral, and that there should be no prior expectation of equivalence (ibid: 318). In the time that had lapsed between the two editions of his book, Wilson had taken a teaching post in Toronto, Canada, where he had been exposed to the practices of the native Americans. He became familiar with the use of a cradle board and provided a detailed account of its use and anatomical consequences:

"But in the ordinary use of the cradle-board by other Indian tribes, all that is aimed at is facility of nursing and transport, and perfect safety for the child. It is accordingly provided with a cradle formed of a flat board projecting beyond its head and feet, and with an arch or head-piece so arranged as to protect the face and head in case of a fall. On this cradle the infant is invariably laid on its back, with the head resting on a pillow or mat of moss or frayed cedar-bark, and is secured by bandages which hold the limbs in an extended posture, and necessarily retain the head in a nearly fixed position. The child is not removed from the cradle-board when suckling, so that the head is subjected to no lateral pressure on the mothers breast. At other times it is slung over her back, suspended from the branch of a tree, or placed leaning against any convenient rest, with the head constantly affected in the same direction. The consequence necessarily is, that the soft and pliant bones of the infants skull are subjected to a slight but continuous pressure on the occiput, during the whole protracted period of nursing incident to nomad life, and when the occipital and parietal bones are peculiarly susceptible to change. The only modifying element is the pillow. When, as is the practice with many Indian tribes, the infant is thrown back, and the consequent flattening affects the parietal bones, extending nearly to the coronal suture; but where a broad and high pillow is used, the weight of the head rests chiefly on the occipital bone, producing the vertical occiput."
(Wilson 1863: 273-274.)

Wilson suggested that the signs of compression to be seen in the parieto-occipital region of many of the brachycephalic crania he had studied might have resulted from the use of such a cradle-board during infancy (ibid: 273). He even went so far as to suggest that the change in head form seen in early historical times might have been, in part, due to the abandonment of such cradling practices, although maintained that the difference in shape between the prehistoric dolichocephalic and brachycephalic crania was altogether too great to be explained entirely by such a conjecture (ibid: 275).

In the second edition of the *Prehistoric Annals of Scotland* reference was made to the *Crania Brittanica* of J.B. Davis and J. Thurnam, which was published in five parts between 1856 and 1865. Upon completion it comprised two volumes. The first volume contained chapters relating to the ancient history, archaeology, ethnology and craniology of Britain. The second volume presented a series of 56 lithographic prints of individual crania with associated descriptive text and discussion of their archaeological and anatomical significance; also collected together were metrical data obtained from 307 skulls, largely British Neolithic and Bronze Age but also some Romano-Britons, Anglo-Saxons and Neolithic Scandinavians. Despite the dual authorship of this work there appears to have been some disagreement over interpretation (Thurnam 1863: 125). Thurnam published a supplementary series of 3 papers (1863, 1864, 1867) wherein he provided some extra data and discussion, but also presented conclusions radically different to those expressed by Davis in the *Crania Brittanica*.

Throughout his discussion in *Crania Brittanica* Davis took pains to deny that there was any evidence for a prehistoric succession of races, or at least cranial types, arguing instead that dolichocephalic and brachycephalic skulls were present in Britain throughout both the Neolithic and the Bronze Age. He supported his position by refusing to accept that the small, round barrows did, in fact, post-date the larger and more elaborate Neolithic chamber tombs:

"But to regard the colossal mound of Newgrange, and the elaborate galleries and chambers of Wellow, Uley and other barrows of this kind as the most primeval is difficult, if not impossible, unless the support of other very convincing evidence could be adduced."
(Davis, in Davis and Thurnam 1865: 229).

In his discussion of the skull from Wetton Hill barrow he says:

".... in this stone barrow on Wetton Hill, presenting only rude flint implements, British pottery, primitive flexed position of the skeleton, and the rude short cist; therefore with every mark of the primeval period, and no element of remote antiquity wanting."
(Davis, in Davis and Thurnam 1865, Volume II: Wetton Hill.)

The British pot in question was a Food Vessel, but a relative chronology of prehistoric pottery would not be constructed for another fifty years. In maintaining this position, Davis was able to claim that the brachycephalic skull form was of indigenous origin, thereby refuting the Scandinavian claim that the Bronze Age was instituted by an immigrant race carrying with it the rudiments of metallurgy. He suggested that bronze weapons had been obtained from Phoenician traders.

Davis' refusal to accept the archaeological evidence for cranial differentiation may perhaps have been motivated by his views on racial origins. He was a member of the Anthropological Society of London, a society founded in 1863 by the polygenist J. Hunt as an alternative to the more orthodox, monogenist, Ethnological Society (Stepan 1982: 45). Polygenism was a theory of racial uniqueness. It proposed that individual races constituted separate species, that racial characteristics were immutable and that interracial marriage would be infertile (ibid: 42). It seems possible therefore that Davis would have been predisposed to deny the existence of two, successive, prehistoric races. To accept them would have necessitated the concomitant acceptance of either racial evolution or racial intermixing, both anathema to the polygenist.

Davis thought that dolichocephalic skulls might be pathological, the result of premature synostosis of cranial sutures (Davis, in Davis and Thurnam 1865: 230), but he was at a loss to explain the recurrent association of dolichocephalic skulls with chambered tombs. His discussion of cradle-boarding, and its role in the genesis of occipital flattening, was more secure although he admitted that brachycephalic skulls of a similar configuration were known to him from societies that did not practice cradle-boarding (ibid: 233). He was also unhappy with the idea that a dolichocephalic race should suddenly cease to exist and be replaced by a brachycephalic one; he made the valid point that the tendency would be for them to blend into one another (ibid: 230). In a separate monograph (1862), Davis suggested that cradle-boards would have been made from a thin, light, wood, perhaps willow. He thought it possible that such boards may have been included with infants at burial, but that they would be unlikely to survive, although a few traces might remain for the discerning observer. He argued that cradleboarding would not be the ultimate cause of brachycephaly however, preferring to consider it as an exacerbating factor.

Thurnam seems to have possessed a rather more sophisticated understanding of archaeology than did Davis, or else a rather less doctrinaire view of racial origins. He agreed with Bateman and Wilson that round barrows and long barrows formed chronologically distinct groups, and that as the former occasionally contained bronze whilst the latter never did then long barrows were the more ancient type (1863: 120). He proposed the axiom: long barrows, long skulls; round barrows, round skulls (1863: 158); and pointed out that although brachycephalic skulls had indeed been recovered from long barrow mounds they were always secondary interments, they had never been found at the base of a barrow (1867: 57). He agreed with Davis that, in many cases, the degree of brachycephaly appeared to have been exaggerated by artificial means (ibid: 156), but disagreed that dolichocephaly might be caused by premature fusion of the sagittal suture, pointing out that equally often the coronal or lambdoid sutures were also found to be fused (1867: 70). For his racial identifications Thurnam turned to classical sources. The brachycephalic/round barrow race he assumed to be the Belgae as they appeared to constitute the final tradition of prehistoric burial to have existed before the Roman conquest. The dolichocephalic crania he thought might belong to the ancestors of the people described by Caesar as being those of the interior, who he equated with the Silures, described by Tacitus in the *Agricola* as being of Iberian ancestry, and therefore, by comparison with the Basques, a pre-Indo-European race (ibid: 77-79).

While Wilson, Bateman and Thurnam had between them established and confirmed the Neolithic date of the dolichocephalic crania and the Bronze Age date of brachycephalic ones, it disturbed Thurnam that this sequence was not consistent with that of the European mainland where brachycephalic skulls had been recovered from Neolithic burials in both Denmark and France. The Scandinavian, Retzius, and the Frenchman, Broca, had both claimed that the brachycephalic crania recovered from these contexts belonged to a pre-Indo-European race (Thurnam 1863: 123). To solve this problem Thurnam took it upon himself to study and measure a series of 61 crania, obtained from prehistoric, mainly Neolithic, tombs in France. He reported a mixture of skull types (1864: 508), with both dolichocephalic and brachycephalic crania being found frequently in the same tomb. He concluded that, in France, two races had come into contact at a very early date and had subsequently blended. He accepted that a similar process of racial blending might also explain the mixture of cranial types to be found in the megalithic tombs of Scandinavia (1864: 508). Thurnam felt forced to conclude that there was no such thing as an identifiable "Celtic" skull, and that instead the individual language groups of the "Celtic" family might, in themselves, constitute distinct races, each with a distinctive cranial morphology (ibid: 515).

With hindsight, it is possible to see that the embryonic nature of prehistoric chronology had led Thurnam and his contemporaries astray. It was assumed that the use of bronze must have been introduced throughout Europe at an approximately synchronous chronological horizon and that, therefore, all Neolithic burials must be of a similar date. This mistake was compounded by the absence of any method of accurately measuring the duration of the Neolithic, estimates tended to err on the side of brevity. It is now known that the Bronze Age commenced at an earlier date in Britain than in either Scandinavia or north/central France. From his descriptions of their burial contexts, it is evident that the majority of French crania Thurnam studied were in fact of late Neolithic date, obtained from tombs of the S.O.M. culture:

"They consist usually of a quadrangular chamber, into which opens a narrow gallery, or allee couverte. In no instance, so far as I know, are there sets of chambers opening on each side of a central gallery, as in several of the English tumuli."
(Thurnam 1863: 133)

The S.O.M. was a relatively long lived culture, currently thought to have run from 3350 calBC to 1750 calBC (Howell 1983: 62), thus much of the French Neolithic material studied by Thurnam may in fact have been contemporary with that of his British round barrows.

Thurnam finally compared the prehistoric crania of Britain to those known from contemporary, 19th century, societies. He thought that the Bronze Age crania were, on average, larger than Alpine or eastern European brachycephalic types, and argued that the Neolithic crania were also longer and narrower than those of any European dolichocephalic people (1867: 64).

In 1877, Rolleston contributed to the volume *British Barrows* a report on the crania excavated by Greenwell. He described in detail a sample of 13 individual crania, providing metrical data, and also presented an overall discussion of the complete collection. He suggested that, in Bronze Age contexts, two distinct cranial morphologies were present - dolichocephalic and brachycephalic - and that they were not the extremes of a continuous population. However, it was not realised at the time that some of the Yorkshire round barrows were in fact of Neolithic date, and of the five skulls chosen by Rolleston as being typical of the dolichocephalic type two were actually from Neolithic barrows. He also noted that both types of skull were obviously distinct from those of the Anglo-Saxons (1877: 645). He followed Thurnam in equating the dolichocephalic long barrow race with the Silures of Tacitus, but preferred to see the round barrow race as being of the same stock as the Cimbri, on account of the similarity in cranial dimensions between British and Scandinavian material (ibid: 680,630). He saw evidence for artificial deformation in some crania, although did not think it would have been intentional (ibid: 593). He also thought that the Neolithic crania bore some resemblance to those of modern Australians, but more so to those of the Inuit (ibid: 717).

J. Mortimer had excavated large numbers of crania from the round barrows of the Yorkshire Wolds during the closing years of the 19th century. They were studied by W. Wright, who published a descriptive catalogue of 62 specimens in which he included metrical data (1904, 1905). From this data, he deduced that the "round barrow, round head" part of Thurnam's axiom was not even approximately correct (1904: 120) since his sample of skulls contained brachycephalic, dolichocephalic and intermediate types. He concluded that the race that had migrated into Britain at the beginning of the Bronze Age was of a mixed type, pointing out that it was an unlikely circumstance for a "pure" brachycephalic race to have arrived:

"To grant this conclusion one must believe that a pure round headed race could have made its tardy progress across Europe unmixed - an assumption which to my mind is unwarranted and incredible." (1905: 442).

Wright's conclusion was a sensible one but unfortunately it was based upon a faulty data set. Again, like Rolleston before him, he was unaware that many of the crania he examined were of Neolithic date, and these accounted for much of the dolichocephalic end of his distributional range of Cranial Index.

The final large corpus of cranial data to be published was by Schuster (1905/6), who examined and measured the collection of 222 crania which was then housed at the Department of Comparative Anatomy at Oxford. This collection contained some material which had been excavated by Thurnam but was largely composed of the crania recovered from the excavations described by Greenwell in his *British Barrows*. Again, there was the occasional Neolithic cranium, and an Iron Age one, mixed in with the round barrow sample, while included in the long barrow lists were several Anglo-Saxon crania belonging to secondary interments in a barrow

at Crawley, Oxfordshire (Crawford 1925: 159). As Schuster refrained from making any synthetic analysis of his data, however, these oversights did not cause any confusion.

By the end of the 19th century most anthropologists were in agreement that, in Britain, during prehistoric times, a brachycephalic race had succeeded a dolichocephalic one but there was no consensus regarding their respective identities. Abercromby put a stop, in part, to this speculation in 1902 when he identified the continental antecedents of the ancient British "Drinking Cup", to be known henceforth, in accordance with German and Scandinavian terminology, as a "Beaker". He also observed the recurrent association of brachycephalic crania with Beaker accompanied burials and proposed that the brachycephalic race had passed over into Britain at the beginning of the Bronze Age bringing with them their Beaker pottery. The "Beaker Folk" had been born. T.H.Bryce (1902) provided further support for this synthesis by pointing out that the central European origin of Beaker pottery proposed by Abercromby accorded well with the known geographical distribution of brachycephalic crania.

In 1917, Turner published and summarised all cranial data obtained up to that time from Scottish burials. He reconfirmed the dolichocephalic - brachycephalic succession initially proposed by Wilson, but observed that the presence of dolichocephalic crania in some early Bronze Age short cists would suggest that the morphological separation of Neolithic and Bronze Age crania might not be so clear cut as had so often been assumed (1917: 209). Nevertheless, he followed what had, by then, become the conventional wisdom of assigning to the Neolithic dolichocephalic race an Iberian origin, but he overlooked Abercromby's contribution when assigning to the brachycephalic race a French or Danish origin, although he did credit them with the introduction of bronze metallurgy. He agreed with Thurnam that there was no stereotypically Celtic cranial type (ibid: 235-254). Turner's paper was perhaps the final example of the 19th century genre of cranial studies in which the data and description of physical anthropology had been combined with observations derived from ethnographical and archaeological sources to arrive at an evolutionist or, later, historical synthesis. Such studies were accepted as legitimate archaeological activity and were influential in shaping contemporary interpretations of prehistory. This situation was changing, however, with physical anthropology becoming increasingly marginal to the archaeological mainstream.

Biometrics and Population Genetics

The dogma of polygenism had survived the publication of Darwin's *Origin of Species* in 1859 by substituting the concept of race for that of species. The origins of racial variety were assumed to be of great antiquity and the defining biological traits of race very slow to change. Therefore, it was maintained that racial inequality was immutable and that races of "inferior ability" could not benefit from the "advantages" of European education or culture. Within Europe itself, the rise of nationalist sentiment during the latter part of the 19th century resulted in the expenditure of much effort by the "scholars" of various countries in describing ideal types of national head forms and expounding upon their, supposedly, superior characteristics. In Britain, however, the limitations of such a typological approach were realised by Galton and Pearson who pioneered the use of quantitative techniques in the study of cranial variation. They emphasised the importance of studying the crania from large, representative, samples of a population and establishing the degree of variability present in a population. Variations of cranial form seen to exist between different population groups were still considered to be immutably racial in aetiology however, with the extra-somatic environment having no influence whatsoever upon the developmental process. Boas' observations of limited heritability (1910-1913) were specifically rebutted (Pearson & Tippett 1924: 119). Although the methodologies of statistical analysis benefited greatly from this approach, the anatomical or archaeological significance of the results were rarely discussed. It was regarded as being sufficient to establish the degree of morphological (equated with racial) similarity extant between groups using a variety of statistical distance measures. Publications became increasingly statistical in content and ceased to appear in the mainstream anthropological or archaeological literature, being placed instead with newly established specialist journals, notably *Biometrika*. During the 1930s, the quantitative approach of the biometricians was integrated with the Mendelian theory of particulate inheritance to establish the present day discipline of population genetics. The theoretical principles of population genetics continue to inform most comparative studies of cranial morphology. Thus, it is assumed that variations in cranial form which exist both within, and between, populations are genetically determined, and as such can only change by the processes of evolution or microevolution.

Working within this theoretical milieu, Morant (1926), as part of a larger study, gathered together and synthesised all of the previously published data relating to prehistoric crania which was available to him. He calculated the means and variances of the numerous measurements and indices in order to compare the two groups objectively. Although taking care to exclude crania of uncertain context from his analysis, he remained unaware of the Neolithic crania in the round barrow series of Wright and Schuster, and also included the data obtained from the Neolithic crania of Duggleby Howe in his Bronze Age Group. As a result, the distribution he produced of the Cranial Indices of Bronze Age male crania showed a greater variation than comparable Neolithic and 17th century samples, the distribution also departed from normality, being skewed towards higher values of Cranial Index. Morant concluded that his Bronze Age crania must therefore be constituted of two racially pure groups (dolichocephalic and brachycephalic) and some hybrids. He then manipulated the results to produce a "pure" Bronze Age group - essentially, he extrapolated a theoretical normal distribution from the data to the right, brachycephalic, side of the modal value (ibid: 63). Although, in so doing, Morant fortuitously excluded the Neolithic skulls in his sample, he also excluded many long headed Bronze Age types. From a sample of 151 crania, 60 were ultimately excluded. If it is assumed that 21 were of Neolithic provenance (Table 6.1) then the remainder must have been Bronze Age; their exclusion renders inaccurate Morant's mean Bronze Age Cranial Index of 82 - it is too high. Two years after his study of English crania, Morant collaborated with Reid in a similar study of Scottish short cist crania (1928), and showed them to more closely resemble the English Bronze Age material than recent Scottish material. The Scottish skulls were also compared with a number of recent European samples, although the value of this exercise was lessened by the omission of any dating information for the European material.

Table 6.1.

Probable Neolithic skulls included in Bronze Age series of Morant.

(Prefix and number refer to original craniometric report; W = Wright (1904/5), S = Schuster (1905/6)).

W2   - Garton Slack 37, burial 8.
W3   - Garton Slack 37, burial 11.
W4   - Garton Slack 37, burial 9.
W5   - Garton Slack 37, burial 10.
W7   - Garton Slack 37, burial 12.
W17 - Wold Newton 284, burial 2.
W18 - Wold Newton 284, burial 7.
W44 - Callis Wold 275, burial 3.
W56 - Hedon Howe 281, burial 5.
W57 - Painsthorpe Wold 118

S99 - Sherburn Wold 7.
S149 - Cowlam 57.
S150 - Cowlam 57.
S151 - Cowlam 57.

Garson (1904) - Duggleby Howe; C,D,G,I,J,K,L.

Morant's study was criticised by Fereday (1956) in a short paper which provided a statistical summary of metrical data obtained from 95 English Neolithic crania. She pointed out that Morant had included 47 skulls from Staffordshire in his Neolithic series without clearly indicating their provenance. With only two chambered tombs excavated in Staffordshire by Bateman, it is not altogether clear from what source Morant derived this body of data. Nevertheless, his mean Cranial Indices, at 72 for males and 74 for females, exceeded Fereday's figures by only one unit in each case. The identity of the Staffordshire crania remains a mystery.

Despite the unsatisfactory nature of Morant's study, based as it was on previously published data of uneven reliability, it remained definitive for over thirty years. The only (comparatively) recent studies of the crania of the prehistoric Britons have been those of Brothwell (1960, 1974) who, by and large, confirmed previous findings. As part of a general study of the palaeodemography of early Bronze Age Yorkshire it was again shown that, although largely brachycephalic, the Bronze Age crania were heterogeneous with respect to their Cranial Indices, affinities with the Neolithic populations of France and Denmark were also restated. This study was impaired, however, by the, still unrealised, bugbear of the Neolithic round barrows. In a later, more wide ranging, study, Brothwell utilised previously published metrical data in conjunction with that from more recent, unpublished, sources in a canonical variate analysis of 11 cranial measurements. Again, morphological separation of Neolithic and Bronze crania was achieved, but it was also suggested that, in Yorkshire, the crania belonging to male Beaker burials might be morphologically distinct from those of Food Vessel or other early Bronze Age burials.

Archaeological Doubts

If prehistorians found the specialist literature of the biometricians difficult to digest it was of little consequence; in response to the overt racism of Kossinna and his successors, with their theories about the inherent superiority of an Indo-European race, moves were afoot to uncouple the concept of race from those of ethnicity and culture. Childe (1933) accepted the theoretical possibility of a race as a biologically discrete entity, but doubted that it had any practical meaning in Europe or the Near East given their shared heritage of chronic migration and population dispersal. He also argued that, while the Cranial Index might be a relatively stable hereditary character, it would be a poor indicator of racial identity, pointing out that in contemporary Europe the apparently distinct "Nordic" and "Mediterranean" racial groups were both dolichocephalic. Childe argued that an archaeological culture could not be indicative of race but should instead be considered to be representative of a people, or ethnic group. He defined an ethnic group as being a population with shared language, customs and peculiarities of material culture. Thus it was a legitimate exercise to characterise the archaeological culture that represented an Indo-European speaking people, but not a genetically segregated Indo-European race. Measures of racial affinity derived from samples of crania were therefore rendered meaningless to the prehistorian. Childe was, in fact, stating a view shared by many of his contemporaries in other disciplines. The Nazi thesis of Aryan supremacy had, during the 1930s, prompted the Royal Anthropological Institute and the Institute of Sociology to issue a joint statement in which a committee of distinguished biologists and anthropologists developed much the same theme. There was no general consensus as to the biological definition of a race, but all were agreed that no pure races existed, and that race did not in any case equate with culture (Stepan 1982: 168).

Nevertheless, despite Childe's rejection of any equivalence between an archaeological culture and a racial group, in the case of the "Beaker Folk" he felt it necessary to make an exception:

"In this instance therefore it looks as if culture and race coincided and one might legitimately speak of a Beaker race."

(Childe 1939: 218).

With this apparent conjunction of an intrusive archaeological culture with a novel racial type, there seemed little need to consider any alternative explanation for either occurrence other than that of straightforward immigration. It was this amalgam of archaeology and physical anthropology that contributed to the "Beaker Folk's" survival in the face of Clark's (1966) scathing attack on the "invasion hypothesis" and it is still seen by proponents of a migrationist model of Beaker culture spread as constituting irrefutable support for their position. Once doubts were expressed about the cultural component of this amalgam, however, it was realised that the evidence of physical anthropology was not quite so clear cut as had always been assumed. The underlying cause, or causes, of variation in cranial morphology remained unknown and factors other than direct inheritance might be influential (Harrison 1980: 160-163). There was also a chronological gap of several hundred years between the early Neolithic chamber tombs and long barrows, from which dolichocephalic crania were recovered, and the early Bronze Age contexts of the brachycephalic types, a period of time sufficient, perhaps, for a process of indigenous change to have taken place (Burgess 1976: 321). Whittle suggested that the practice of artificial deformation may have been overlooked (1981: 302) and indeed it had for over seventy years, although in the 19th century it had generated much discussion, as previously described. In consequence of these uncertainties, the proponents of Beaker culture diffusion felt safe in ignoring the challenge presented to their theories by the evidence of the crania.

Yet pointing to potential weaknesses in a theory, to its possible flaws, is not a procedure to be considered analogous to its decisive refutation. Nor yet is ignoring a body of evidence any substitute for offering a coherent thesis of explanation. It remains the case that, time and again, both subjectively and objectively, marked differences in form have been observed to exist between examples of Neolithic crania and their early Bronze Age comparanda, an unsavoury "fact" perhaps, and one that has been left to languish in the unfashionable backwaters of archaeology. Still, unfashionable or not, explanation remains wanting. It is the purpose of this study to make the first, perhaps tentative, steps in such a direction. It will attempt to answer the following three questions:

1) Are the anatomical differences reported to exist between crania of the Neolithic and early Bronze Age real?

2) Assuming the answer to question (1) to be affirmative, then what are the possible aetiologies of such differences?

3) In the light of the answers to questions (1) and (2), is it possible to apprehend the intrusive presence of a "Beaker Folk" from amidst the human crania of prehistoric Britain?

Chapter Seven

THE HUMAN CRANIUM: FORM AND DEVELOPMENT

Introduction

The idea that the human skull may be used as a stable indicator of genetic distance is a legacy of the cranial studies performed during the late 19th and early 20th centuries. It is disconcerting to discover that since then there has been no concerted programme of research initiated to investigate the veracity of this idea and, perhaps also, to explode a myth. Nevertheless, several hypotheses have been developed in the literature that provide the basis for a more systematic investigation of cranial form and its genesis. There follows in this chapter an attempt to gather together these hypotheses in order to produce a more coherent framework of investigation. In so doing tentative models of morphological change might

be suggested and utilised to explain the reasons for the morphological dissimilarity thought to exist between the excavated crania of Neolithic and Bronze Age Britain.

The Human Cranium

The cranial skeleton surrounds and protects the brain whilst also providing the structural template for the face. In the young adult it is composed of 22 individual bones which are formed, after fusion, from 45 embryonic precursors. As a simplification the cranium can be considered to consist of three functional/structural units: the calvarium, the naso-maxillary complex and the mandible (Figures 7.1, 7.2). The calvarium is the braincase, the collection of bones that encloses and protects the brain. It consists of an upper portion, or

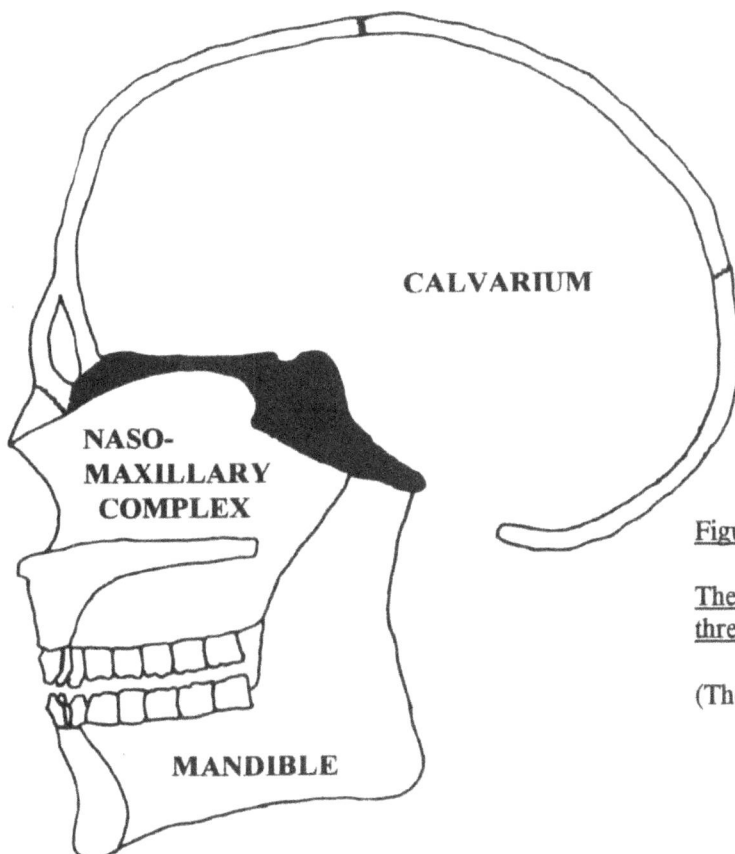

Figure 7.1.

The human cranium in sagittal section, showing its three major structural/functional components.

(The shaded area represents the cranial base).

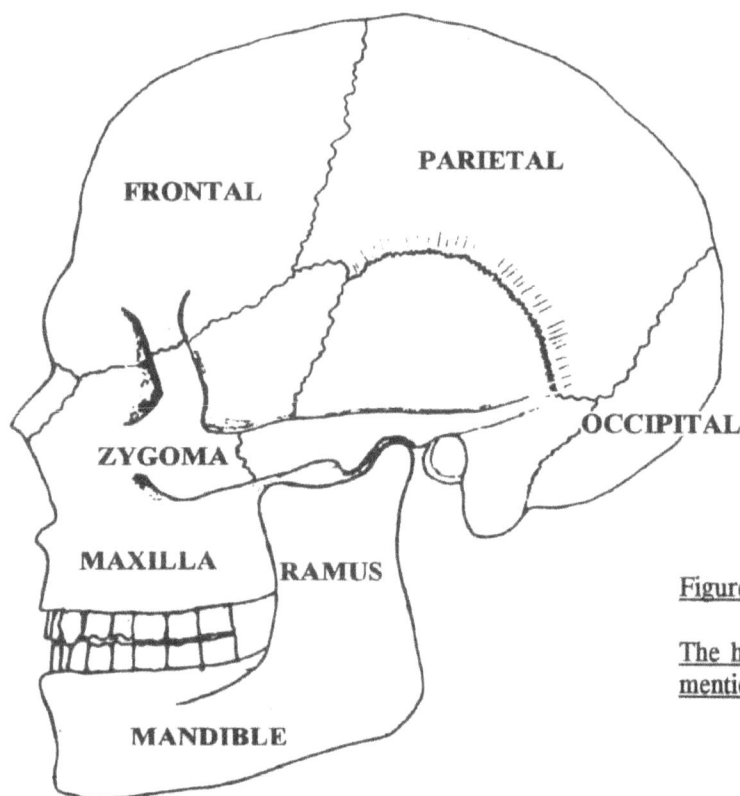

Figure 7.2.

The human cranium, showing the positions of bones mentioned in the text.

cranial vault, and a lower portion, the cranial base. The cranial base is divided into two parts, anterior and posterior, by the sphenoccipital synchondrosis and is angled around this cartilage in the sagittal plane. The naso-maxillary complex encloses the nasal air passages and supports the palatal dentition while the mandible, or lower jaw, contains the basal dentition.

Structurally differentiated skull forms do not form discrete populations, morphologically they are a continuum. However, for descriptive purposes, it is convenient to dichotomise skulls into two extreme forms: dolichocephalic and brachycephalic. These forms have been defined metrically using the ratio between head length and head breadth to provide the Cephalic Index for head form, or Cranial Index for skull form. These indices are estimated as follows:-

maximum skull/head breadth * 100
maximum skull/head length

Dolichocephalic skulls are defined as having a Cranial Index of less than 75 while the brachycephalic Index is in excess of 80.

A dolichocephalic skull is built around a relatively narrow, but elongated, cranial base with an open, flat cranial flexure in association with an antero-inferior positioning of the naso-maxillary complex and a corresponding downward and backward rotational alignment of the mandible. The resultant facial profile tends towards being convex, or retrognathic. The cranial base of the brachycephalic skull is shorter but wider than

that of the dolichocephalic skull, with a more acute and upright cranial flexure in conjunction with a more protrusive lower jaw. There is a tendency towards a concave, prognathic, facial profile. The reduced lateral dimensions of the dolichocephalic head are associated with close set eyes and a thin, long nasal cavity. The eyes of a brachycephalic individual are further apart and the nasal cavity is wider, but shorter. The convex and concave profile tendencies of the different skull types carry inbuilt dental malocclusion patterns but in both cases compensatory mechanisms exist to produce a straighter, orthognathic profile. Thus in the dolichocephalic skull there may be a broader mandibular ramus to push the lower jaw forward while in the brachycephalic a more open gonial angle might act to lower the mandible (Enlow 1990).

The sex of an individual has some effect upon cranial morphology. In relative terms, the male lungs are larger than the female as they need to serve the respiratory demands of an increased muscle mass. This results in a larger airway with a larger nose and naso-pharynx. Thus the nasal region of a male tends to be more protuberant, males having a tendency towards a retrognathic type face while females tend towards a flatter, more orthognathic, face. In females, facial development begins to slow after about 13 years of age but in males the puberty related increases in body size necessitate that the maturation process of the face continues through adolescence. Male skulls on average tend to be more robust than female skulls due to the demands of the more substantial cranio-facial musculature.

44

The structural/functional units of the cranium do not develop in isolation. There is an underlying balance provided by the cranial base which accommodates regional adjustments in anatomy so as to maintain the overall functional integrity of the skull. The face cannot vary in shape or size independently of the cranial base or else it would be necessarily deformed. Alterations in the configuration of the brain and cranial base therefore cause secondary changes in facial morphology, and vice versa.

The Use of Cranial Morphology as an Indicator of Biological Distance

It has long been known that human crania are morphologically variable. Numerous statistical studies of craniometric data have shown that it is possible to produce phenetic classifications that possess either geographical or chronological validity, studies of British Neolithic and Bronze Age crania have already been discussed in the previous chapter. On a global scale, statistical analyses are exemplified by that of Howells (1973) who successfully discriminated between samples of crania drawn from 17 populations using a suite of 57 measurements. The interpretation of these classifications in many, if not the majority, of craniometric studies is based on the premise that adult cranial form is realised after rigid conformation during growth to an inherited genetic blueprint - the genotype. The genotype itself is assumed to have evolutionary roots which reach down deep into the Pleistocene. Skull form is therefore considered to be an adaptive feature, the result of natural selection (see Appendix One).

As the timing of natural selection is dependent upon the rate of genetic mutation it is a long term process in humans, proceeding over spans of "evolutionary time" that may be considered in terms of tens of thousands of years. Humans anatomically modern in form are now thought to have a history of about 100,000 years (Lewin 1989). Natural selection is unlikely to significantly alter anatomical form in what might be termed "historical time", that is to say periods of several millennia or less. It is this short term immunity to the effects of natural selection which has engendered the concept of anatomical, and thus cranial, immutability and encouraged the belief that skull form may act as a stable indicator of biological distance. Thus morphologically distinct, or at least statistically separable, groups of human crania are considered to be synonymous with breeding populations. When such a theoretical position is adopted then changes, or differences, in cranial morphology are viewed as being consequences of microevolution (see Appendix One).

Microevolution is a principle, or set of principles, used by population geneticists to explain differences or changes in allele frequencies which they may observe to occur between populations. Microevolution operates at the level of the genotype, not the phenotype. Nevertheless, by using these principles to construct explanatory models it becomes possible to consider anatomical distance, or change, in terms of the presence or absence of contact between populations. Before such models are deployed, however, there are three simplifying assumptions which must be made. These are:

1) That the cranial phenotype is a faithful reproduction of the cranial genotype. The environment must be assumed to exert no significant effect upon ontogeny.

2) That a multivariate craniometric data set is an accurate representation of cranial form.

3) That a statistical measure of multivariate distance may be used as an analogue of genetic distance.

The validity of the first of these assumptions is examined during the remainder of this chapter, that of the second and third will be considered in subsequent chapters.

Phenotypic Plasticity and Genetic Diversity

It has been noted that in studies of craniometric data episodes, or trajectories, of morphological change are often considered entirely in terms of the microevolutionary processes of genetic drift and gene flow. It has been argued however that it is not clear what, if any, empirical data can be mustered to support this assumption of genetic determinism - the assumption may be, as a major proponent of such studies has admitted, unfounded:

"One school of anthropologists, in fact, holds that such characters are too responsive to effects of selection and of the environment to be reliable indicators of the genetic sources or relations of a population. Indeed, we have no proof to the contrary."
(Howells 1988: 98).

This statement is not surprising. It is no longer credible to regard the biological process of ontogeny as being the victim of a strict genetic control. It is becoming increasingly clear that a single genotype is often able to produce a range of different, environmentally suited, phenotypes, a phenomenon known as phenotypic plasticity (Stearns 1982). Thus, the structural or functional characteristics of a biological system may, in the first instance, be genetically determined but its ultimate physical manifestation is modulated by the environment. The genes, in effect, provide an outline plan. They define the mechanisms by which ontogeny must proceed and the limits within which morphogenesis might occur. Within the confines of this outline plan, however, there remains much scope for variable development and the manifestation of environmental effects. The achieved age and size of humans at maturity onset, for instance, are not genetically pre-determined parameters, independent of the pre-pubertal environment. They are plastic in their expression and are influenced by levels of childhood nutrition.

It must also be borne in mind that there is a large amount of genetic diversity maintained within the gene pool of a human population. It is a corollary of this fact that there must also be a range of different phenotypes expressed within a population, some of which will be better adapted to the environment than others, and which will therefore constitute the majority type, although there will always be present a range of less well adapted phenotypes. If the environment should change in any way, however, the relative fitness of the various phenotypes might alter accordingly, so that a previously minor type acquires better survival characteristics and becomes the predominant type. This process of genetically-based, morphological change is not absolute but, rather, it is a statistical phenomenon of changing allele frequencies. It is not dependent upon ongoing chromosome mutation but instead shifting patterns of environmental selection act upon a range of pre-existing variation; it is therefore a potentially more rapid process of change than that of natural selection in its true, evolutionary, sense.

When it is realised that phenotypic plasticity may, in itself, be an attribute of the phenotype, and thus variable in its expression, then the complexity of the mechanisms which underlie cranial morphogenesis is better appreciated. Any genetic influence upon cranial form might be remote and, in part, indirect. This is reflected in the relatively low correlations observed in heritability studies.

Heritability of Cranial Form

There have probably been hundreds of craniometric studies that have explained differences or changes in cranial morphology as being the visible manifestation of microevolutionary process. It is notable, however, that there have been significantly fewer studies of cranial heritability - studies which have attempted to assess the extent to which cranial form is heritable, and therefore genetically determined. Heritability studies commonly use a suite of measurements to represent skull form and the assumption is made that if the morphology of the cranium is determined by polygenic inheritance alone, with no environmental effects registered, then it is possible to arrive at a theoretical estimate of the degree to which morphology, expressed metrically, should correlate between genetically related individuals. By comparing observed with expected correlations the relative heritability of the cranial dimensions measured may then be assessed. Correlation coefficients between parent/child and sibling/sibling have been calculated, but rarely approach the theoretical norm (Susanne 1975; Bernhard et al 1980). In an attempt to reduce environmental interference to a minimum Paganini-Hill et al (1981) carried out a study of 784 members of a religious isolate with a common lifestyle and reported a value of 60% expected correlation. But heritability studies such as this have been criticised as they are performed in relatively stable environmental conditions and marked changes in environment may induce correlative anatomical changes that completely override any heritability considerations. Thus the significance of a 60% correlation in conditions of environmental stability is doubtful. The relative importance of the contributions made by the genotype and the environment to the final expression of cranial form remains to be defined.

Bone Remodelling and Cranial Morphogenesis

The low estimates of correlation produced by heritability studies are easier to understand when considered within their physiological context. Bone is popularly conceived of as being a functionally inert, structural tissue - resembling in many ways its vegetative counterpart, wood. This conception is far removed from the truth, however. Bone is a living tissue and exists in a state of flux, it is continually renewing itself, or remodelling (see Appendix Two), and in so doing has the potential to alter its shape. This mutability provides bone with the ability to morphologically "track" any changes in the conditions of its matrix, and a fuller understanding is fundamental for any comprehensive study of skull form, and its genesis. The process of growth remodelling, which is well established in the foetal skull by the 14th week (Enlow 1990), undermines any concept of bone which characterises it as being as a static, inert, tissue; its ability to respond to changes in its microenvironment has enabled Moss to construct his "functional matrix" hypothesis (1969). This hypothesis suffers from a shifting terminology but essentially postulates that the size, shape and location of a cranial bone are determined in response to its physiological matrix. This matrix includes "soft" tissues such as the brain, eyes, muscle and teeth, but also "functioning spaces" - the oral and nasal cavities and the pharynx. Thus, although cranial bones would be continually displaced in space by alterations in the size parameters of their matrices, it is envisaged that they maintain their overall cohesion and correct anatomical configuration by growth remodelling (Figure 7.3). The functional matrix hypothesis, if accepted, has important implications for any study of cranial form and its heritability. It suggests that the adult cranium must be considered as the end product of a continuous sequence of morphological adjustments that began in the foetus. If this is the case then adult cranial form cannot be considered to be a strict interpretation of a genetic "blueprint", it would not be significantly heritable and metric analyses would be of no value for estimating biological distance.

There is a broad measure of agreement that the functional matrix theory provides an accurate model of calvarial growth; as the neural capsular matrix expands outward the flat bones of the cranial vault are carried with it, maintaining contact with each other by appositional growth at sutures and conforming to alterations in brain shape by remodelling. However, although Moss denies bone-forming cartilage any primary role in the growth process his view is disputed (van Limborgh 1972; Johnston 1979), for it is apparent that the cranial base retains the facility for independent growth and development and might therefore be subject to more stringent genetic regulation. Its growth remains relatively normal in cases of congenital malformations of the brain such as hydrocephalus and anencephalus and furthermore it has been shown experimentally that chondrocranial growth is only slightly influenced by mutilating other cranial structures. In contrast, syndromes which affect cartilage development may result in the underdevelopment of midline cranial base structures. Latham and Scott (1970) have pointed out that although several cartilage synchondroses are operational in the foetal and early post-natal chondrocranium they rapidly diminish in number, that although the sphenooccipital synchondrosis may play a principal role in cranial elongation, there is a progressive increase in the importance of cranial growth by matrix displacement, which might include muscle "pull" as well as the expansionary "push" of growing soft tissues. Thus, overall, cranial morphology is to some extent predetermined by the genetic control of chondrocranial growth, but it is also sensitive to the requirements of its tissue matrix.

It is overly simplistic, therefore, to consider inter-generational transformations of cranial form in terms of microevolution alone, there may also be immanent the effects of a changing environment. There now follows a consideration of some environmental "morphogens", aspects of the extra-cranial environment that may play a significant role in the realisation of cranial form.

Artificial Cranial Deformation

The physiological requirement for the calvarium to adapt to the conformation of its surrounding matrix renders it peculiarly vulnerable to deformation in response to the application of external pressure during childhood. Such deformation may be intentional or unintentional and may persist into adulthood. Intentional deformation is produced by tightly binding the head with bandages to produce a circumferential depression, or else inserting

small hard boards to flatten particular areas of the skull, often the frontal and occipital bones (Ubelaker 1989: 96). Unintentional deformation usually occurs as a result of cradle-boarding, when an infant is bound to a flat board and kept immobile for long periods of time. The continual pressure of the board against the back of the head leads to occipital flattening. It has been observed that a round head, with a natural tendency towards brachycephaly, is more prone to this type of deformation than one with a projecting occiput (Ehrich & Coon 1948: 183). It has also been demonstrated that the crania of infants born prematurely have a tendency to dolichocephaly. The underdeveloped state of their neck musculature, together with their relatively large head mass predispose these infants to lay with their heads resting on their sides, and which are thus compressed laterally. Again, the dolichocephaly so produced persists into adulthood (Baum & Searls 1971).

The Effects of Cultural Innovation upon Cranial Morphology

Human teeth are functionally dimorphic. The incisors and canines, which comprise the anterior dentition, are used primarily to grip and to tear while the molars and premolars, the posterior dentition, are used more for actual mastication. A continuing process of dental reduction has been demonstrated to have occurred throughout the later Pleistocene and the Holocene (Brace et al 1987; Frayer 1977), a process which has affected the

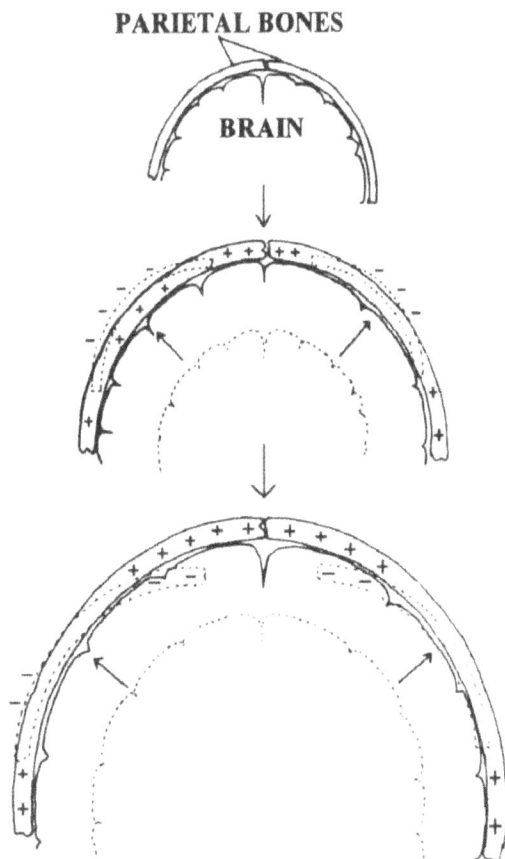

Figure 7.3. Growth remodelling.

Schematic sections of the growing cranium which illustrate the simultaneous reconfiguration and growth, by processes of selective resorption and deposition, of the two parietal bones in response to the expanding tissue mass of the brain.

(+ = deposition; - = resorption).

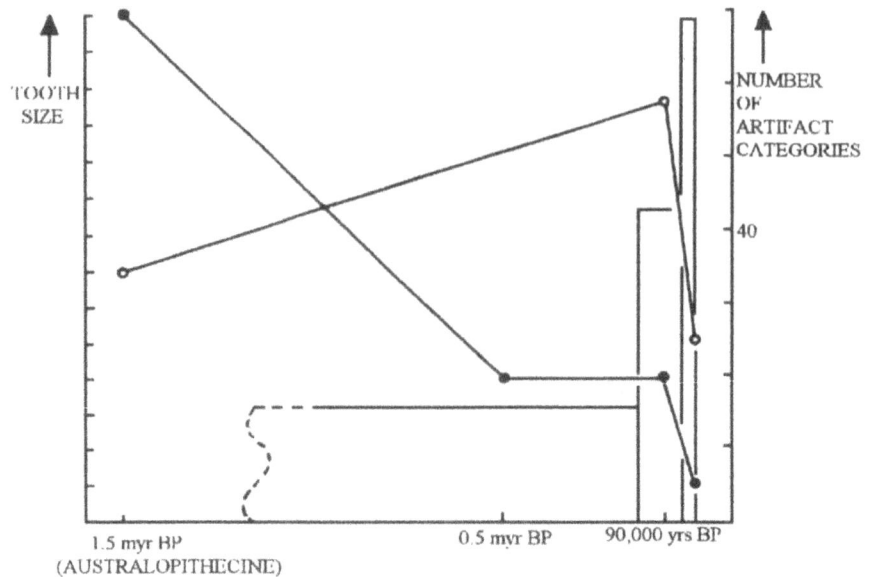

Figure 7.4.

Dental reduction and technological elaboration.

Line graph - relative change in tooth size.

Filled circles = molars;
Open circles = incisors.
(After Brace & Montagu 1978: 361).

Histogram - number of distinct implements comprising cultures in Atlantic Europe.
(After Lewin 1989: 118).

size of each individual tooth of both the lower, and upper, dental arcades (Figure (7.4). However, the aetiology of posterior dental reduction appears to have differed from that of anterior reduction. Molar diminution has been a long term evolutionary trend, a characteristic feature of hominid phylogenesis. It is thought that this is a consequence of the increasingly important role played by meat in the hominid diet, meat requires less preparative grinding by the molars than poorer quality plant foods. In contrast, the anterior dentition tended to increase in size throughout the earlier Pleistocene, this trend of incisor size increase reached its apogee with the Neanderthal, thereafter incisor size decreased at a similar rate to that of the molars (Figure 7.4).

For earlier hominids, the anterior dentition had probably functioned as a "third hand", it is known from ethnographic sources that the incisors may be used for a variety of manipulative purposes including the holding of bone drills, straightening wooden spear shafts and stripping hides (Wolpoff 1980: 178). It has been argued that, from the beginning of the Upper Palaeolithic, the continuing elaboration of evermore specialised tool kits would have progressively reduced the need to use the front teeth for such purposes (Wolpoff 1980: 278; Brace et al 1987). The post-Neanderthal acceleration of incisor reduction is, therefore, best viewed as an epiphenomenon of increasing cultural complexity. At the same time, innovations in the field of food preparation , such as the adoption of "earth oven" cooking techniques and of ceramic vessels to boil or pulp food, would have reduced the need to intensively chew food and thus have allowed further molar diminution (Frayer 1977, Brace et al 1987).

Large tooth size would perhaps possess a selective advantage in that primitive methods of food processing would be associated with high rates of dental attrition. Small teeth would rapidly wear down and, without teeth, it would be difficult to orally macerate food. Additionally, once dental enamel is worn away the underlying pulp would be exposed and life threatening infection might ensue. It might even lead to suicide -

dental abscesses are the only reported cause of suicide in some south seas communities (Davies 1972). In consequence, it has been suggested that an increasingly elaborate cultural repertoire allowed the relaxation of selective pressure acting to maintain large tooth size as a necessary adaptation, with concomitant dental reduction (Brace et al 1987). Not all workers agree with this hypothesis, however. The rate of dental reduction that occurs from the Upper Palaeolithic onwards does not appear to be constant, there seems instead to be periods of more rapid reduction between the earlier and later upper Palaeolithic, and again between the Mesolithic and Neolithic (Figure 7.5) (Calcagano 1986; Frayer 1977). These periods of rapid reduction were coincident with horizons of cultural innovation (Frayer 1977: 118). An alternative proposal, therefore, is to see the trend to smaller teeth as being a selective adaptation (Frayer 1977: 118).

Although significant, dental reduction in itself is unlikely to have had a remarkable effect upon cranial morphology. Smaller roots, it is true, would allow accommodation within a mandible or maxilla of reduced dimensions, but the absolute volumes involved are small. However, the cultural advances which rendered teeth increasingly redundant for purposes of mastication and manipulation would also have caused a parallel redundancy of the cranial musculature, which would require less development for the efficient mechanical operation of the jaws. Alterations in muscle mass and size would be expected to exert a marked influence on cranial morphology, although dental dimorphism would again elicit a differential response.

Molar grinding is powered by the masseter and medial pterygoid muscles, which attach to the lateral and medial aspects, respectively, of the mandibular ramus (Figure 7.6). The two medial pterygoid muscles originate on each side of the sphenoid bone, a central component of the cranial base, while the origins of the masseters are to be found on the zygomatic, or cheek, bones. The

48

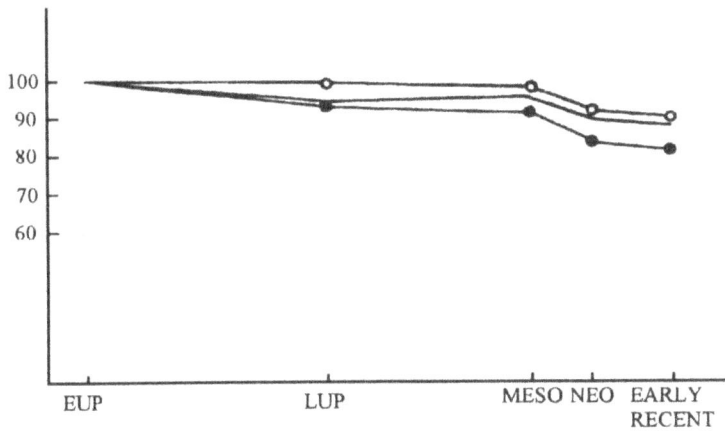

Figure 7.5.

Reduction in tooth size during the later Pleistocene and the Holocene.

Filled circles = total occlusal area;
Open circles = maxillary incisor breadth;
Solid line = maxillary incisor length.
(Information from: Calgano 1986; Frayer 1977; Brace et al 1987).

dwindling of this musculature allows a corresponding gracilization of its supporting skeleton. There is a trend towards reduction in both size and lateral extension of the zygomatic arch to which the masseter is attached. Thus crania with a set of muscles suitable for prolonged and heavy chewing will have broader and heavier, perhaps also shorter, faces than those confronted by a soft food diet (Brace & Montagu 1978: 453). This has been confirmed by animal experiments where it has been shown that moderate differences in the hardness of diet provided for rats during their growth period affects the medio-lateral dimensions of the adult maxilla. It was suggested that the wider maxilla of the animals fed on a hard diet resulted from increased muscular stimulation during more prolonged, or more difficult mastication (Beecher & Corruccini 1981).

There is a different set of muscle relationships serving the needs of the anterior dentition when it is used to grip and to pull (Wolpoff 1980: 178). To counteract the anterior loading produced by a pulling action large forces are generated by the temporalis, particularly posteriorly, and also by the neck, or nuchal, musculature. Consequent enlargement of these muscles is accommodated by a backwards extension of the cranium, thus producing a longer, and narrower, skull (Figures 7.7 & 7.8). In addition, large forces are produced by enlarged masseters

Figure 7.6.

Schematic frontal section of the human cranium showing the major muscles of mastication.

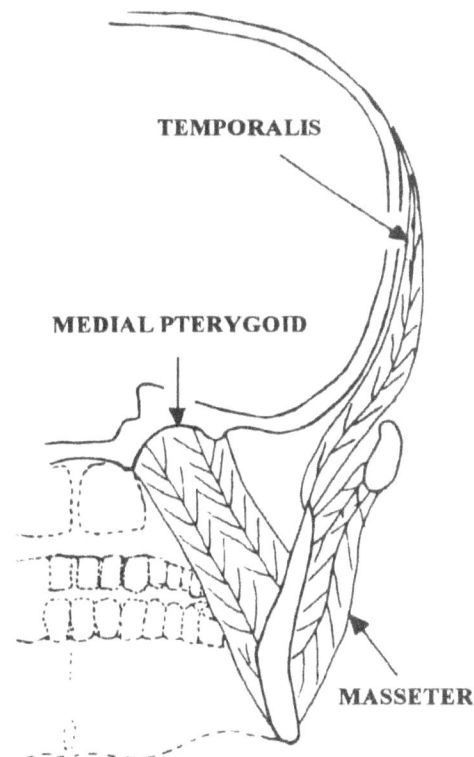

49

Figure 7.7.

Temporalis and masseter muscles.

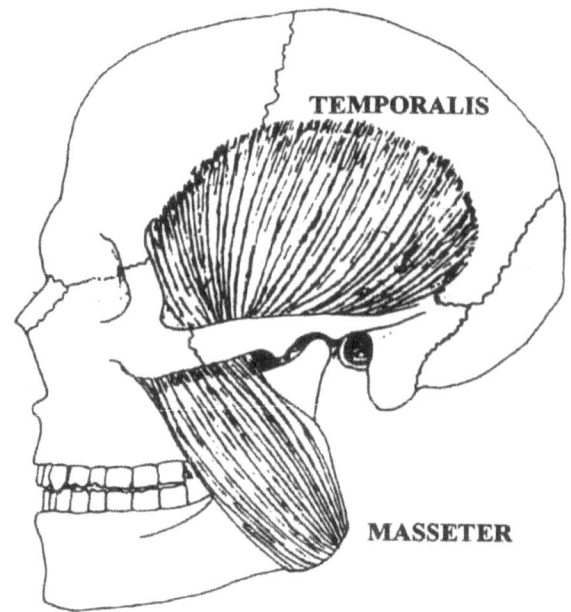

and anterior temporales to counteract the vertical loading produced by frontal bite. Again, any anterior enlargement of these muscles produces a larger, and more forwardly positioned, zygomatic arch. Although the diagram reproduced here is of an early hominid, the same set of mechanical/skeletal relationships has been used to explain the unique morphology of the present day Inuit cranium. Despite their arctic habitat, the Inuit possess one of the most dolichocephalic crania in the world - the legacy of the unusually large size of their temporales muscles. Their prominent zygomas are, similarly, associated with enlarged masseters and temporales. The Inuit habitually use their anterior dentition as a "third hand" and their well developed musculature enables them to generate a bite force double that of modern Europeans (Hylander 1977). Despite their powerful jaws, however, Inuit teeth are not particularly large, probably because of their high quality, largely meat, diet. This confirms that although reductive trends presenting in teeth and muscle may be parallel, they are not necessarily associated.

It is evident from the fossil record that, in the long term, the progressive decrease in both tooth and muscle size has been associated with an increasing gracilization of the human cranium. Weidenreich (1945: 17) has shown that the differences between ectocranial and endocranial measurements, an estimate of bone robusticity, have decreased through time (Table 7.1). There has also been a corresponding anatomical modification of the cranium with a reduction in the size of the maxilla and mandible resulting in their more infero-posterior placement relative to the cranial vault which has, in turn, become relatively shorter, but broader (Wolpoff 1980: 299). Again, the relevance of these observations to more recent populations may be questioned but studies of Nubian material have monitored this process in crania dating from the Mesolithic period

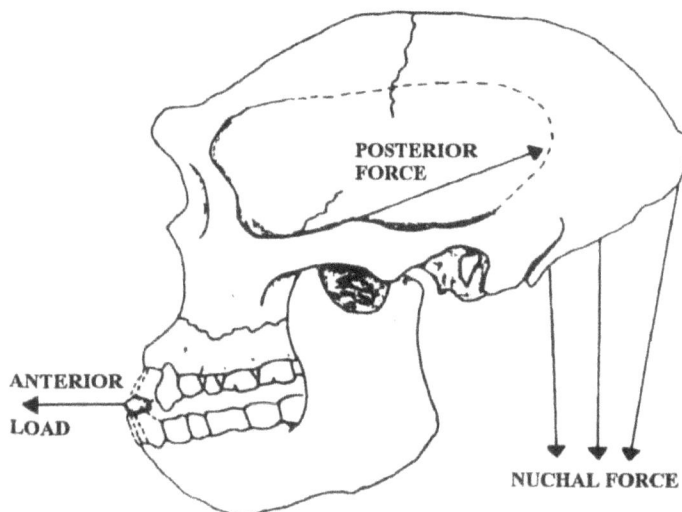

Figure 7.8.

Muscle forces generated by using anterior dentition to pull.

(After Wolpoff 1980).

50

Table 7.1.   Cranial gracilization. (After Weidenreich 1945: 17).

	Homo erectus.	Early Homo sapiens.	Modern Homo sapiens.
% difference between endocranial and ectocranial:			
length	30.3	24.1	12.8
breadth	13.3	9.8	7.2

(c9000 BC) through to the early Christian period (c1100 AD) (Carlson & van Gerven 1977). These diachronic changes in both the structure and the morphology of the human cranium are no doubt propelled by a combination of genetic modification and developmental plasticity as suggested earlier. The rate at which these changes might occur remains uncertain, however, there is no clear indication of how long a "lag phase" might exist between cultural innovation and physiological response. The empirical data necessary for establishing this rate of change remain largely unavailable although the observation that the adult facial skeletons of Inuit who are raised on a soft, "western" diet are less robust than those of their parents (Waugh 1937), when taken together with the animal studies of Beecher & Corruccini (1981) referred to previously, provide some indication that the effect of dietary change upon cranial shape may be expressed inter-generationally.

Climate and Head Shape

Cephalic, or Cranial, Index has been shown to covary with climate on both a continental and a global scale (Beals 1972; Beals et al 1983, 1984; Hiernaux 1977; Guglielmino et al 1979; Crognier 1981), with Cephalic Indices ranging from 76 in hot, dry, climates to 81 in glacial areas (Figure 7.9). Known distributions would suggest that both humidity and temperature are important determinants of cranial shape and this has been confirmed by a reanalysis , carried out by Guglielmino et al (1979), of the craniometric data collected by Howells (1973). Howells had used discriminant function analysis to organise his data set (derived from 17 populations from a variety of locations distributed globally) and had found that the first discriminant function (DF1), which produced maximum discrimination between samples, separated European, American and East Asian populations from Africans and Australians. This was in contradiction of genetic data derived from blood group, enzyme and other

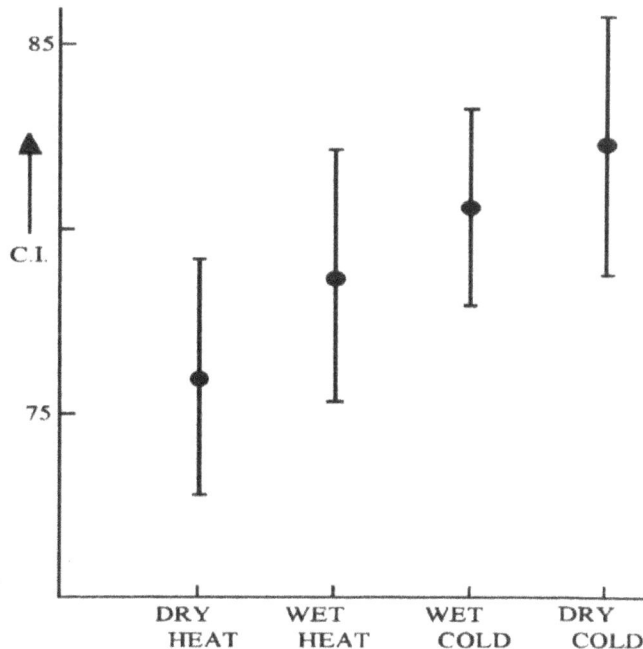

Figure 7.9.

Positive correlation of Cephalic Index with climate.

(After Beals 1972: 89).

Figure 7.10.

Cranial Indices Of European populations and their neighbours during the early twentieth century.

Cross-hatching = brachycephalic (Cranial Index >81).
Horizontal line shading = mesaticephalic (Cranial Index 78-81).
No shading = dolichocephalic (Cranial Index <77).

(After Coon 1939: 258; Weidenreich 1945: 32).

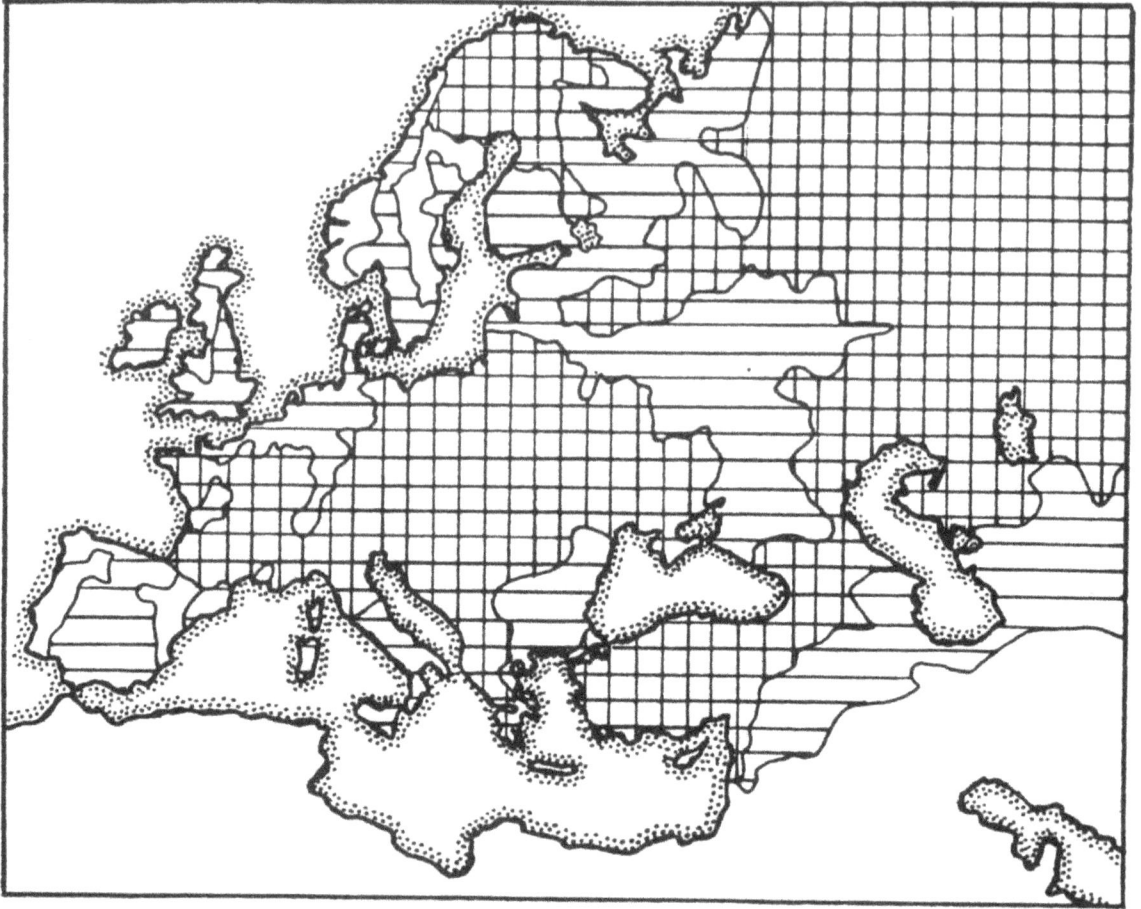

protein polymorphisms which suggested that African and European populations were more closely related to each other than to either Australians or Americans. Guglielmino and his co-workers showed that, in fact, DF1 was strongly correlated with temperature and that a subsidiary DF, number 9, was correlated with humidity. Thus dividing up the populations by means of DF1 was, in effect, grouping them together on the basis of climatic association. By using DF2 instead the structure of craniometric similarity that emerged matched that of genetic similarity. It was also demonstrated in this study that temperature was negatively correlated with vault breadth and facial height but positively correlated with alveolar prognathism. Humidity was positively correlated with cranial length. These findings are partly in accord with the distribution of Cranial Indices known to have existed in early 20th century Europe - when inhabitants of warmer/wetter areas were more dolichocephalic than those of colder/drier areas - but the maritime distribution of the dolichocephalic skull form would suggest that humidity is a more important determinant of cranial form on a continental scale than it is on a global scale (Figure 7.10).

Altered head shape may, in part, be representative of a more general, climate induced, somatic mutability (Brace et al 1978: 432; Hiernaux 1977; Ruff 1991). Human metabolic integrity is preserved by enzyme systems which achieve maximum activity at 37°C. Body temperature is maintained at this optimum both by overall shape and by a series of physiological mechanisms, a combination which acts to increase thermal output after the catabolism of stored energy reserves during episodes of strenuous physical exercise or else decrease thermal output in conditions of low ambient temperature. Considerations of shape generally revolve around alterations in the mass:surface area ratio of the body. Thus, in hot climates, the surface area is maximised to promote heat loss through direct radiation, air current convection and perspiratory evaporation. Conversely, in cold climates, these mechanisms are retarded by a reduced surface area. The effects of temperature on body shape may be confounded by those of humidity, however, with drier climates favouring a lower mass:surface area ratio than wetter climates.

If the body and head are considered as straightforward energy conserving/dissipating structures, then changes in their mass:surface area ratios can be explained as simple anatomical adjustments towards geometrical optima. The relationships that exist between head shape, overall body shape and climate are complex, however. Realised cranial morphology is probably best considered as an expression of compromise, a compromise reached between two, contradictory, processes of climate-induced, anatomical, shape change. Ruff (1991) has argued that, when considered in its entirety, the human body most closely approximates a cylinder in shape, and it is a property of cylindrical objects that their volume:lateral surface area ratio is a positive correlate of cylinder breadth, it is independent of height. Thus, in order for the human populations of colder climates to increase their body mass:surface area ratios, an increase in breadth-related body dimensions is required, expressed both antero-posteriorly and laterally. The bodies of people living in cold climates tend to be, on average, bulkier than those belonging to individuals from hot climates. However when the head, particularly the calvarium, is considered in isolation it is not cylindrical in shape but instead more closely resembles an ovoid sphere. As the highest possible volume:surface area ratio of any object is that achieved by a sphere, it is a prior expectation that, in cold climates, there would be a tendency for the calvarium to adjust in shape towards greater sphericity. This would require equalisation of the three linear dimensions of the calvarium, which remain unequal however in all human populations. The antero-posterior breadth (cranial length) exceeds the lateral breadth which, in turn, is greater than the height. Thus, to approach the proportionality of a sphere there would be a requirement for decreased length, increased height and an unchanged breadth. There is a conflict of geometry, therefore, between the morphological optima needed to be achieved by, on the one hand, the calvarium as a unique structure, and, on the other, by the calvarium as an integral component of the body. In consequence, there follows a morphological compromise which, in cold climates, permits lateral expansion of the calvarium with a smaller degree of longitudinal shortening and, perhaps, an increase in height. The resultant trend is towards brachycephaly. The opposite, of course, holds true for individuals living in hot climates.

It has long been maintained that the nose is, in itself, an anatomical structure which is responsive to climatic variation (Thomson & Buxton 1923; Brace & Montagu 1978: 427-431; Franciscus & Long 1991; Weiner 1954; Wolpoff 1968). Nasal regulation of somatic heat and moisture exchange with the environment is thought to be important, not only for the maintenance of body temperature at an optimal 37°C, but also for the protection of the mechanisms of gas exchange which proceed in the pulmonary alveoli and which are sensitive to departures of ambient temperature and humidity from physiological norms. The external nose and interior nasal fossa together provide a mucous secreting epithelial surface which serves to warm and humidify inspired air. A narrow, projecting, nose provides a relatively greater surface area of epithelium and is thus often present amongst the populations of cold, or arid, climates. By contrast, in hot, or humid, climates a broader, but shorter, nose presents a proportionately reduced amount of epithelial surface which acts to retard the recovery of heat and moisture from expired air. Alterations in the size or shape of the internal nasal fossa would need to be accommodated by a change in the conformation, or flexure, of the cranial base and might therefore be a contributory factor in the overall cranial response to an exigent climate.

In theory, nasal breadth should cline in association with climate, being positively correlated with heat and/or humidity, negatively correlated with cold and/or aridity. Several regional studies have indeed shown this to be the case (Wolpoff 1968; Hiernaux 1977), as have a number of more wide ranging ones (Weiner 1954; Thompson & Buxton 1923, Franciscus & Long 1991; Crognier 1981). However, when viewed globally the position is less clear, across the Eurasian land mass a reversal of the expected cline is revealed. The nasal breadth of the inhabitants of central Asia tends to be greater than that of those dwelling in more temperate, and thus warmer and wetter, areas of Europe. The reason for this is not clear, but the suggestion that the inhabitants of central Asia are but recent arrivals, having been resident for a few millennia only (Brace & Montagu 1978: 430), has more the appearance of special pleading than of explanation. There is then, at present, little evidence to suggest, in northern latitudes at least, that nose form can be considered to react to the vagaries of climate in an anatomically consistent manner, and its effect on cranial morphology must therefore remain questionable.

Beals (1984) has suggested that 30-40% of the variance known to exist between the Cranial Indices of various populations might be attributed to thermoregulatory response and has suggested that this variation in morphology is adaptive in nature and that the rate of change can be measured by reference to the New World, first colonised about 15000 years ago. Thus, the difference in Cranial Index between populations of the polar and tropical zones will have occurred within that timespan and a rate of change can be estimated. However work with migrant populations has suggested that the response of head shape to climate may well be a developmental, not adaptational, feature. Kobyliansky (1983) has convincingly demonstrated that in Israel the first generation offspring of immigrants from eastern and central Europe are more dolichocephalic than their parents and that their Cephalic Indices approximate the values found amongst Israelis of Middle Eastern extraction. In the eastern European case there was a shift in mean Index from 83.6 to 77.7. A similar process may underlie Boas' (1910-13) observations that, in the United States, children of south Italian immigrants were more brachycephalic than their parents while the reverse was true of children with parents of east European origin. (There may have been other factors at work however. Keith observed that the head shapes of third generation immigrants of both western and eastern European descent were indistinguishable, and suggested it was the result of a uniform, American, diet (Keith, quoted in Davis 1972: 42)). Thus the rate of climatically associated cranial change is also uncertain, although immigrant data strongly suggests that it might be rapid, and should perhaps be considered as an inter-generational event.

Conclusion

The anatomy of the human cranium represents a structural compromise to the spatial demands of three autonomous physiological processes: respiration, mastication and neural function. An alteration in the operational characteristics of any one which necessitates a change in the physical dimensions of its skeletal support will necessarily result in compensatory changes to the entire cranium. Thus, overall cranial morphology is sensitive to a variety of environmentally derived modifiers which exert their influence both directly, during ontogeny, and indirectly, by altering the relative fitnesses of varying genotypes. In this chapter three aetiologies of morphological change have been discussed, these are:

1) artificial constraint,
2) cultural innovation,
3) thermoregulatory response.

It is unlikely, however, that all such modifiers have been identified. The effects of childhood malnutrition on developing cranial form are not known, although studies on rats have suggested that muscle development might be sacrificed in order to maintain the integrity of the brain. There is an associated underdevelopment of the facial skeleton with reorientation of the cranial base and calvarium (Pucciarelli 1980, Pucciarelli & Oyhenart 1987). The possible influence of geology, transmitted through diet, on cranial form also remains to be investigated since Kobyliansky has, somewhat enigmatically, referred to a Russian study in which significant correlations were shown to exist between head shape and the soil concentrations of various elements.

Without a detailed catalogue of environmental morphogens, and in the absence of any substantial body of empirical evidence relating to the rates of morphological change, it might be claimed that any study of cranial variability is flawed from the outset, perhaps fatally so. Indeed, Renfrew has recently suggested as much:

'Craniometry, the study and measurement of human skulls, has in recent years enjoyed about as much prestige in scientific circles as phrenology.'
(Renfrew 1987: 4).

In the following chapters, it will be shown that such a suggestion is unduly pessimistic and that, on the contrary, it is possible to derive some meaningful, if limited, conclusions from a craniometric study of the prehistoric inhabitants of Britain.

Chapter Eight

CRANIOMETRY: METHODS AND RESULTS

Measurement Technique

There is a wide range of internationally defined and standardised measurements available for use in the definition of cranial morphology, but it was realised from the outset of this study that selection from the available repertoire would be severely constrained by the generally poor state of preservation of the material under study. A suite of 20 measurements was eventually chosen which provided overall description of the calvarium and naso-maxillary complex. The choice of measurements was influenced both by their discriminatory potential (Sokal et al 1987: 18) and by the survival characteristics of the necessary landmarks in the material under study (Brothwell & Krzanowski 1974). In multiple inhumation deposits the cranium and associated mandible are often separated and it is difficult to ascertain correct, matching, identities; measurements of the mandible were therefore not included in this study.

To achieve comparability with previously published studies of British crania the measurements taken were as described in Brothwell (1981). To facilitate the computer handling of the data the abbreviations used in describing the measurements follow the system introduced by Howells (1973) although they differ in their details. The accepted British equivalent is given in parentheses after each measurement definition. The measurements used were as follows:

GOL - maximum cranial length (L).

XCB - maximum breadth (B).

WCB - minimum frontal breadth (B').

ASB - bi-asterionic breadth (Biast.B.).

BBH - basi-bregmatic height (H').

BNL - basi-nasal length (LB).

FRK - frontal arc (S1).

PAK - parietal arc (S2).

OCK - occipital arc (S3).

FRC - frontal chord (S'1).

PAC - parietal chord (S'2).

OCC - occipital chord (S'3).

BAL - basi-alveolar length (GL).

NAH - upper facial height (G'H).

NLH - nasal height (NH').

NLB - nasal breadth (NB).

OH - orbital height (O2).

OB - orbital breadth (O'1).

PAL - palatal length (G'1).

PAB - palatal breadth (G2).

It was often the case that landmarks formed by sutural conjunction were obscured by the presence of a wormian bone or a complex suturation pattern. Where this occurred the correct position of the landmark was estimated by extending the lines of the relevant sutures to an intersecting point.

Measurements were obtained by the use of either vernier callipers, spreading callipers or tape measure, whichever was most appropriate. Precision was shown to be acceptable by remeasuring 10 skulls after intervening lapses of time which varied from a few days to several months. It was not possible to establish the accuracy of the measurement techniques used but comparisons with measurements taken by more recent workers were generally good.

As a result of post-depositional damage or decay a major proportion of the crania studied proved to be lacking in some of the anatomical landmarks necessary for obtaining a complete set of measurements. Several strategies were adopted in an attempt to surmount this problem, some methodological and some statistical. If a landmark was missing as a result of localised injury then its position was estimated. Although this might diminish the accuracy of the individual measurement the approximation would be good and likely to be better than any provided by subsequent statistical manipulation of the data. The values of ASB for crania 025, 086, 170 & 228 were estimated by their regression on XCB. The values of measurements OH and OB for skull 098 were assumed to be the group means. More often however damage to a skull was widespread so that a limited "fallback suite" of measurements was obtained. These measurements described the anatomy of the calvarium and were as follows: GOL, XCB, WCB, FRK, PAK, OCK, FRC, PAC, OCC. From badly damaged skulls, where possible, the measurements GOL and XCB only were obtained, these measurements being necessary for the calculation of Cranial Index.

Cranial Grouping

For purposes of comparison the crania were divided into several chronological and/or cultural groups. Group identity was determined by either burial practice or artefact associations, more rarely by stratigraphy. The major groups constructed were as follows:

Early Neolithic - All crania recovered from primary deposits in long barrows and chambered tombs. (EN).

Later Neolithic - All burials with associations of a Grooved Ware or Peterborough type. Specifically, these include jet sliders, antler maceheads, edge ground "Seamer" axes and "Duggleby" adzes and transverse arrowheads. This group corresponds largely to Kinnes' (1979) stages D and E. (LN).

Other Neolithic - Neolithic burials not able to be included in either of the two preceding groups. Although, in the main, corresponding to Kinnes' (1979) stages A, B and C it might be mistaken to attribute to them all an earlier Neolithic date as they are often distinguished solely by the association of a leaf-shaped arrowhead, an artefact type which continued in use for the duration of the Neolithic (Green 1980: 92). (ON).

Bell Beaker - Burials associated with either a Beaker, tanged copper dagger or arm bracer. Burials with barbed and tanged arrowheads only were not included in this group as the artefact is often associated with ceramic types other than Beaker. (BB).

Weapons Group - After Piggott (1963: 82). This is a late Beaker group of burials furnished with either late Beaker vessels (Clarke's S3,S4), bronze or copper flat axes,

stone shaft-hole battle axes (Roe's III, IV, V) or rivetted bronze daggers (Piggott's II, III, IV; Gerloff's Masterton, Butterwick, Milston, Merthyr Mawr). (WG).

Food Vessel - Burials accompanied by either a Food Vessel, plano-convex flint knife, jet bead necklace or single pointed copper or bronze awl. The inhumations from Folkton with Collared Vessels are included in this group, as is the burial from Mill Hill which was provided with an Armorico-British B bronze dagger (Gerloff's Cressington). (FV).

The chronological and cultural relationships of the preceding three groups remain to be fully defined but they can regarded as forming an approximate, if overlapping, chronological sequence with the Bell Beaker group being the earliest and the Food Vessel latest. This particular interpretation of early Bronze Age chronology is not currently accepted by all workers in the field but the supporting evidence is fully described and discussed in Appendix 3.

Bronze Age - All apparently early Bronze Age burials not able to be accommodated in any one specific group. This might be because of the absence of any grave goods or else the presence of non-specific, long lived, items such as double pointed metal awls and single jet buttons or beads. (BA).

A descriptive catalogue of all crania measured is presented in Appendix 4, with the craniometric data in Appendix 5.

Statistical Methods

There are a number of statistical methods available which may be used to facilitate the display and analysis of a multivariate data set. They fall into two categories, depending upon the nature of the data set to be analysed. If the data are derived from two or more predefined groups, groups whose membership criteria are external to the data under consideration, then methods are available which may define the extension of group structure into the data set. If, on the other hand, no external grouping information is available then exploratory methods may be used to search the data set for any structure that may be present. Although the craniometric data collected in this study were open to prior grouping by reference to cultural or chronological criteria, it was not a necessary concomitant that such generated groups would find expression in the craniometric data. It might be, as diffusionist explanation demands, that the different cultural groups are to be considered as the material detritus of changing patterns of cultural expression, projected into the archaeological record by a biologically steady-state population. A null hypothesis was adopted therefore: that the cranial morphology of the inhabitants of prehistoric Britain remained relatively stable from the beginning of the Neolithic through to the late Bronze Age. The craniometric data could then be analysed using exploratory methods to ascertain the presence, or absence, of any morphological groupings, independently of external, archaeological, information. The two, separate, grouping structures, archaeological and craniometric, would then be available for comparison. The exploratory methods chosen were principal components analysis and cluster analysis, both available within the commercial SPSSX software package.

Univariate Statistics

Before submitting the craniometric data to multivariate analysis the differences between the mean values of each individual measurement obtained from the Bronze Age and Neolithic series were first tested for significance, using Student's T-Test. Included in the Neolithic series were all crania from groups EN and ON. Those from groups BA, BB, FV and WG were included in the Bronze Age series. For male crania, most significant differences occurred between measurements of the calvarium, both longitudinal and lateral. The pattern was consistent, no matter whether only those crania which possessed a complete set of measurements were chosen for testing (Table 8.1) or else if all crania were included (Table 8.2). The Neolithic skulls were significantly longer than those of the Bronze Age, the major contribution to this increased length being derived from the central and posterior parts of the calvarium as measured by PAK, PAC and, to a lesser extent, OCK and OCC. Bronze Age crania were wider than Neolithic ones, both anteriorly as measured by WCB and posteriorly as measured by XCB.

However, this increased width of Bronze Age skulls was not demonstrated by the measurement ASB. The differences between the mean nasal breadths (NLB) of both series achieved significance when all available measurements were considered. A similar pattern of differences was revealed when the measurement means of female skulls were inspected (Table 8.3). The Cranial Indices for all individuals were calculated when the requisite measurements were available. The results are presented in Table 8.4 and the distributions shown in Figure 8.1. The mean Cranial Index of the Bronze age series was significantly higher than that of the Neolithic series, and also than that of the Late Neolithic sample. Female crania displayed the same pattern of differences for both single measurements and the Cranial Index (Table 8.4, Figure 8.2).

Size and Shape

Shape may scale with size either allometrically or isometrically. That is to say, shape can alter in a consistent fashion in conditions of increasing absolute size (allometric scaling) or else it may remain constant (isometric scaling) (Corruccini 1987). To test for evidence of allometry in the prehistoric crania under investigation a simple measure of cranial size, the Cranial Module (Sankas 1930), was computed as follows:

$$\text{Cranial Module} = GOL + XCB + BBH/3.$$

Table 8.1   Univariate statistics.

All male crania with a full set of measurements available for analysis one.

Neolithic -17 crania.
Bronze Age - 39 crania.

	Neolithic	Bronze Age	Significance
GOL	196±6	186±7	<0.005
XCB	139±5	146±7	<0.005
WCB	98±3	101±4	0.008
ASB	115±4	113±6	N.S.
BBH	140±7	139±6	N.S.
FRK	135±8	132±7	N.S.
PAK	136±7	127±8	<0.005
OCK	129±11	118±8	<0.005
FRC	117±6	114±5	0.025
PAC	123±4	114±6	<0.005
OCC	105±7	96±6	<0.005
NAH	69±3	70±5	N.S.
BNL	105±4	106±6	N.S
BAL	99±5	98±6	N.S.
OH	33±2	33±3	N.S.
OB	40±2	41±2	N.S.
NLH	52±3	53±3	N.S.
NLB	23±2	25±2	N.S.
PAL	45±3	46±3	N.S.
PAB	40±4	41±3	N.S.

Table 8.2.   Univariate statistics.

All male crania with all available measurements included. Figures in parentheses refer to the number of crania available for each particular measurement. Measurement

	Neolithic (Mean ±1SD)	Bronze Age (Mean ±1SD)	Significance
GOL	197±6 (42)	187±8 (109)	<0.005
XCB	138±5 (42)	145±7 (109)	<0.005
WCB	98±4 (34)	100±4 (103)	0.029
ASB	114±5 (30)	114±6 (78)	N.S.
BBH	139±6 (21)	139±7 (58)	N.S.
FRK	134±7 (34)	132±7 (103)	N.S.
PAK	136±7 (34)	128±7 (102)	<0.005
OCK	127±10 (34)	118±7 (97)	0.042
FRC	116±5 (34)	114±6 (95)	N.S.
PAC	123±5 (34)	115±6 (95)	<0.005
OCC	103±7 (34)	96±6 (92)	N.S.
NAH	69±4 (20)	69±5 (74)	N.S.
BNL	105±4 (21)	106±6 (58)	N.S.
BAL	99±5 (17)	98±6 (51)	N.S.
OH	33±2 (21)	33±3 (61)	N.S.
OB	40±2 (21)	41±2 (60)	N.S.
NLH	52±2 (21)	53±3 (69)	N.S.
NLB	23±2 (21)	25±2 (66)	<0.005
PAL	46±3 (20)	46±3 (64)	N.S.
PAB	40±4 (20)	40±3 (65)	N.S.

Table 8.3.   Univariate statistics.

All female crania with all available measurements included. Figures in parentheses refer to the number of crania available for each particular measurement.

	Neolithic (Mean ±1SD)	Bronze Age (Mean ±1SD)	Significance
GOL	186±7 (28)	179±8 (49)	<0.005
XCB	133±6 (28)	141±5 (48)	<0.005
WCB	93±5 (24)	97±5 (45)	<0.005
ASB	108±6 (14)	108±5 (25)	N.S.
BBH	132±7 (14)	133±6 (32)	N.S.
FRK	127±4 (22)	126±7 (46)	N.S.
PAK	130±6 (23)	124±8 (46)	<0.005
OCK	121±7 (20)	114±8 (44)	<0.005
FRC	110±3 (22)	109±4 (39)	N.S.
PAC	117±4 (23)	110±6 (39)	<0.005
OCC	98±6 (20)	94±6 (38)	0.024
NAH	64±4 (12)	63±4 (29)	N.S.
BNL	98±2 (11)	101±7 (29)	N.S.
BAL	93±7 (8)	95±7 (24)	N.S.
OH	32±2 (11)	32±2 (27)	N.S.
OB	40±2 (11)	39±2 (26)	N.S.
NLH	49±3 (12)	48±3 (29)	N.S.
NLB	23±2 (12)	24±2 (27)	0.03
PAL	44±5 (9)	43±3 (21)	N.S.
PAB	38±3 (9)	40±4 (23)	N.S.

Table 8.4. Mean Cranial Index.

Figures in parentheses refer to the number of crania available for the calculation of each mean index.

Neolithic Male: 70.1 ±3.2 (42)
Neolithic Female: 71.3 ±3.7 (28)

Late Neolithic Male: 71.5 ±4.8 (11)

Bronze Age Male :   78.1 ±5.3 (109)
Bronze Age Female: 78.8 ±4.2 (48)

Figure 8.1.

Histograms of male Cranial Indices.

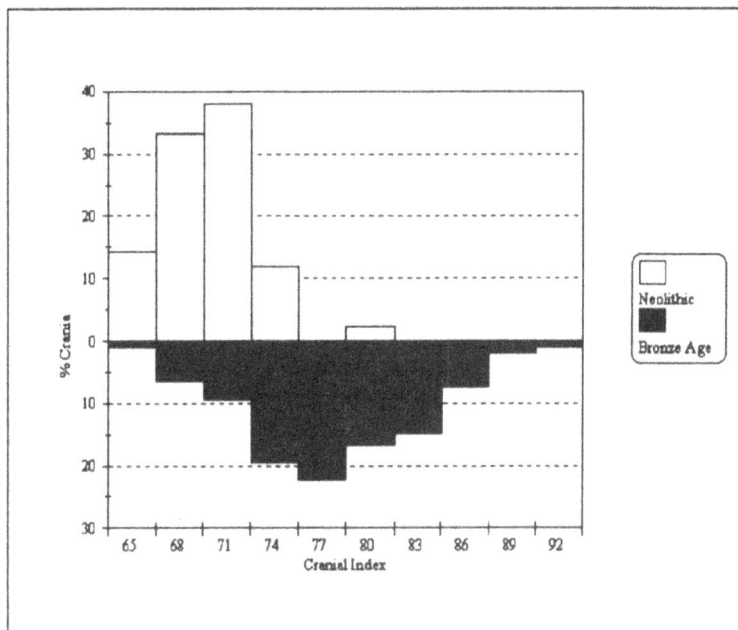

Figure 8.2.

Histograms of female Cranial Indices.

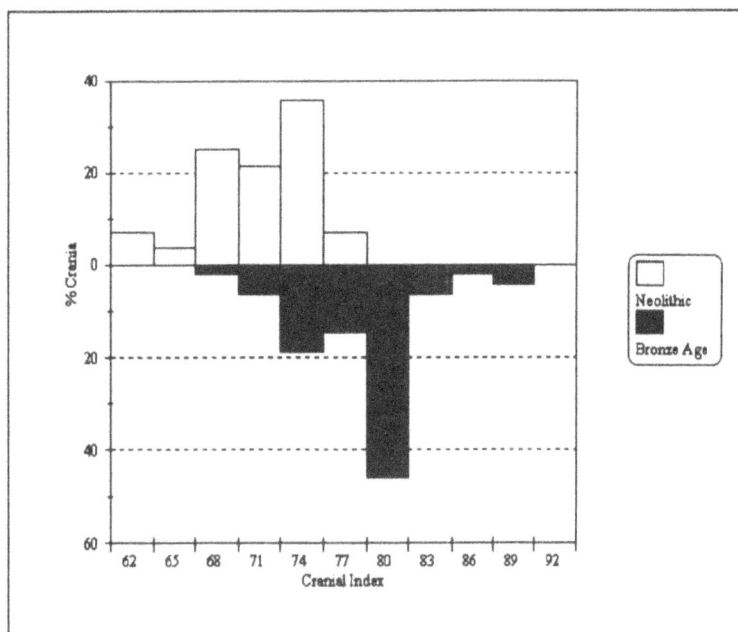

Table 8.5.   Mean Cranial Module.

Figures in parentheses refer to the number of crania available for the calculation of each mean module.

Neolithic male - 158.2 ±4.0 (21)
Bronze Age male - 156.9 ±4.1 (58)

Table 8.6.   Cranial Index/Module Correlation.

Neolithic males: r = 0.088
r^2 = 0.008   Not significant.

Bronze Age males: r = -0.237
r^2 = 0.056   Not significant.

The mean Cranial Module of the Neolithic Series was not significantly different from that of the Bronze Age one, suggesting that the crania of both series were of a similar size (Table 8.5). Furthermore, when compared to Cranial Index, which is a measure of proportionality and hence shape, there were no intra-sample correlations (Table 8.6). Thus, any effect size might have upon the crania under study would be isometric - the stature of an individual would not affect the shape of the cranium. This conclusion is supported by the close agreement between the mean Cranial Indices of both sexes within each series; assuming in each case that the females would, on average, be smaller than males. An important corollary of this property of isometry is that, in future, it would prove possible to standardise cranial measurements against an overall measure of body size, thus removing any size-related variance from the data set. This was not possible in the present study as there was not sufficient reliable information available pertaining to the stature of the skeletons from which the cranial measurements were obtained.

Although the relationship between size and shape was isometric for both of the cranial series studied, it might be expected that absolute body size would intrude into the statistical analyses by causing all measurements to correlate in a positive manner, each size-associated increase in any single measurement would be associated with similar size associated increases in all other measurements. To assess the extent to which this phenomenon might have interfered with the collected data the correlation matrices of the male samples were inspected, as shown in simplified form in Tables 8.7 and 8.8. If absolute size was influential there would be a large number of positive correlations. This was not the case with the Neolithic series, only 26 pairs out of a total of 190 were positively correlated. For the Bronze Age series the situation was less satisfactory, with 50 pairs of measurements being positively correlated. A large number of these correlations appeared to possess an underlying anatomical rationale, however; for instance the positive correlations seen amongst measurements of length, or else the nasal measurements which were correlated with supero-anterior measurements from adjacent areas. As in the Neolithic series there were several negative correlations. This suggests that the majority of correlations reveal relationships of shape, not size, and that the interference of size in the data analysis would not be too marked.

Multivariate Analysis One

In this analysis all male crania which possessed a complete set of measurement data were submitted to principal components and cluster analyses. Seven of the extracted principal components had eigenvalues in excess of 1, although inspection of the scree plot suggested that only the first four of these components were significant (Figure 8.3), together they accounted for 55.3% of the total variance exhibited by the sample. The principal component loadings are shown in Table 8.9.

Principal component 1 (PC1) was, in effect, a measure of cranial length. It had high positive correlations with all longitudinal measurements, particularly overall length (GOL) and, to a lesser extent, the chord and arc measurements (FRC, PAC, OCC, FRK, PAK, OCK). PC1 was also positively correlated with vault height (BBH) and negatively with palatal breadth (PAB).

PC2 was harder to interpret, demonstrating both positive and negative correlations. There was a moderate degree of positive correlation with most measures of the facial skeleton, particularly upper facial height (NAH). The minimum frontal breadth (WCB) was also positively correlated with this component, perhaps on account of its close association with the zygomatic, or cheek, bones. PC2 therefore seems to be a measure of facial height, or robustness, although there are also negative correlations with measures of parietal length (PAC, PAK).

PC3 measured calvarial breadth, correlating positively with both maximum biparietal breadth (XCB) and biasterionic breadth. Both of these measurements are taken posteriorly but the measure of anterior calvarial breadth (WCB) was not correlated with this component. On the other hand, frontal arc (FRK), which is a composite length/height measure of the anterior calvarium was. PC3 also demonstrated strong negative correlations with basi-nasal length (BNL) and basi-alveolar length (BAL), both of which are measures of maxillary prognathism. PC3 seems, therefore, to be a measure of the relations of brachycephaly. Crania with high scores on PC3 would be characterised by lateral enlargement of the calvarium in association with retrusion of the maxilla as a result of an increased angle of flexure of the cranial base, and perhaps with a compensatory lengthening, or at least curvature, of the frontal bone.

Table 8.7.   Neolithic male crania: correlation matrix.   (Simplified, only significant correlations shown).

	GOL	XCB	WCB	ASB	BBH	FRK	PAK	OCK	FRC	PAC	OCC	NAH	BNL	BAL	OH	OB	NLH	NLB	PA	PAB
GOL	0																			
XCB		0																		
WCB			0																	
ASB		+		0																
BBH					0															
FRK						0														
PAK							0													
OCK	+						-	0												
FRC	+	+			+	+			0											
PAC							+	-		0										
OCC					+	-	+		-		0									
NAH	+											0								
BNL	+		+										0							
BAL	+					+			+					0						
OH												+	+		0					
OB																0				
NLH												+			+		0			
NLB																		0		
PAL												+							0	
PAB																	+		+	0

Table 8.8.   Bronze Age male crania: correlation matrix.   (Simplified, only significant correlations shown).

	GOL	XCB	WCB	ASB	BBH	FRK	PAK	OCK	FRC	PAC	OCC	NAH	BNL	BAL	OH	OB	NLH	NLB	PA	PAB
GOL	0																			
XCB		0																		
WCB	+	+	0																	
ASB		+		0																
BBH	+				0															
FRK	+	+	+	+	+	0														
PAK	+		+			+	0													
OCK	+							0												
FRC	+	+	+	+	+	+	+		0											
PAC	+		+			+	+		+	0										
OCC	+				+				+		0									
NAH	+							+	+		+	0								
BNL	+	-			+							+	0							
BAL	+	-			+								+	0						
OH												+			0					
OB	+								+			+				0				
NLH			+		+							+			+		0			
NLB			+		+		+	+										0		
PAL																			0	
PAB									-		-	-								0

61

Table 8.9. Multivariate analysis one: component loadings.

	PC1	PC2	PC3	PC4
GOL	.88630	.04210	-.16143	.11021
XCB	-.22422	.30479	.67579	.35369
WCB	.01488	.44662	.23114	.20290
ASB	.34437	.05399	.42897	.08755
BBH	.41131	.36180	-.25286	-.10058
FRK	.58150	.19689	.48989	.03409
PAK	.51273	-.44681	.24663	-.40247
OCK	.65139	-.03047	-.30035	.56400
FRC	.72768	.21709	.34562	-.03261
PAC	.65228	-.43590	.19777	-.31818
OCC	.66427	-.01783	-.36491	.49755
NAH	.01548	.76414	.08878	-.17647
BNL	.24434	.57220	-.54772	-.36284
BAL	.18287	.42874	-.61875	-.18046
OH	.21649	.47616	.23200	-.39507
OB	.05547	.40344	.11763	.19691
NLH	-.06380	.65638	.25612	-.19936
NLB	-.25976	.39070	.08504	.39517
PAL	-.16690	.23014	-.22480	.21984
PAB	-.41356	.10659	-.20170	-.08549

Figure 8.3.

Multivariate analysis one: scree plot.

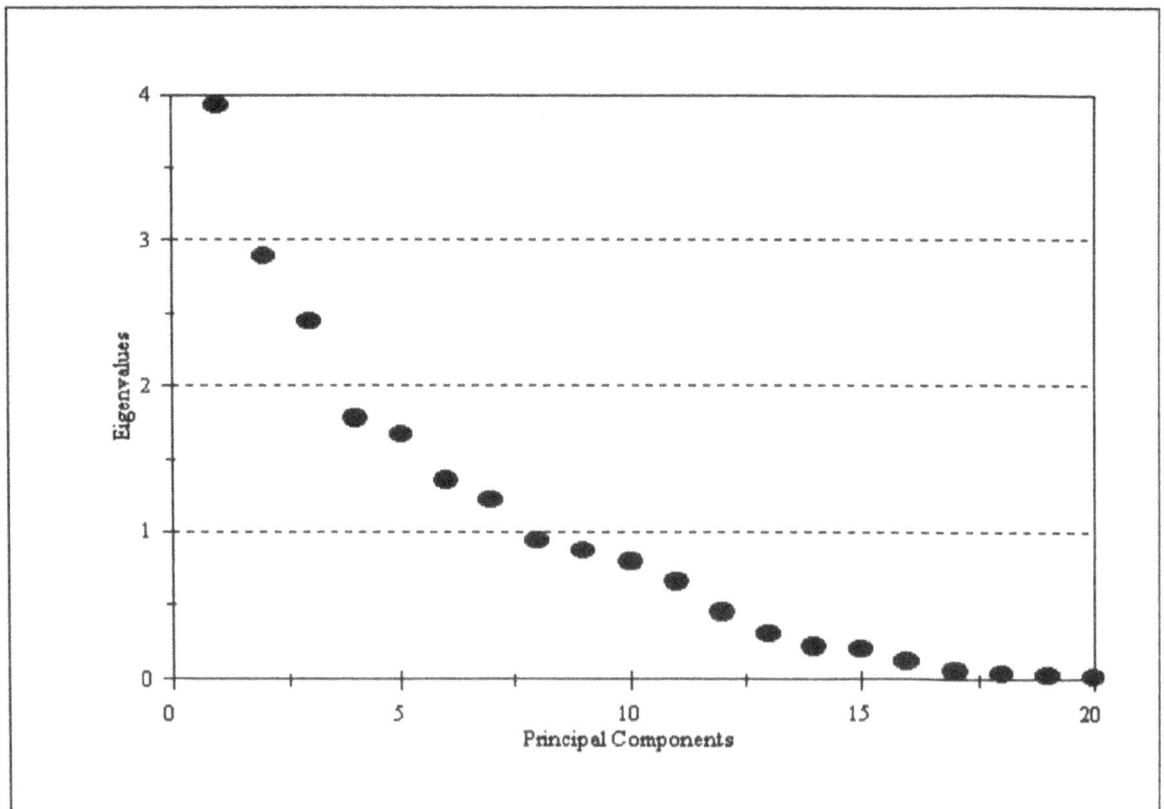

62

Figure 8.4. Multivariate analysis one: principal components plot.

Open circles = Neolithic series.
Filled series = Bronze Age series.

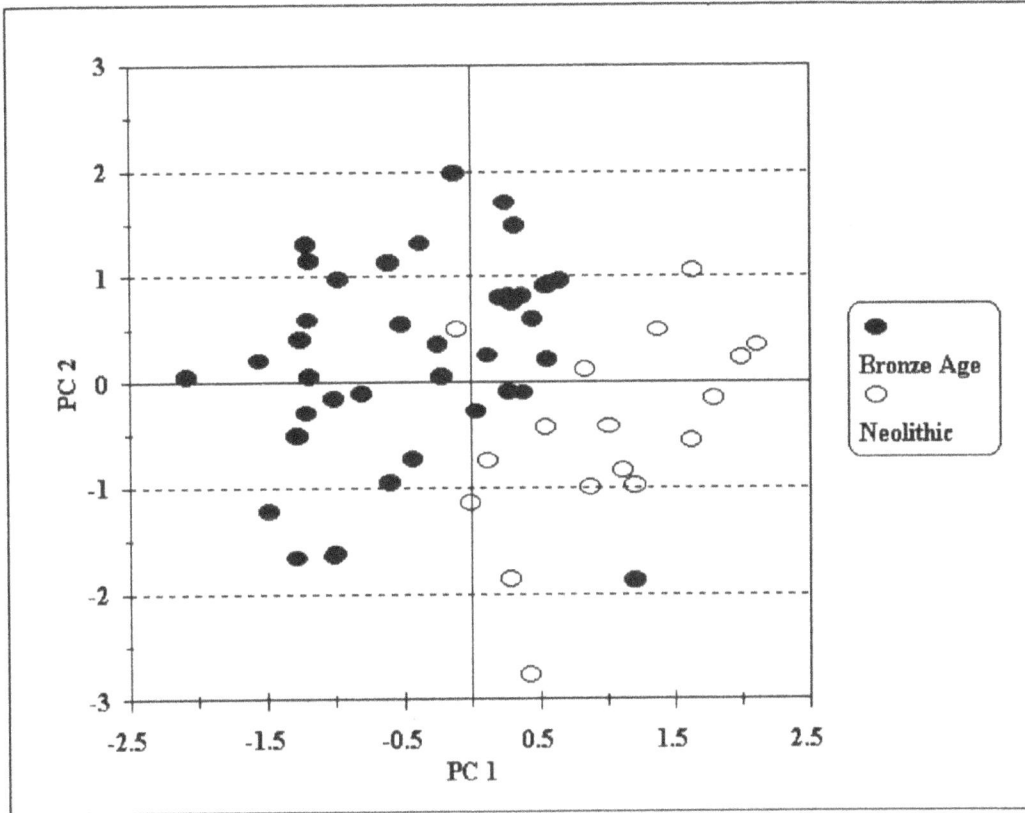

Figure 8.5. Multivariate analysis one: principal components plot.

Open circles = Neolithic series.
Filled circles = Bronze Age series.

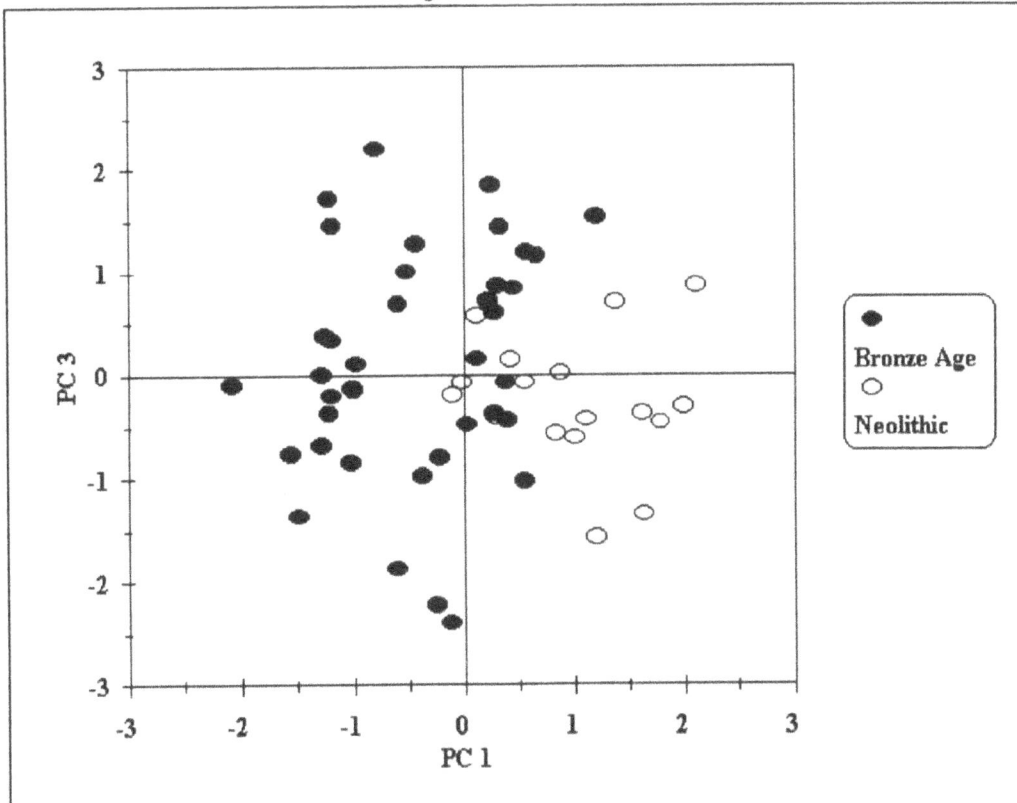

Figure 8.6.

Multivariate analysis one: superimpositon of cluster structure onto principal component plot.

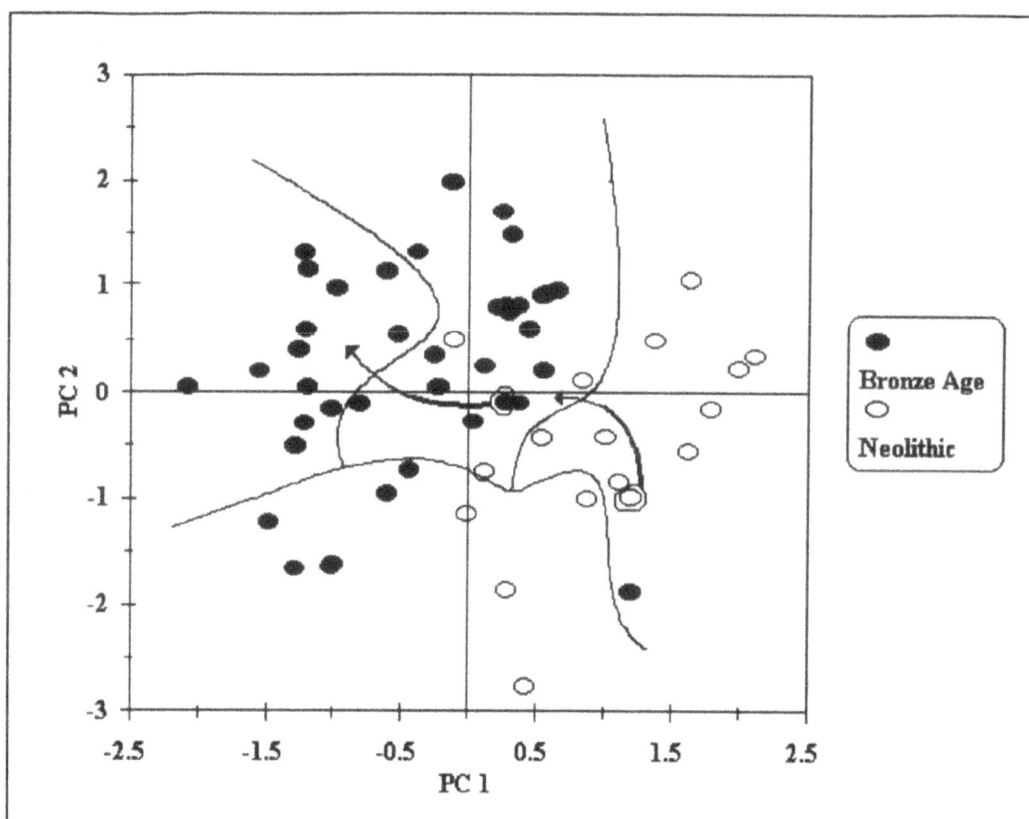

PC4 is a measure of cranial vault proportions, positively correlated with the occipital measurements (OCC, OCK) while being negatively correlated with parietal measurements (PAC, PAK). PC4 was also negatively correlated with basi-nasal length (BNL) and orbital height (OH), positively correlated with nasal breadth (NLB). It is unfortunate that NLB did not achieve a high correlation with any one particular principal component but instead demonstrates low levels of correlation with several different components, thus making its contribution to cranial morphology difficult to assess.

When the component scores of individual crania are projected onto the principal component axes it can be seen that the greatest separation of Bronze Age and Neolithic crania is provided by the first three components (Figures 8.4 - 8.5). Neolithic crania tend towards higher scores on PC1. Where their scores on PC1 are equal to those of Bronze Age examples the Neolithic crania have lower scores on PC2. Bronze age crania are equally distributed along PC3 while those of Neolithic date have mainly negative scores. Thus, in relative terms, the tendency is for Neolithic skulls to have higher scores on PC1 with lower scores on PC2 and PC3. Overall however, Bronze Age crania are distinguished by a greater degree of morphological heterogeneity. This analysis suggests that, on average, Neolithic skulls are more dolichocephalic than those of the Bronze age, but that if crania of equivalent length are compared then those of Bronze Age date have higher, or more robust, faces together with shorter parietal bones.

The results of the cluster analysis are presented in Figure 8.6. Although a clear-cut structure emerges using the method chosen the clusters do not appear to possess an absolute reality, they instead represent a partitioning of a continuous morphological distribution. Thus, if four well defined clusters are recovered by dividing the dendrogram at the rescaled distance of 20, and their membership superimposed upon a plot of PC1 vs PC2, it may be seen that the clusters effectively divide up the distribution into four parts, apparently using information derived only from PC1 and PC2. Important information from PC3 is disseminated between clusters. This exercise highlights the dangers inherent in the use of an uncorroborated cluster analysis for the exploration of an unknown data set. The cluster analysis did not provide any information not already available, in more useable form, from the principal components analysis. The apparent failure of the cluster analysis may have been due, in part, to the correlated nature of the craniometric data set. It is possible to compensate for these correlations by performing a cluster analysis on extracted principal components, which are by definition orthogonal; but as this then assigns equal weight to all PCs it is not at all clear that the remedy is in any way superior to the malady. More sophisticated measure of distance, such as that of Mahalonobis, may have improved the resolution of clusters but were not available in the SPSSX software package.

Table 8.10. Multivariate analysis two: component loadings.

	PC1	PC2	PC3
GOL	.90131	-.10245	-.09467
XCB	-.20976	.28243	.72517
WCB	.14137	.33499	.44682
FRK	.61518	.32917	.51118
PAK	.64035	.52173	-.48481
OCK	.65086	-.67604	.14014
FRC	.70892	.18427	.47076
PAC	.73760	.42094	-.44395
OCC	.61045	-.71009	.11920

Figure 8.7. Multivariate analysis two: scree plot.

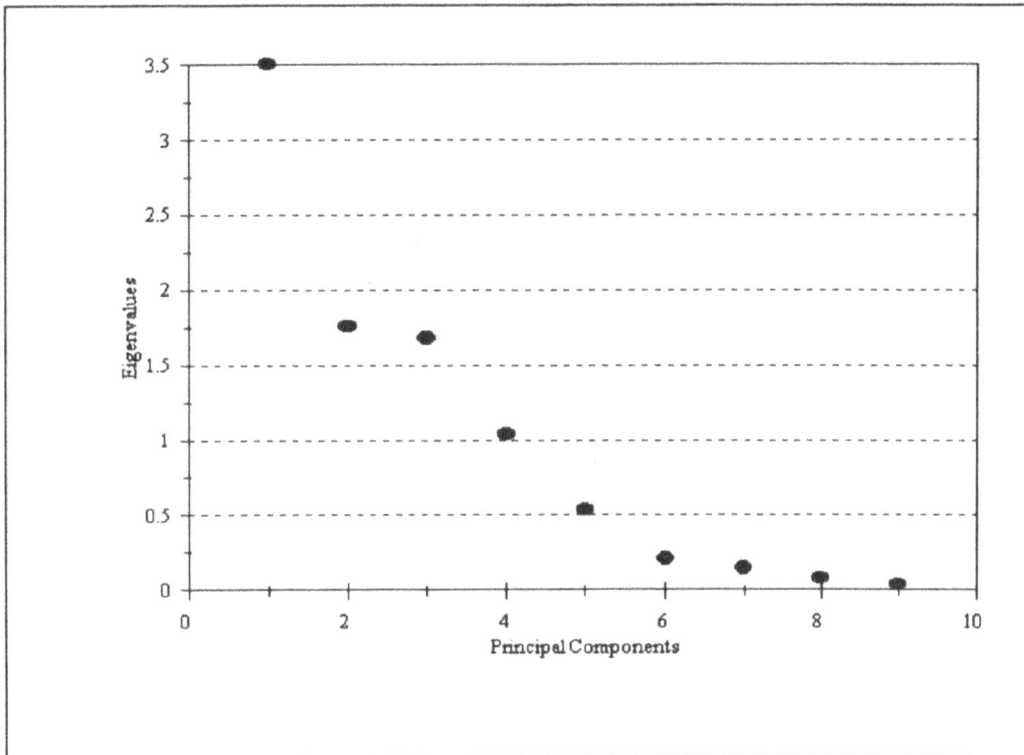

Multivariate Analysis Two

In this analysis, all male crania with a reduced set of measurements were examined. These measurements were GOL, XCB, WCB, FRK, OCK, PAK, PAC, and OCC; which, together, provided overall coverage of the calvarium. Although this reduced set of measurements diminished the descriptive potential of the analysis, this was compensated for by the increased number of crania able to be included.

Four of the principal components extracted from the data had an eigenvalue in excess of 1, although the scree plot suggested that only the first three were of any significance (Figure 8.7). The principal component loadings are presented in Table 8.10.

PC1 was, as in analysis 1, a measurement of length.

PC2 was marked by strong negative correlations with both measurements of occipital length (OCK, OCC) and by corresponding positive correlations with the

65

Figure 8.8. Multivariate analysis two: principal components plot.

Open circles = Neolithic series.
Filled circles = Bronze Age series.

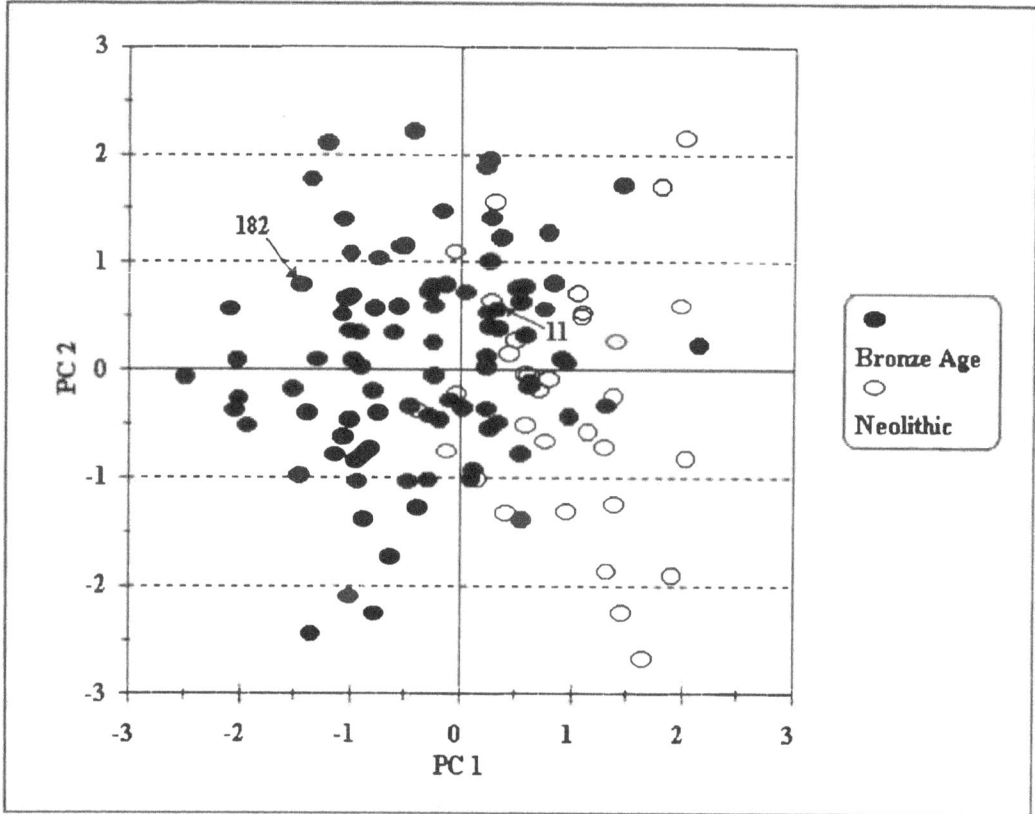

Figure 8.9. Multivariate analysis two: principal components plot.

Open circles = Neolithic series.
Filled circles = Bronze Age series.

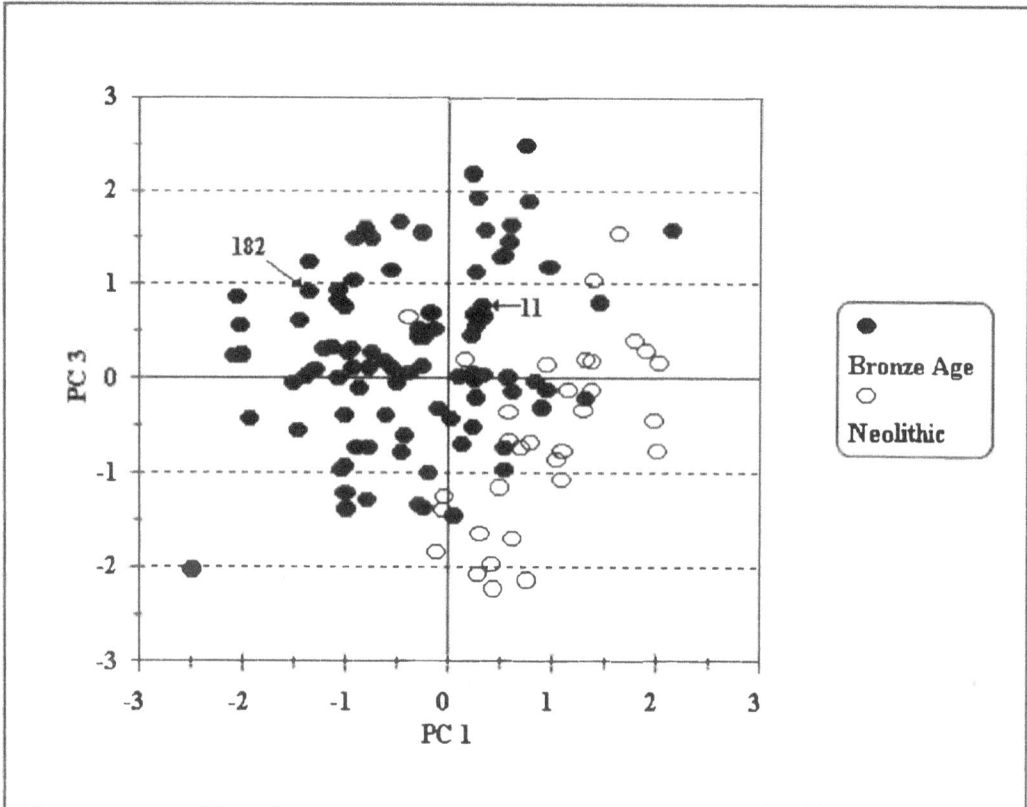

Figure 8.10. Multivariate analysis two: principal components plot.

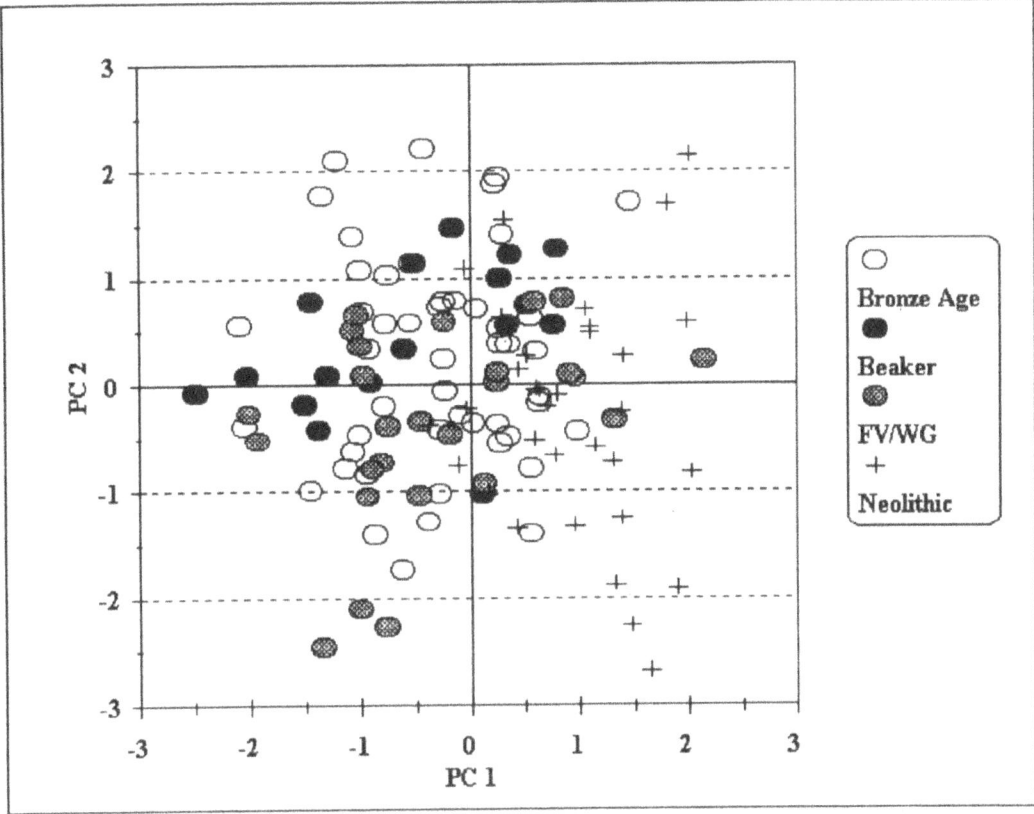

Figure 8.11. Multivariate analysis two: principal components plot.

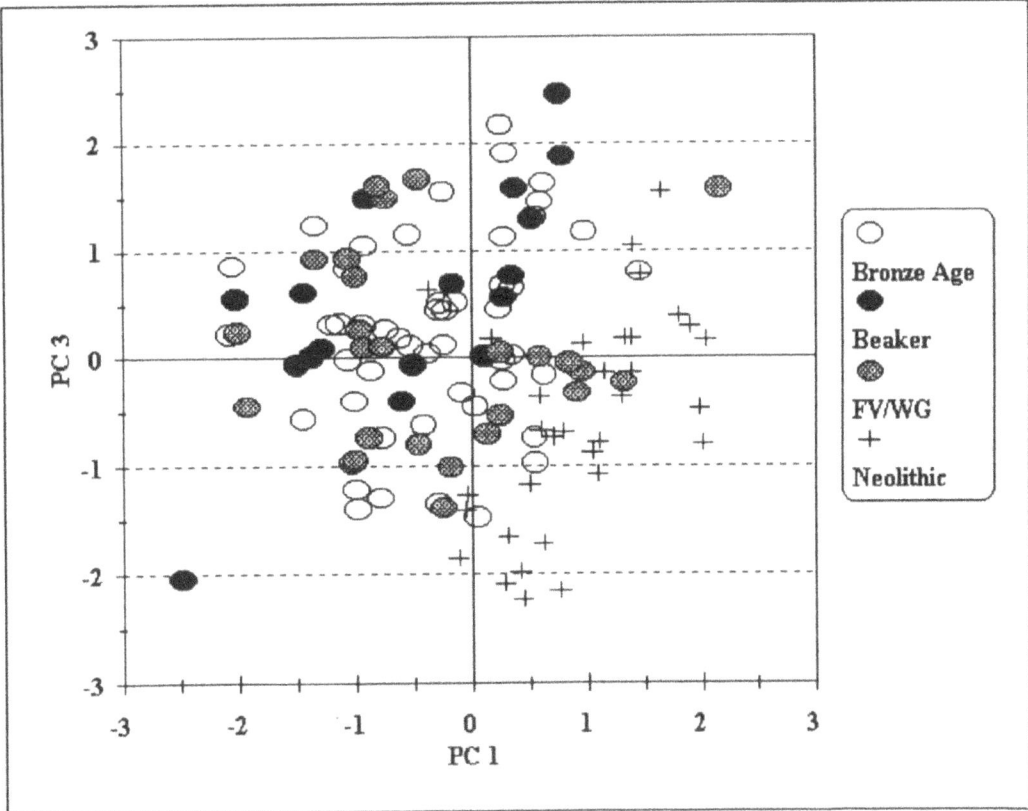

measurements of parietal length (PAC, PAK). It was probably the equivalent of PC4 as extracted in analysis 1.

PC3 had a marked positive correlation with maximum breadth (XCB), it was also positively correlated with WCB, FRK and FRC. This pattern is similar to that represented by PC3 in analysis 1 and interpreted there as being representative of brachycephaly.

The projections ot the component scores of individual crania onto the principal component axes are shown in Figures 8.8 - 8.9. As in analysis 1, separation of Bronze age and Neolithic series was achieved by PC1 and PC3, albeit with a greater degree of overlap. PC2 did not discriminate between samples, both sets of calvaria demonstrated a balanced distribution although the

Neolithic examples were marked by a trend not apparent within the Bronze Age series. The Neolithic skulls tended towards a negative correlation between PC2 and PC3, that is between length of the parietal bone, as measured along the sagittal suture, and cranial width. This relationship, hinted at in analysis 1, was not present in the Bronze Age series.

Figures 8.10 and 8.11 show the principal component scores of the constituent groups of the Bronze Age series. They do not form discrete clusters, but there is a suggestion that groups FV and WG have positions on the PC2 axis midway between the EN and BB groups. This positioning will be discussed more fully in the next chapter.

Table 8.11. Multivariate analysis three: component loadings.

	PC1	PC2	PC3
GOL	.87595	.07749	-.06018
XCB	-.25120	-.19517	.69161
WCB	-.03130	.36370	.56062
FRK	.56531	-.26917	.58950
PAK	.55327	.78079	-.04592
OCK	.66728	-.55336	-.28759
FRC	.63580	-.12409	.61518
PAC	.69512	.66086	-.14822
OCC	.66068	-.60026	.24226

Figure 8.12.

Multivariate analysis three: scree plot.

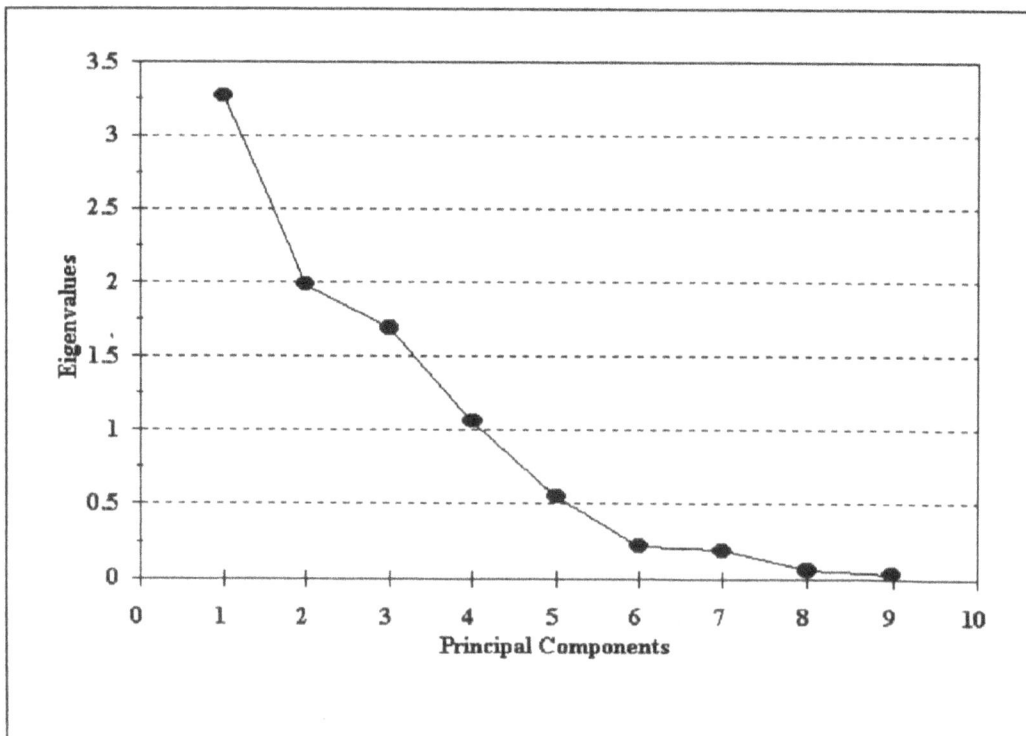

68

Figure 8.13. Multivariate analysis three: principal component plots.

Open circles = Neolithic series.
Filled series = Bronze Age series.

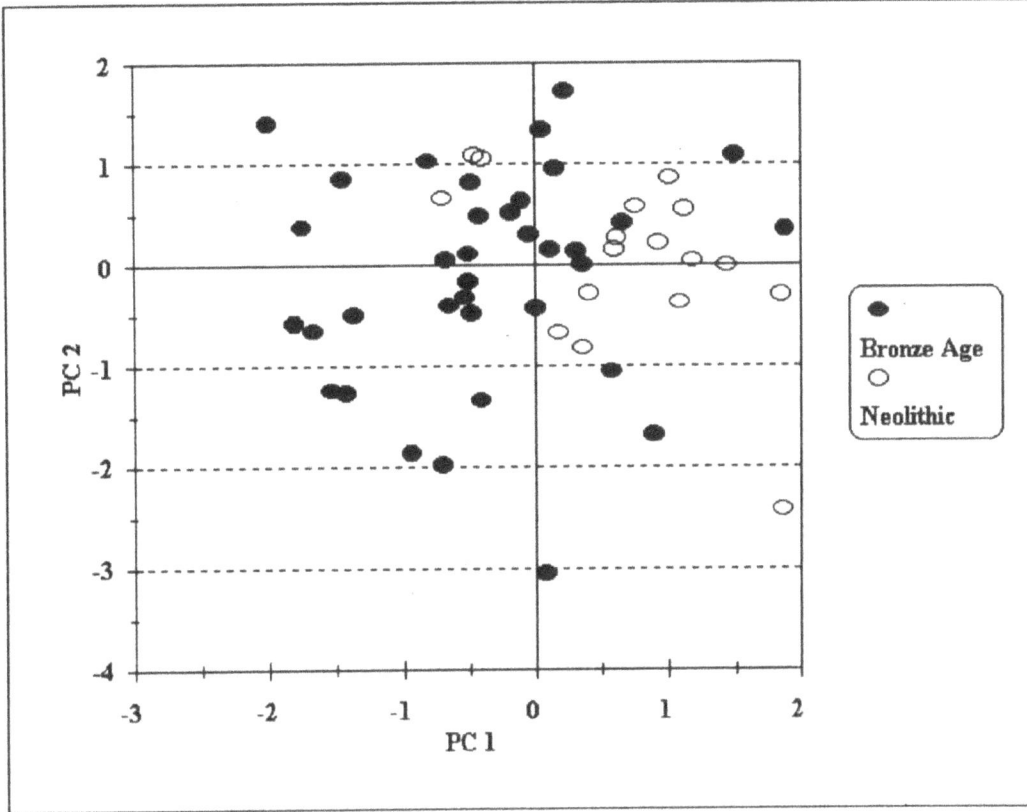

Figure 8.14. Multivariate analysis three: principal component plots.

Open circles = Neolithic series.
Filled circles = Bronze Age series.

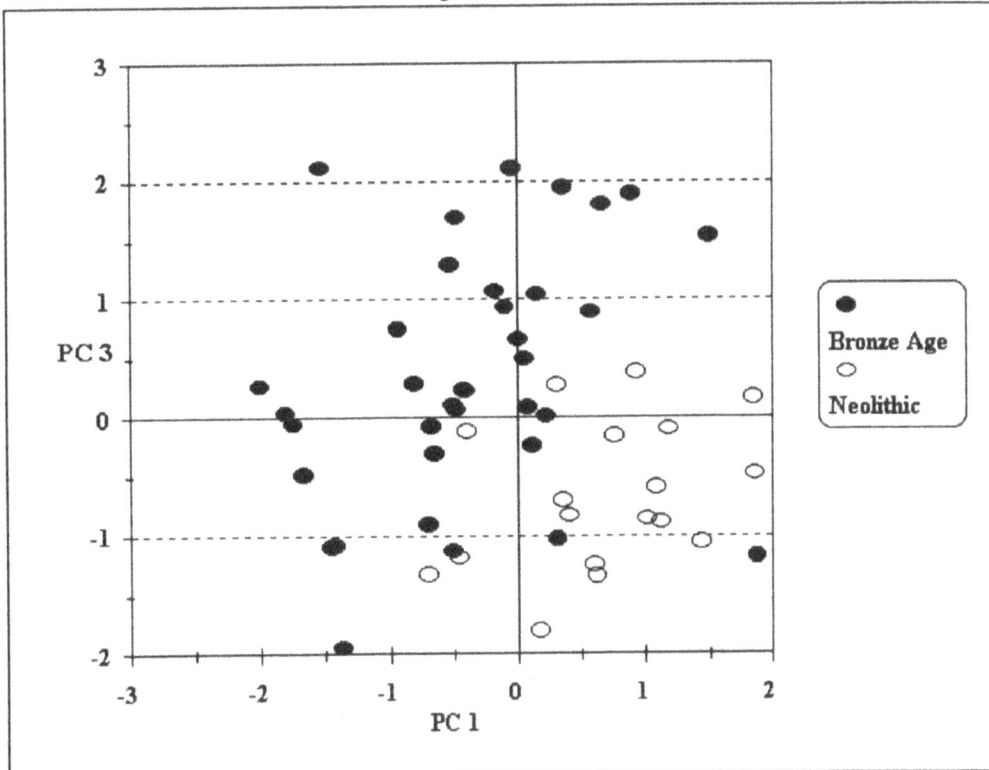

69

Prior visual examination of the crania included in this study suggested that the physical conformation of two, at least, may have been unduly affected by cradleboarding. There was a marked flattening of the posterior surface of the calvarium. These crania were numbers 11 and 182 and might have been expected to show an extreme positioning in relation to other crania, but this was not the case (Figures 8.8 - 8.9), their positioning was not in any way remarkable. This suggests that the measurements used in this study were not ideally suited to the demonstration of cranial deformation arising out of the use of a cradle board, and that the absence of any evidence for this practice in this study should not be considered conclusive.

Multivariate Analysis Three

In this analysis, all female crania with the reduced set of measurements (GOL, XCB, WCB, FRK, OCK, PAK, PAC, OCC) were examined. The results were in broad agreement with those obtained from male crania in multivariate analysis two (Table 8.11, Figures 8.12 - 8.14).

Summary of Results

The statistical analyses presented here largely, perhaps not surprisingly, corroborated earlier work. The main difference between the series was shown to be one of shape, represented in both analyses by PC1, a measure of length or dolichocephaly; and PC3, a measure of breadth or brachycephaly. The skulls of the Neolithic series were markedly dolichocephalic while those of the Bronze Age were more variable but tended towards brachycephaly. This apparently trivial finding is significant as it demonstrates, perhaps for the first time, that the use of the Cranial Index to discriminate between samples of crania drawn from different prehistoric populations is a meaningful exercise. The Index embodies a large amount of real, morphological, information and is not to be viewed merely as a random combination of two, readily available, measurements. The importance of this finding is magnified when it is realised that it allows the comparison of the derived results with a larger body of data drawn from the literature. These comparisons are considered further in the next chapter, and are crucial for the investigation of the patterns, and causes, of diachronic change in cranial morphology.

Further features of anatomical differentiation were noted. The facial skeletons of the Bronze Age crania were shown to be higher, or more robust, than their Neolithic equivalents and associated with increased nasal breadths. The greatest contribution to the increased length of the Neolithic skull was made posteriorly by the parietal bones; within the Neolithic sample itself it was observed that the narrower skulls possessed longer parietal bones. Overall the Bronze Age crania were more variable in morphology than those of the Neolithic. The significance of these findings will be considered more fully in the next chapter.

Conclusion

At the end of Chapter 6 it was proposed that this craniometric study was designed to answer three questions, which were:

1) Are the anatomical differences reported to exist between crania of the Neolithic and early Bronze Age real?

2) Assuming the answer to question (1) to be affirmative, then what are the possible aetiologies of such differences?

3) In the light of the answers to questions (1) and (2), is it possible to apprehend the intrusive presence of a "Beaker Folk" from amidst the human crania of prehistoric Britain?

It has been shown in this chapter that the answer to question (1) is indeed affirmative. The answers to questions (2) and (3) will be considered during the course of the following chapter.

Chapter Nine

THE CRANIA OF PREHISTORIC BRITAIN

Introduction

It has been confirmed that Neolithic skulls do tend to be, on average, longer and narrower than their Bronze Age counterparts. Traditionally, it has been assumed that this difference in morphology was a realisation of a difference in genotype - with a population of Bronze Age "round heads" supplanting one of Neolithic "long heads". Alternative explanations were proposed in Chapter 7, however. It was suggested instead that cranial morphogenesis might be determined, or at least affected, by cultural or natural aspects of the extra-cranial environment. During the course of this chapter it is proposed to assess the relative merits of these two opposed hypotheses of cranial morphogenesis - genetic and environmental - when explaining the results of the craniometric study. Comparative data drawn from the literature will also be used to create synchronic and diachronic contexts within which these hypotheses may be better considered.

Genetic Determinism

At its simplest, genetic determinism assumes that cranial form is determined by the action of a multiple gene system, and that the expression of this gene system is resistant to environmental perturbation. It follows that the range of cranial morphologies present within a population can change only by means of microevolution, and in particular by gene flow. Thus, following population, and therefore genetic, admixture a hybrid cranial morphology should emerge which encompasses that of both parent populations but, on average, presents as intermediate in form.

It has been argued already that there is little hard evidence to support the case for genetic determination of cranial morphology. But if it is accepted for the time being however, and if it is assumed that an immigrant "Beaker Folk" interbred with an indigenous, insular, population, then the results of the craniometric study are perhaps in accord with such a hypothesis. When the individual PC scores which were obtained during Multivariate Analysis Two are projected onto their respective axes there is a suggestion that the crania of the early Bronze Age WG and

FV groups may be separated from those of the BB group and that they may be intermediate in form between groups EN and BA.(Figures 9.1 - 9.4).

This observation is, by itself, relatively inconclusive. It is possible to test the hypothesis of genetic determinism further, however, if Cranial Indices alone are considered, which then allows the utilisation of a large body of comparative data. If the brachycephalic skull type was characteristic of a "Beaker Folk", and if it is proposed that the brachycephalisation of a region's population followed on from the penetration of Beaker migrants, then those regions which did not witness Beaker immigration should not show equivalent evidence of brachycephalisation. This is not the case. Late Neolithic/ early Bronze Age crania have been recovered from two areas of north-west Europe which retain few, if any, traces of the Beaker Culture. These areas are Denmark and the part of north-eastern France that was home to the S.O.M. culture. In both these areas there is a trend towards early Bronze Age brachycephaly. Indeed, the Cranial Indices of the contemporary English, French and Danish groups are virtually indistinguishable (Figure 9.5, Table 9.1). If the English data are in any way remarkable it is for the degree of early Neolithic dolichocephaly - not early Bronze Age brachycephaly.

This trend to brachycephaly which manifests itself in the crania of Neolithic and early Bronze Age north-west Europe suggests further that cranial form is not genetically determined, and that it might alter through time by mechanisms other than those of microevolution. A similar conclusion is reached after inspection of historical British data (Figure 9.6, Table 9.2). It is evident that mean Cranial Index increased from the moderately dolichocephalic Anglo-Saxon-Scandinavian skulls of the early medieval period until a degree of brachycephaly was reached in the later middle ages which equalled, or even exceeded, that of the preceding Bronze Age population. By the 17th century the mean Cranial Index had declined. This oscillation in mean Cranial Index was not accompanied by any major population influx and it is unlikely that any other process of microevolution could effect such a change. There must have been factors other than genes at work. Again,

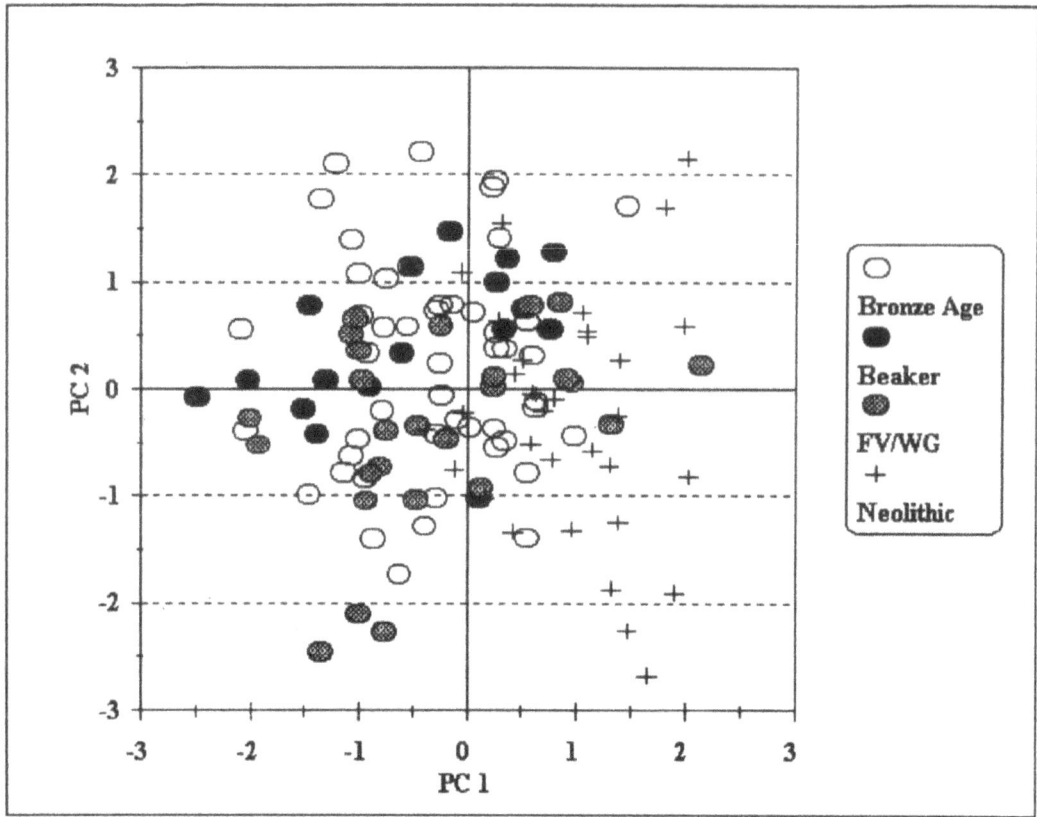

Figure 9.1. Multivariate analysis two: principal components plot.

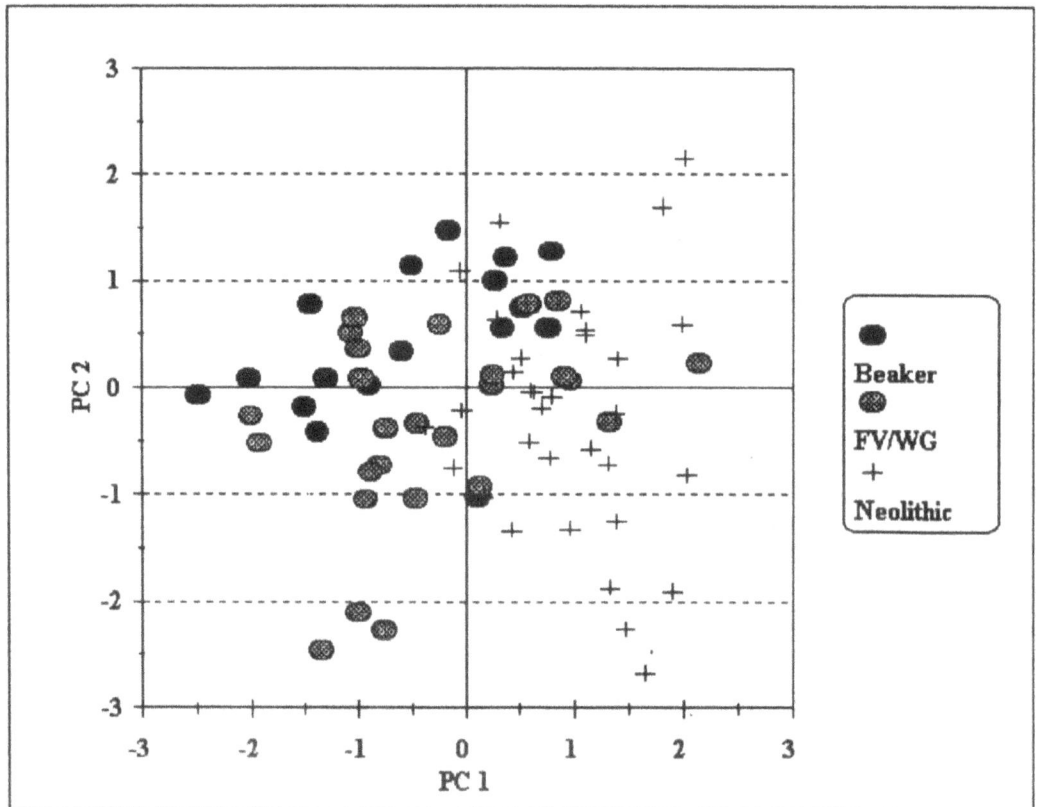

Figure 9.2. Multivariate analysis two: principal components plot with non-specific Bronze Age crania (group BA) removed for purposes of clarity.

Figure 9.3. Multivariate analysis two: principal components plot.

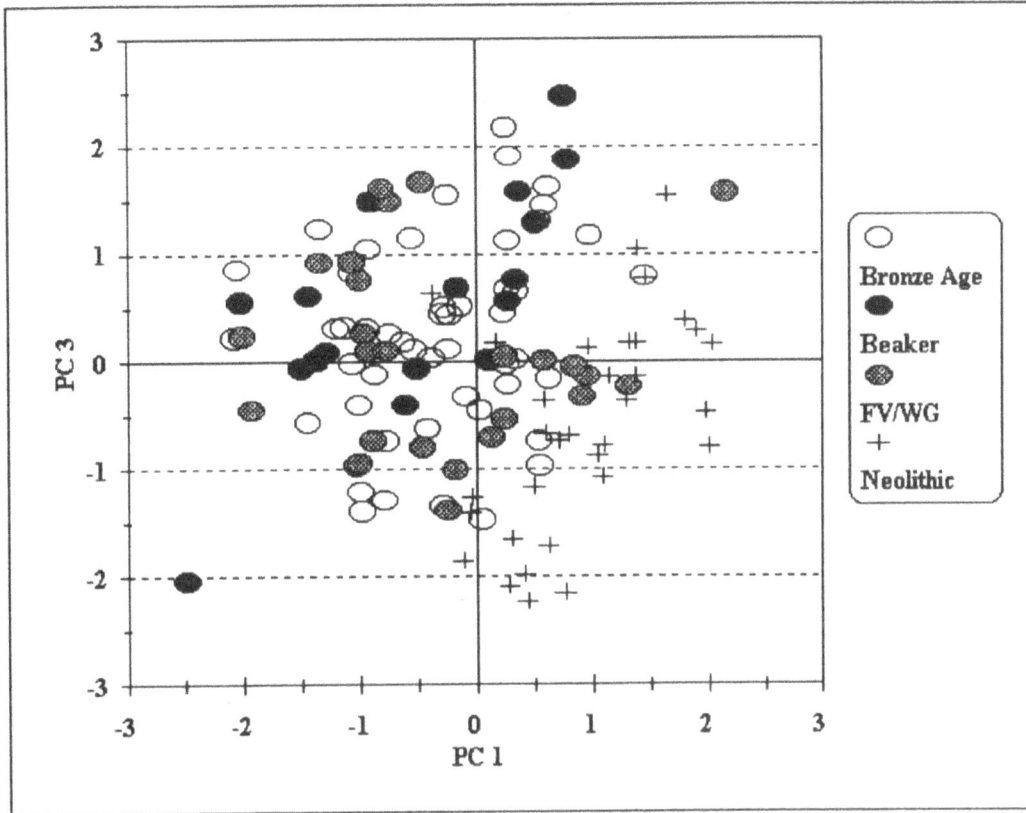

Figure 9.4. Multivariate analysis two: principal components plot with non-specific
Bronze Age crania (group BA) removed for purposes of clarity.

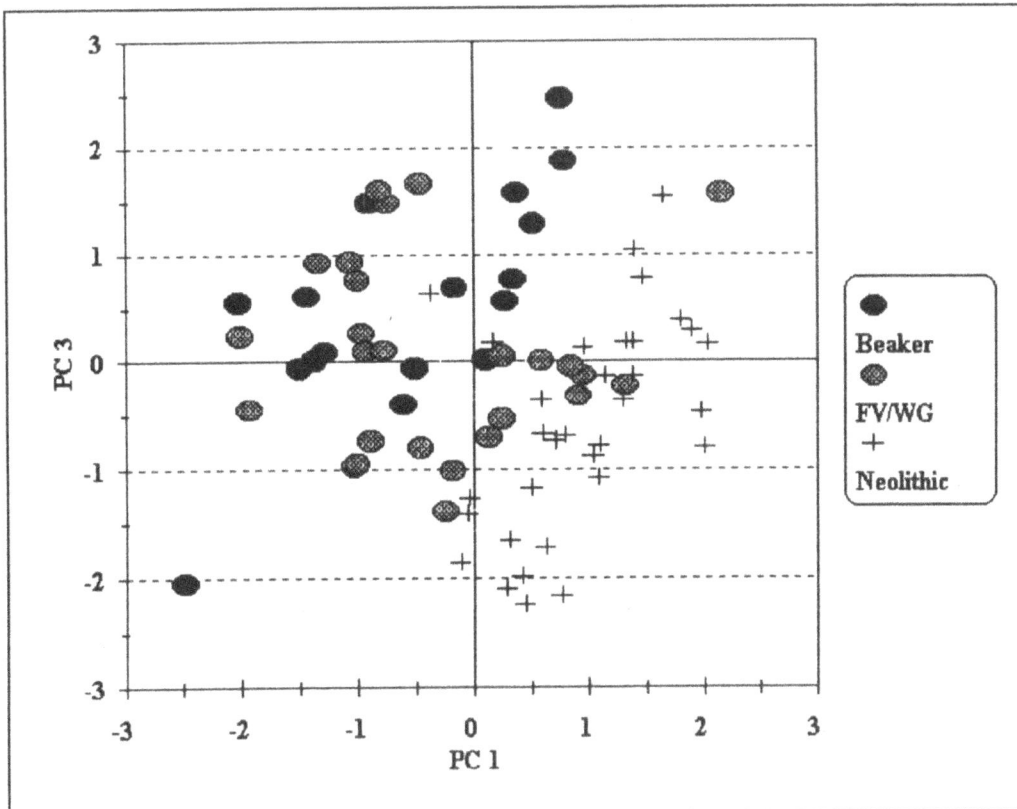

Table 9.1.   European cranial data. (Males only).

Location.	Approximate Date.	Cranial Index. (Mean ±1SD)	Reference.
Northern France	7000BC - 4900BC	73.0 ±2.7	Asmus (1973)
Northern France	4950BC - 4400BC	73.2 ±3.4	Riquet (1973
Northern France	4400BC - 3400BC	73.8 ±4.0	Riquet (1973)
Northern France	3400BC - 1750BC	77.8 ±5.2	Riquet (1973)
Denmark	3400BC - 2600BC	76.0 ±3.8	Jorgensen (1973)
Denmark	2600BC - 1800BC	77.2 ±3.8	Jorgensen (1973)
England	4000BC - 3000BC	70.1 ±3.2	Present study
England	2500BC - 1600BC	78.1 ±5.3	Present study

however, in this long term historical context, it is the extreme dolichocephaly of the early Neolithic crania that excites comment, not the brachycephaly of the Bronze Age.

The Natural Environment: Climate

In Chapter 7, literature was cited to suggest the existence of an intimate association between climate and cranial form. It seems possible, then, that changes in climate might induce corresponding alterations in cranial morphology. Over the past millennium the British climate has been anything but stable and the pattern of its variability is reasonably well known, in outline form at least. This allows comparison of climatic data with the historical cranial data presented in Table 9.2.

The first thing to notice is that there is a long term trend of climatic change apparent against a background of short term fluctuations (Lamb 1988: 27-39). The first century of the present millennium witnessed a gradual warming which culminated in a climatic optimum between 1100 AD and 1300 AD. During this time average temperatures were 0.5°C higher than at present and the period was marked by the relatively frequent occurrence of warm, dry summers and autumns. There was a subsequent deterioration of climate from this optimum until the nadir of the "little ice age" was reached between 1600 AD and 1700 AD. Average temperatures were 2°C cooler than at present and there was an increased incidence of wet, cool summers and autumns. Thereafter there was a recovery which lasted until the middle years of the present century. A graphical summary of this

climatic oscillation is presented in Figure 9.7 with the Cranial Indices of chronologically relevant populations superimposed.

It must be remembered that cranial form at death will reflect the childhood environment, which suggests that the mean Cranial Indices in Figure 9.7 should, in reality, be shifted slightly to the left - by the space of a generation perhaps. Nevertheless, Cranial Index does seem to correlate positively with temperature and negatively with humidity. While the negative correlation with humidity is as expected, the positive correlation with temperature comes as some surprise. It will be recalled from Chapter 7 that several workers have shown Cranial Index to be negatively correlated with ambient temperature. However, it was also shown in Chapter 7 that in early 20th century Europe head shape tended to cline in an east-west direction rather than north-south. At this time dolichocephaly was associated with a maritime climate while brachycephaly was a feature of populations inhabiting more continental areas. If it is accepted that in temperate regions humidity is a more influential determinant of cranial morphology than is temperature then the historical picture clarifies. The brachycephaly of the British late medieval population was a response to the dryness, or continentality, of the climate.

If the brachycephalisation of the medieval inhabitants of Britain was a consequence of the mild desiccation of their environment then the possibility that a similar circumstance may have caused the brachycephaly of the early Bronze Age must be considered. In the absence of written records, however, the prehistoric

Table 9.2.   British Cranial Data.

(Male Crania Only).

Location.	Approximate date.	Cranial Index.	Reference.
England	4000BC - 3000BC	70.1 ±3.2	Present study
England	2500BC - 1600BC	78.1 ±5.3	Present study
Wetwang	400BC - 50AD	73.6 ±4.0	Dawes (1980)
Maiden Castle	100BC - 50AD	76.0 ±2.3	Goodman & Morant (1940)
Danes Graves	400BC - 50AD	73.3 ±3.5	Wright (1903)
Trentholme Drive	150AD - 350AD	76.5 ±8.4	Dawes (1980)
Bidford on Avon	500AD - 550AD	73.6 ±2.7	Brash etal (1935)
Burwell	600AD - 700AD	74.5 ±3.2	Brash et al (1935)
York Minster	?500AD - 1100AD	75.3 ±3.6	Dawes (1980)
York Aldwark	950AD - 1550AD	79.4 ±4.3	Dawes (1980)
York Clementhorpe	1150AD - 1550AD	80.2±3.6	Dawes (1980)
Hythe	1100AD - 1600AD	82.6 ±3.7	Dawes (1980)
Scarborough	1200AD - 1500AD	79.0 ±4.4	Little (1943)
Carmelite Friary	1300AD - 1600AD	79.6 ±3.6	Miles (1989)
Ensay	1500AD - 1600AD	77.1 ±3.3	Miles (1989)
Farringdon Street	1600AD - 1700AD	75.4 ±3.5	Hooke (1926)
Whitechapel	1600AD - 1700AD	74.3 ±3.3	McDonell (1904)
Moorfields	1600AD - 1700AD	75.5 ±3.0	McDonell (1906/7)

Figure 9.5. Cranial Indices of some prehistoric English and French populations.

Mean plus/minus 1 standard deviation range of Cranial Indices of north French crania represented by gray area. Superimposed are the mean plus/minus 1 standard deviation Cranial Indices of the English early Neolithic and Bronze Age series obtained during the present study. The horizontal bars provide an indication of chronological span.

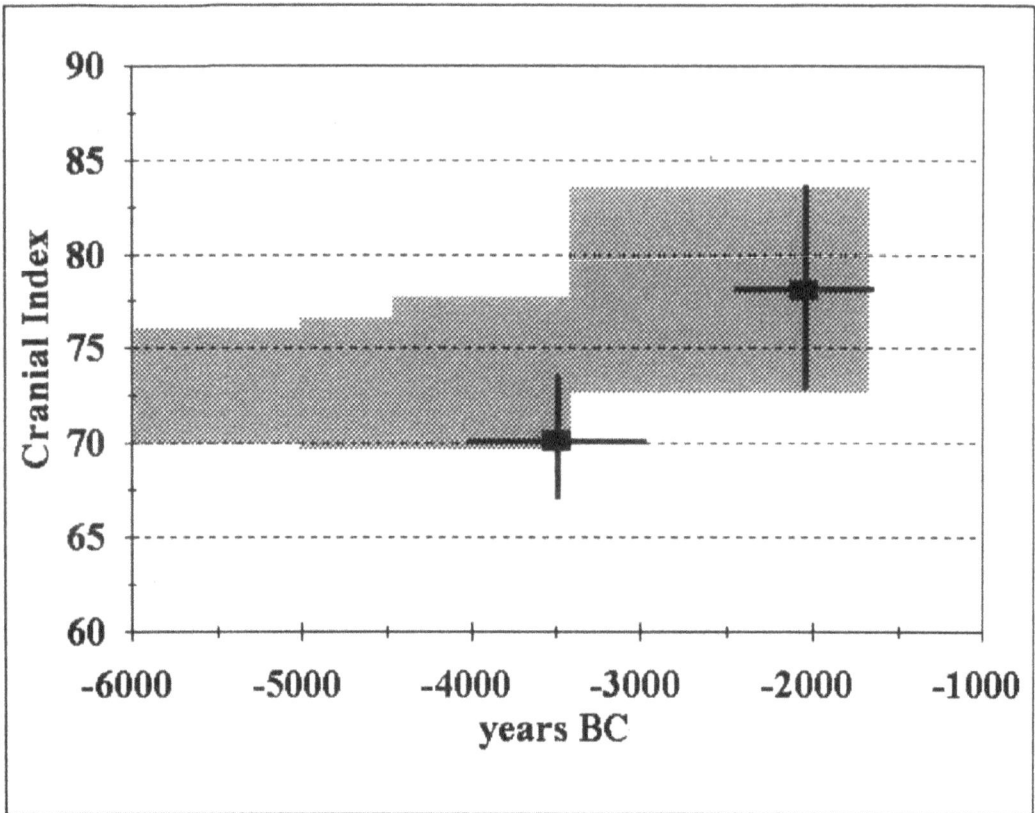

Figure 9.6. Cranial Indices of prehistoric and historic British populations.

Mean plus/minus 1 standard deviation range of Cranial Indices. Horizontal bars indicate approximate chronological span of each buried population.

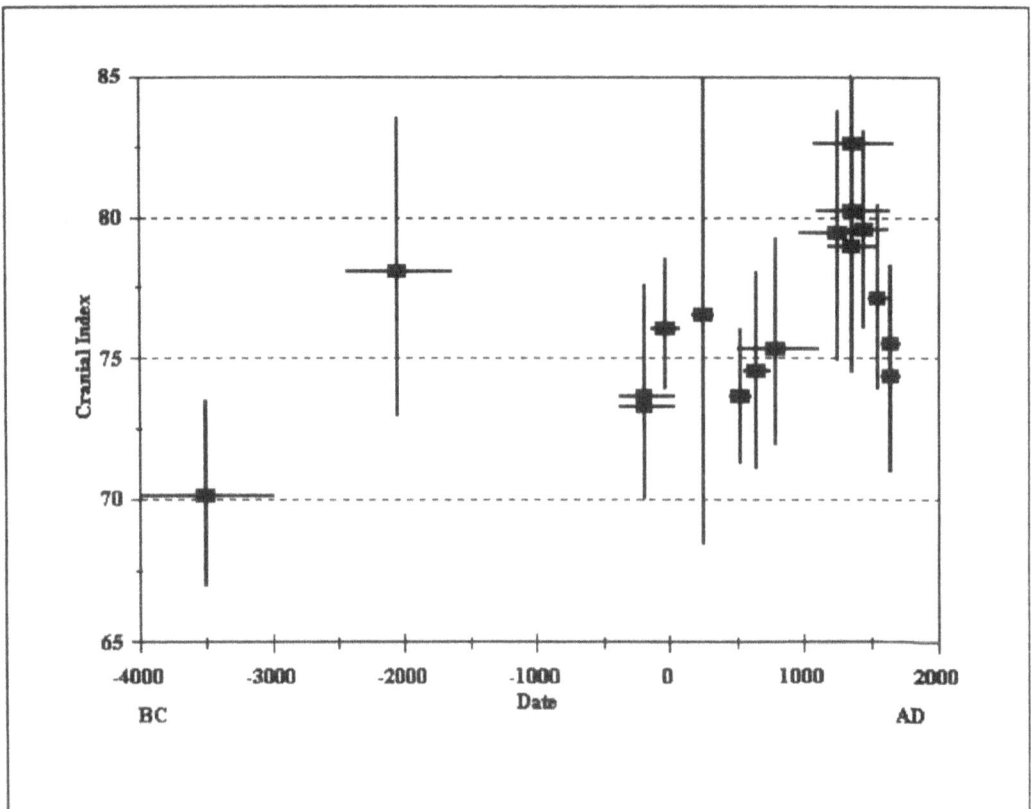

Figure 9.7. Fluctuations in climate and in Cranial Index.

Broken line = potential water surplus in southern Scotland, measured at 50 year intervals (Parry 1985: 43).

Solid line = mean average temperature in central England, measured at 50 year intervals (Lamb 1988: 53).

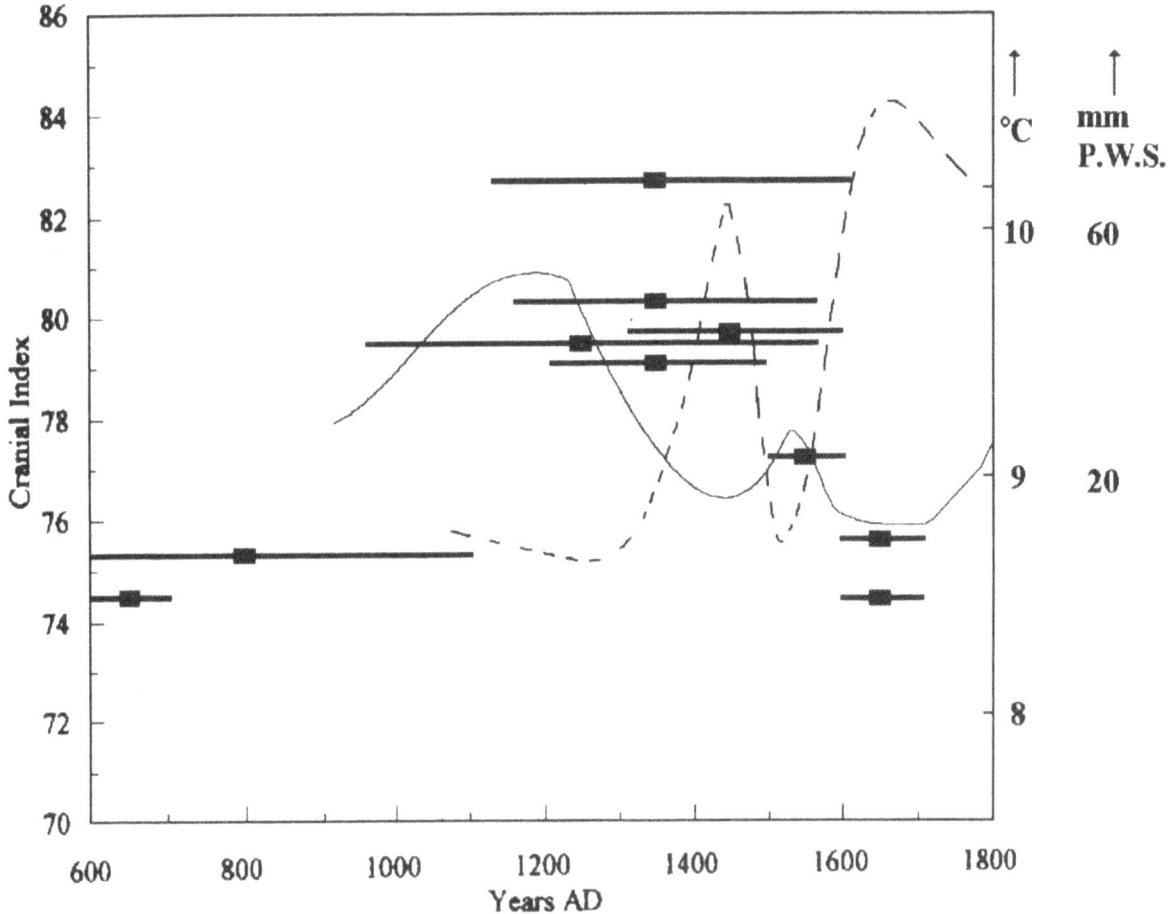

climate is less amenable to investigation than that of the past millennium. It is necessary to rely upon, often inconclusive, environmental data.

The Neolithic and Bronze Age crania examined in this study were all recovered from contexts encompassed chronologically by the period termed Sub-Boreal by Scandinavian palynologists. Lasting from 3800 calBC until 900 calBC, the Sub-Boreal has been classically described as a period of continental climate - drier, and with colder winters, than the preceding Atlantic period. The botanical evidence upon which this climatic succession was based has been criticised, however (Smith 1981), and in any case the evidence of the present millennium cautions against the acceptance of any schemes that posit millennia long periods of climatic uniformity. It seems preferable instead to consider the Atlantic and Sub-Boreal as a single period of post-glacial optimum climate, with temperatures perhaps 2°C higher than today, but subject to periodic oscillations (Smith 1981).

One such oscillation has been termed the "Piora". Pollen analyses and tree ring studies in central Europe have, together, provided evidence of a period of more unsettled weather dated to between 4240 calBC and 3800 calBC. The climate was colder and wetter, but also more variable (Bogucki 1988: 22). There is widespread formation of peat bog throughout Britain at this time, and trackways were built in the Somerset Levels. (Evans 1981: 12; Smith 1981: 141). Perhaps, therefore, the early Neolithic crania might have achieved their adult morphology in cool, damp conditions. On the other hand, there is evidence for drier conditions during the early Bronze Age (2480 calBC - 1450 calBC). Wind blown silt has been recovered from several contexts and there is formation of recurrence surfaces in peat bogs - no trackways were built on the Somerset Levels between 3100 calBC and 1750 calBC (Tinsley 1981: 211; Evans 1981: 17-19). Many marginal areas were also brought under cultivation during the early Bronze Age, only to be abandoned after 1450 calBC and not farmed again until the climatic amelioration of the Romano-British period and then again, significantly, during the medieval warm epoch (Burgess 1980: 118, 238).

There seem sufficient grounds to argue, therefore, that the gradual increase in Cranial Index which occurred throughout north-western Europe during the Neolithic and early Bronze Age could have been in response to climatic improvement. As the nasal breadths (NLB) of the Bronze Age series are greater than those of the Neolithic series, it seems possible that brachycephalisation was secondary to lateralisation of the nasal cavity - perhaps in order to make available a greater surface area of mucosa with which to humidify inspired air. It is less clear that poor climate would have been responsible for the dolichocephaly of the Neolithic Britons, however. This was extraordinary in comparison both to their continental contemporaries and to their insular successors.

Cultural Environment

The significantly greater lengths of the Neolithic parietal and occipital bones (as evidenced by the measurements PAK, PAC, OCC and OCK) suggest that the dolichocephalic morphology of the early Neolithic skull may have been necessary to accommodate posterior enlargement of the temporales muscles. If this was the case then, perhaps like the present day Inuit, the extreme length of the early Neolithic skull might have been a developmental response to certain features of the cultural environment. It is unlikely that these features would have been technological - the English crania are noticeably longer than their continental counterparts but there is no evidence to suggest that the sophistication of their respective household toolkits differed in a comparable fashion. If elements of the cultural environment were responsible for the posterior lengthening of the English Neolithic cranium they must have been behavioural, and specific. The inhabitants of Neolithic England may have chosen to use their teeth for certain tasks - tasks for which other, continental, populations would have preferred to use tools.

The hypothesis that the cultural environment might affect cranial morphogenesis is derived, in part, from the analogy of the Inuit. The Inuit also suggest a test of the hypothesis. Cruwys (1989: 154) has shown that, in comparison to other population groups, the incisors of the Greenland Inuit show a relatively greater degree of tooth wear than do their molars. Thus, if the dolichocephalic form of the early Neolithic cranium was due, in part at least, to the habitual use of the anterior dentition as a "third hand" then their incisor:molar wear ratios should be correspondingly large, and significantly greater than those of Bronze Age crania. Unfortunately, at the present time, it has not proved possible to proceed with such a study. Thus the role of the cultural environment in cranial morphogenesis during the earlier Neolithic remains unknown, although an empirical route to the refutation of the hypothesis is available.

It remains to consider what influence, if any, artificial constraint may have exerted upon the morphogenesis of early Bronze Age crania. As already noted in the previous chapter, it is not at all certain that the measurements chosen in this study were suitable for demonstrating the effects of cradleboarding, or other forms of artificial constraint, on the human cranium. A similar conclusion was reached by Heathcote (1986: 95-102) using a much larger measurement suite than that of the present study, and who reported that the gross measurements of length and breadth (GOL and XCB) were those most likely to be affected, but not to any significant extent. Nevertheless, the increased NLB of the Bronze Age series, a measurement known to be unaffected by cradleboarding, suggests that their brachycephaly was largely independent of this type of constraint, although it might have been a contributory factor in some cases. For any future study of this phenomenon to be successful it would require the utilisation of novel measurements. This would be best accomplished by comparing a set of crania known to be deformed with a normal set, and devising a measurement suite which would provide optimum discrimination between the two.

The Crania of Prehistoric Britain

There are, then, two possible interpretations of the craniometric data:

1) That the appearance of the brachycephalic skull in Britain announces the arrival of an immigrant population.

2) That the different skull morphologies are caused by different cultural or climatic environments.

Neither can be excluded by study of early Neolithic and early Bronze Age crania alone. To choose between the two alternatives it is necessary to examine crania from the late Neolithic. Thus, if the immigrant population interpretation is to be accepted then it would imply that the crania of the later part of the Neolithic would resemble those of the earlier part. On the other hand, for the environmental interpretation to be valid, it would require the late Neolithic crania to be of intermediate morphology. Unfortunately, late Neolithic crania are notable largely on account of their rarity. Those crania that have been assigned a late Neolithic provenance are not precisely dated, it is not clear if they possess a uniform chronological spread or whether they should all be dated to an earlier or later part of the late Neolithic. Still, Cranial Indices from 11 male crania may be compared to those of the early Neolithic and Bronze Age cranial series (Table 9.3). It can be seen in Figure 9.8 that the late Neolithic crania are, morphologically, more diverse those of the early Neolithic, and also tend more towards brachycephaly - but again the pattern is hardly conclusive. Of more interest are data from the tomb of Isbister, where 13 male crania were recovered and their Cranial Indices reported in the excavation publication (Hedges 1983). A series of C14 dates also provide a relatively secure time bracket for the use of the tomb, from 2950 calBC until 2450 calBC. These Isbister crania are indeed of intermediate morphology (Figure 9.8), an observation that would strongly support the second of the above alternatives - that the different skull morphologies arose out of different cultural or climatic contexts. It might be objected that as

Table 9.3. British Cranial Data.

(Male Crania Only).

Location	Approximate date.	Cranial Index. (mean ±1SD)	Reference.
England	4000BC - 3000BC	70.1 ±3.2	Present Study.
Isbister	2950BC - 2450BC	73.4 ±3.3	Hedges (1983).
England	3000BC - 2200BC	71.5 ±4.8	Present Study.
England	2500BC - 1600BC	78.1 ±5.3	Present Study.

Figure 9.8.

Cranial Indices of British prehistoric populations - including Isbister data.
  (Mean plus/minus 2 standard deviation range of Cranial Indices).

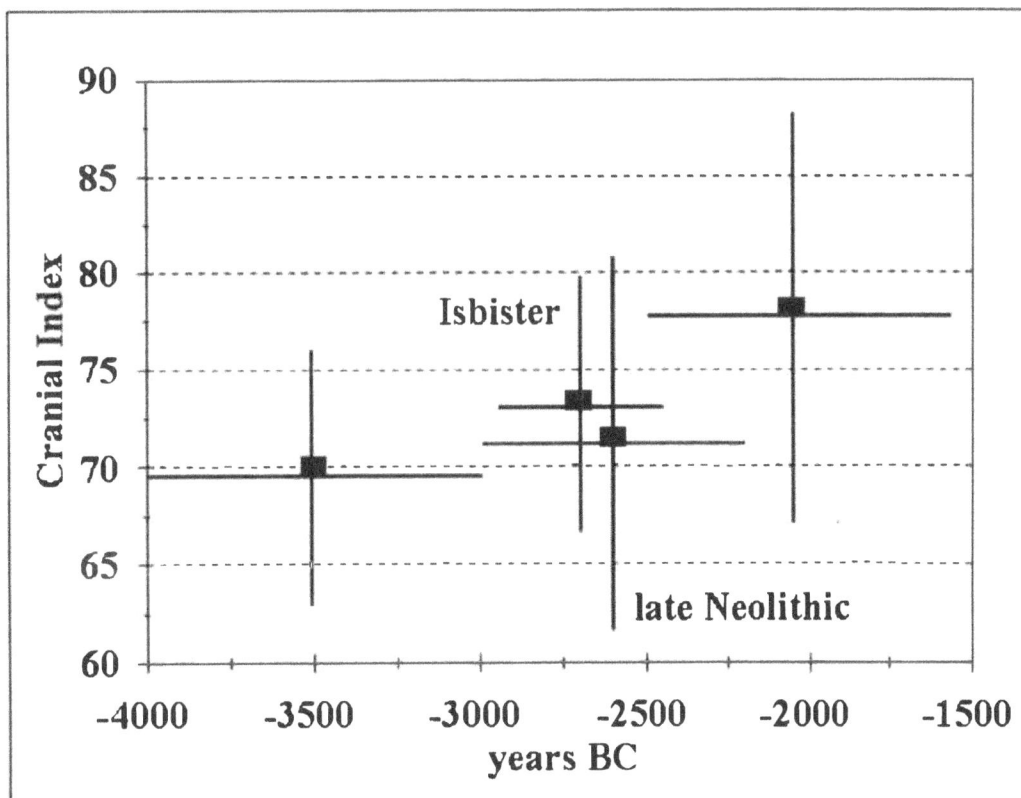

79

the Isbister tomb is situated in the Orkney Islands then the recovered crania are not strictly comparable to those of the English early Neolithic and Bronze Age series. Whilst this is true, it will be remembered from Chapter 6 that the literature describing Scottish crania has consistently reported a morphological dichotomy which is parallel to that of England. There seems no reason, therefore, to doubt the significance of the Isbister crania.

If it may be accepted that changing environments induced correlative anatomical changes in the human crania of prehistoric Britain, then what would be a likely scenario? The brachycephaly of the early Bronze Age seems normal in the context of north-western Europe, and can be explained as a response to the prevailing continental climate. The dolichocephaly of the early Neolithic may have been due, in part, to a wetter climate; but it seems more likely that culturally-specific behaviour also contributed to the extreme dolichocephaly. Climatic amelioration and altering patterns of behaviour then combined to produce the trend to Bronze Age brachycephaly. This scenario remains speculative, of course, but it presents a coherent hypothesis of morphological change that may stand in opposition to the genetic/immigration hypothesis. Future research projects may help to decide between them, some possible avenues of approach have already been suggested during the course of this chapter.

Conclusion

On balance, it seems that there is little need to look for a "Beaker Folk" when attempting to explain diachronic change in cranial morphology. The biological literature suggests that morphological change might occur in response to parallel changes in the extra-cranial environment and be partly independent, at least, of any genetically-driven microevolutionary process. The results of this cranial study and consideration of comparative material do not contradict this suggestion. However, this should not be taken as confirmation of the non-existence of the "Beaker Folk". Rather, it serves to emphasise that the brachycephalisation of prehistoric Britons was a biological phenomenon, and one which cannot be utilised for the investigation of an archaeological entity such as the Beaker culture. Biology cannot provide easy answers to complex archaeological questions.

Several methodological points need to be made. The measurements taken in this study were standard, internationally recognised and have been in use for over 100 years. As such, they were designed to answer 19th century questions and it is not at all clear that they remain universally optimal. A failing of the measurement suite has already been touched upon in the discussion of artificial constraint, but more could have been said during the consideration of the cultural environment. The length of the temporal fossa, for instance, may have provided a useful indicator of temporalis development. Measurement of the superior temporal line, if patent, and which marks the upper margin of the temporalis muscle, may also have

been useful in this respect. Multivariate techniques of data analysis did not prove to be of great benefit to this study - most conclusions were arrived at after comparison of individual measurements or Cranial Indices. It is possible that this failing of the multivariate analyses was due, in part, to the non-specificity of the measurement suite.

The comparative data which was considered towards the end of this cranial study suggested that cranial morphology and climate might fluctuate in tandem. This seems to be a novel observation. Although it is well known that cranial form correlates with climate the correlation is usually assumed to have deep evolutionary roots; but the medieval oscillation of Cranial Index would seem to contradict this and point instead to a cranial reaction which is developmental in origin. It has further ramifications as it exposes a fundamental weakness of climatic studies. These generally assume that head shape has been stable over the last millennium - thus many alleged "recent" crania studied are in fact of medieval date. Inclusion of these medieval crania acts to obscure more subtle patterning of morphology within climatic zones and Europe appears to be more uniformly brachycephalic than is actually the case.

Overall, the conclusions that can be drawn from this cranial study are disappointing. This is not surprising, perhaps, given the lack of any real understanding of cranial morphogenesis. This has been compounded by the relative paucity of reliable data available from more recent excavations. It is unfortunate that the study of cranial morphology has fallen into such disrepute that many human bone reports do not now include even the most basic measurements of cranial length and breadth. Nor yet do the determinants of cranial form warrant more than a passing mention in most textbooks. This reluctance to measure, and to discuss, is no doubt a product of the legitimate desire of bone specialists to distance themselves from the distorted racism of past decades; but it serves only to impede the formulation of anything other than simplistic explanations based only on genetics - on race. In the absence of new hypotheses, with firm foundations of fresh data, then the old ones persist. This cranial study will have been worthwhile if it has persuaded some, at least, that such a study is not taboo, but rather that it is a necessary endeavour if the myths of yesteryear are to be finally dispelled.

Chapter Ten

CONCLUDING THOUGHTS

This study reviewed the changes in interpretation of the Neolithic - Bronze Age transition that have taken place over the last twenty years.

The first part of the study critically examined the case put forward for a diffusionist explanation of Beaker culture spread; and concluded that its theoretical basis - that Beaker assemblages had acted either as a symbol or as an agent of social change - was unfounded. Furthermore, a structured model of long-distance migration seemed better suited to address the complex archaeology of the period. It became clear that the refutation of the "migrating Beaker Folk" hypothesis during the 1970s had been facilitated by the use of outdated Childean definitions of culture, people and migration; definitions which Childe himself had discarded before the end of his career. No effort had been made to construct alternative models of migration from out of the more detailed material available within the literature of anthropology, geography and demography.

Paradigms in Prehistory

It was described in Chapter Two how it is possible to discern in the various works of Childe a gradual elaboration of theory - from his early, optimistic, definitions of culture in the 1920s through to his more cautious, indeterminate statements of the 1950s, and to his increasing concern with processes of long term change, both social and technological. It was claimed that his ultimate theoretical stance was not so different from that of Clarke (1968) or Renfrew (1977). However, this view of a gradual and continuous development of archaeological theory is not generally accepted, or realised. It was suggested in Chapter Two that the attack on the dual concept of Beaker culture and "Beaker Folk" had been facilitated by use of Childe's early, simple, definitions of culture and migration. This omission seems to be a feature of the "New", or processual, archaeology generally. Thus, in two recent textbooks, *Prehistoric Europe* (Champion et al 1984) and *Neolithic Europe* (Whittle 1985), the only general works by Childe listed in their bibliographies are his earliest: The Dawn of European Civilisation (3rd ed. 1939) and The Danube in Prehistory (1929). His later works, books such as Social

Evolution (1963) and Piecing Together the Past (1956), are passed over in silence. Whilst not deliberate, the effect of this omission is to emphasise the theoretical originality of the New Archaeology, and to create a vision of prehistoriography which is revolutionary, as opposed to evolutionary.

Revolution is a word much used in the writings of archaeologists. It was used by Childe between the wars in a subversive fashion - with its connotations of Bolshevism it was unsettling to the academic establishment. More recently, however, the word revolution has been used to describe apparent changes in the aims and epistemology of archaeological theory, following closely the revolutionary model developed by Kuhn (1970) to describe theory change in the natural sciences.

Kuhn suggested that all scientific research proceeds within the confines of a series of disciplinary frameworks which are constructed from agreed sets of methodologies and theoretical assumptions. He chose to call these disciplinary frameworks "paradigms" and argued that scientists will never make a concerted effort to refute the basic tenets of their supporting paradigm. He thus disagreed with Popper's "conjectures and refutations" model of scientific progress. Nevertheless, the history of science is littered with abandoned paradigms, and Kuhn took pains to explain why this should be.

There will always be anomalous observations, observations inexplicable within the orthodox paradigm. Their number will tend to increase through time, engendering dissatisfaction with the paradigm. Ultimately a new, different, paradigm is articulated, one that is able to accommodate all known observational data, including anomalies. The new paradigm is not a logical outgrowth of the first, however, but presents instead a new way of representing and investigating reality. It has a different epistemology. It is a change in scientific viewpoint that Kuhn likened to a gestalt switch. A period of "extra-ordinary" science ensues, during which time the new paradigm gathers adherents while the old one falls into disrepute and its supporters, like old soldiers, just fade away. Kuhn termed this process a paradigm shift, the classic example is held to have occurred in physics when the Einsteinian view of a relative universe replaced the absolutism of the Newtonian one.

Kuhn provided a model of scientific progress that was discontinuous. Periods of consolidating "normal" science are punctuated by intervals of rapid, revolutionary, advance - by periods of "extra-ordinary" science. This model is at variance with the received wisdom of gradual, evolutionary, growth, but has proved attractive to recent generations of theoretical archaeologists, particularly those of the New Archaeology that emerged during the 1960s and 1970s. However, although providing an attractive analogue for the development of archaeological theory, it rather falls down when there is no general agreement about the timing of paradigm shifts. Often, and predictably, the scholar proposing a paradigm shift is holding forward his or her own work as being exemplary of the new paradigm. One candidate for the appellation "new paradigm" was the New Archaeology, as its name suggests. It was discussed by one of its leading British protagonists, writing in Kuhnian inspired prose, as follows:

"Several commentators have spoken recently of a 'revolution' in prehistory, of the same fundamental nature as a revolution in scientific thinking. It has been suggested, indeed, that the changes now at work in prehistory herald the shift to a 'new paradigm', an entire new framework of thought, made necessary by the collapse of the 'first paradigm', the existing framework in which prehistorians have grown accustomed to work."
(Renfrew 1973: 15).

But to a younger, uninvolved, generation the revolutionary significance of the New Archaeology begins to fade away, it is perceived to be a constituent of the orthodox mainstream. New, "revolutionary" developments clamour for attention:

"If one wishes to talk about paradigms in archaeology, where the term 'paradigm shift' means a fundamental change in the way in which archaeologists actually see the world of material culture, the decisive break occurs not in 1962 with the substitution of one form of empiricism with another (Binford 1962), but in 1982 with the appearance of Symbolic and Structural Archaeology."
(Tilley 1989: 185).

It is too soon to judge the revolutionary claims of the post-processualists but, with hindsight, it now seems possible to judge the extent to which the New Archaeology really was new - and the verdict seems to be, in theoretical terms at least: not very (Trigger 1989: 289-328; Courbin 1982). New Archaeologists undoubtedly benefitted from the development and application of new scientific techniques, C14 dating in particular; they were also to the fore in producing large bodies of novel data after the development of new methodologies, notably surface survey and the systematic recovery of floral and faunal remains. Theoretically, however, much was derived from social anthropology - both the social evolutionism of the 19th century and the structural-functionalism of the early 20th. Palaeoeconomic studies were founded on the work of Clark (1952).

The example of the New Archaeology seems not to support Kuhn's model of revolutionary progress, therefore. It is possible to trace an evolutionary scheme of theory development with any "newness" or "revolution" being derived from technical, and not theoretical, advances. Since the second world war, at least, processual/evolutionist and culture-historical prehistories had co-existed, were even articulated, notably in the various writings of Childe, but also by others (Daniel & Renfrew 1988: 92). The co-existence of different archaeological approaches within the archaeological mainstream seems to offer a better description of archaeology than a revolutionary succession of paradigms. Kuhn himself doubted that his model was applicable to the social sciences or humanities. What seemed to distinguish science, for Kuhn, was the absence of multiple paradigms, a situation common in the arts (Kuhn 1970: 209). Nevertheless, Kuhn's model seems to have left a deep impression upon those who seek to theorise, and see fit to categorise themselves with labels of chronological exclusion - whether it be "new" or "post".

It is a fundamental of the Kuhnian model that an outdated explanatory paradigm is no longer of any value for either the acquisition or the interpretation of data - it can no more ask the right questions than it can supply the right answers. The concept of "paradigm shift" lends itself to misuse as an instrument of academic closure. Claims of new paradigms carry with them the unstated proposal that all previous work, in the form of the replaced paradigm, is no longer relevant. It discourages the study of large sections of the pre-existing archaeological literature, the outcome being under-informed and often repetitive explanations. Strident claims of new paradigms should therefore be viewed with suspicion, and resisted. Clarke has warned that to restrict archaeological research to a single paradigm implies a:

".....deliberate relinquishment of certain freedoms and an inevitable narrowing of intellectual focus."
(Clarke 1972: 9).

Explanatory Modes

In a philosophical sense most archaeologists are realists. They believe that the world is a physical entity whose existence is independent of any knowledge thereof, and that theories which relate to its existence may possess a greater or lesser degree of correspondence to material reality. This realist orientation is virtually unavoidable given the nature of the subject matter with which the archaeologist works. Nevertheless, not surprisingly perhaps, there are dissenters:

"....we abandoned any attempt to create a privileged or foundational discourse which would suggest that it is "in the true" by virtue of internal logical coherency or by means of reference to, or correspondence with, realities standing outside discourse...."

(Shanks & Tilley 1989: 7).

Ultimately, perhaps inevitably in an archaeological context, such an idealist stance is untenable - the realities standing outside of discourse await confrontation:

"The data set used to investigate some aspects of the theoretical perspective put forward above consists of 70 completely restored or restorable vessels attributable to the southern Swedish middle neolithic funnel neck beaker (TRB) tradition, dateable to between circa 2600 bc and 2280-2140 bc..."

(Shanks & Tilley 1987: 155).

There is an objective reality then, a material past, and it invites investigation. It is not conducive to simple description, however; it is complex and may be approached by many descriptions, or explanations, which are not necessarily exclusive (Piggott 1965: 6, Clarke 1968: 643). Throughout this study reference has been made to two alternative approaches to the material reality of the archaeological record, two different "modes" of archaeological explanation: culture-historical and processual/evolutionist.

The choice of the word mode was deliberate, it was to emphasise that an "explanatory mode" was not to be equated with a Kuhnian paradigm, and also that it represented a distinct way, or fashion, of approaching the past. Thus the processual/evolutionist mode is used to explain long term sequences of change that present in the archaeological record by reference to an underlying mechanism, or regularity, adumbrated as a general theory. The culture-historical mode, on the other hand, is used to explain short term, often unique, patterns of change. The processual/evolutionist mode is more suited to the study of prehistory while that of culture-history is the preserve of the historical archaeologist. These two modes of explanation are structurally dissimilar. The processual/ evolutionist subsumes a number of alternative theories for explaining change, foremost amongst which are Marxism, Systems Theory and Neo-Darwinism. These theories are close parallels to Kuhn's paradigms in that they contain their own theoretical assumptions and dictate the use of different categories of data. Clarke referred to them as "supermodels" (1972: 5) while Trigger termed them "high level theories" (1989: 22). (Trigger was mistaken to equate his high-level theories with Clarke's controlling models. These were more fully termed controlling mind models by Clarke and they referred to the, not fully perceived, social environment of the archaeologist which helped to form his or her world view. As such, the controlling models controlled the archaeologist, not subsidiary set of models or theories).

The two modes of explanation are dissimilar, therefore, and because they are structurally dissimilar it is not possible to derive one from another. Thus a diachronic stack of culture-historical explanations will not form a processual explanation in the absence of any articulating theory. Their dissimilarity does not imply incompatibility, however. Each mode may be used to "frame" a certain aspect of reality, but neither one enjoys priority. Different explanatory aims require the use of different explanatory modes, although it is not at all clear that this point has been generally realised.

Revolution and the Beaker Culture

Before a theory can be considered to be new, or revolutionary, it must displace an old, discredited theory. This is why Renfrew spoke of the collapse of the "first paradigm". It is also why Champion et al (1984: 156) looked forward to the:

"...development of an acceptable alternative framework for European prehistory..."

to replace the inadequate:

"...traditional normative model."

Thus, before any revolutionary, processual, explanations could be deployed by the New Archaeologists it was first felt necessary to thoroughly discredit previous explanations, and show them to be devoid of any explanatory potential. This was achieved by ignoring anything that was processual or evolutionist in the writings of "pre-processual" archaeologists and by characterising the, admittedly predominant, culture-historical scenarios as sterile. Ultimately, this is why the concepts of Beaker culture and "Beaker Folk" were attacked, not because of any irreconcilable asymmetry of theory and data, but because there was no room for them in the new scheme of things. Yet, as the preceding discussion of explanatory modes made clear, they are not mutually exclusive alternatives, they are complementary, and describe different aspects of reality. The utilisation of one does not require the prior refutation of the other. Thus, the denial of archaeological cultures or ethnic groupings is not a prior requisite of a study of the evolution of social ranking in western Europe. As a procedure it is analogous to arguing that lions and tigers do not exist before proceeding with a study of the evolution of mammalian carnivores. The dangers inherent to such an approach were emphasised towards the end of Chapter Two. Although the culture-historical mode might seem unsuitable, or inappropriate, for the study of prehistory, the entities it defines really exist, and lie in wait, ready at all times to mislead the unwary processualist. The inability, or at least unwillingness, to realise this has been a major failing of the British New Archaeology.

The Subjective Archaeologist

It seems that the interpretations of archaeologists may often be, unwittingly and unwillingly, influenced by realities other than those contained within the archaeological record. This is not a novel observation. Nor is it the intellectual property of the critical theorists. The controlling models of Clarke have already been alluded to; Piggott, following Collingwood, was more specific:

"...we interpret the evidence in terms of our own intellectual make-up, conditioned as it is by the period and culture within which we were brought up, our social and religious background, our current assumptions and presuppositions, and our age and status."
(Piggott 1965: 5).

It was the laudable aim of many new archaeologists to circumnavigate these shoals of subjectivity, although some would claim that they foundered in the attempt. This study has suggested as much. The differing morphologies of prehistoric crania were a well known "fact", but in the shadow of the second world war it was considered to be an unsavoury one, deemed to be unworthy of investigation. Renfrew's characterisation of craniology as phrenology was symptomatic, prehistorians generally were content to overlook or to summarily dismiss the evidence of the crania whilst constructing theories based upon more up to date, more fashionable, bodies of data. Similarly, the availability of improved models of migration and ethnicity seems not to have been recognised, or even desired, by those wishing to be part of a "processual revolution". There certainly does not appear to have been any attempt to seek them out.

Trigger has argued that the social concerns and aspirations of archaeologists will be those of their larger peer group - the middle classes (1989: 14). He suggested that, in America at least, the revival of interest in cultural evolution during the 1960s may have been borne out of the desire of archaeologists qua middle classes to present their privileged position as the natural outcome of an evolutionary process that was beyond their control (1989: 289). On the other hand it has been argued that the 1960s and 1970s were a time of withdrawal from empire, of relinquishment of imperial ambitions, and alternatives to nationalist, culture-historical explanations were sought for (Ammerman 1989). But why New Archaeologists, or their successors, should desire an "archaeology of discontinuity" is not altogether clear, unless motives of personal advancement are suspected. However, it seems probable that the adoption of a revolutionary polemic by the New Archaeologists of the 1960s was a response to the political environment of their academic adolescence. In western Europe and north America the children of the middle classes had embarked upon a crusade to establish a new world order, to meet the challenge archaeology needed to be both ambitious and iconoclastic - the times demanded nothing less.

It seems more honest then to admit to subjectivity, and perhaps in so doing to diminish its effects. The self-reflexive subjectivity of Piggott seems, in the end, to present a more certain route to objectivity than do many attempts at strict theoretical legislation. Hypotheses and interpretations may multiply as a result, and entail a continuing process of evaluation. Interpretations must be open to constant scrutiny as facts and theories shift around within their social formers. This is no bad thing, a fuller understanding of the past can only follow. But it seems desirable that any process of critical evaluation should proceed by means of a logical and structured discourse, polemical exchanges from theoretical bunkers serve only to retard progress and ultimately vitiate the discipline.

Appendix One

ADAPTATION AND MICROEVOLUTION

Natural Selection and Adaptation

The physiological configuration of an individual organism - the sum of its structural and functional characteristics - is known as its phenotype. The phenotype is the physical expression of the underlying genetic code, the genotype, after modification by environmental factors during growth and development. Modern evolutionary theory emphasises the role played by natural selection in acting upon the heritable variation contained within the total available genotypes, or gene pool, of a population to produce more environmentally suited individuals. Genetic variation is maintained by random mutations which constantly occur as chromosomes are damaged during meiotic division. These mutations produce novel gene variants, or alleles, most of which are lethal in effect and thus will not be retained within the species. Others appear to be selectively neutral. However, upon occasion, a mutation will occur which confers upon its owner a relatively increased chance of survival that may be translated into reproductive success, thereby ensuring that the mutant allele will spread through the circumjacent population. This process of mutation and selection is recurrent, and may effect many physiological traits, with differential mortality acting as a "filter", weeding out less fit individuals to produce a population with a range of phenotypic, ultimately genotypic, variation better adapted for survival within its particular, exigent, environment. The genotype of an individual organism becomes adapted to the environment by virtue of the superior survival characteristics of its "carrier", its reproduced phenotype.

Microevolution: Genetic Drift and Gene Flow

Ideally, an equilibrium distribution of alleles will occur within an infinite, random breeding, population. However, natural populations are finite entities and may be delineated by geographical or socio-cultural boundaries. Relative differences in allele frequencies may develop between regionalised populations as a result of genetic drift. Genetic drift occurs as genetic information is lost in a random fashion through failures of inter-generational transmission. There is a resultant decrease in intra-populational genetic variation. There is also, however, a corresponding decrease in inter-populational genetic similarity as allele frequencies are differentially maintained. This process is most marked in populations which are descended from a small group of individuals who carried only a portion of the genetic information available within a larger parent population. Such a situation may arise after a small scale migration (founder effect) or result from a drastic reduction in population after a natural disaster (bottleneck effect).

Genetic drift is a microevolutionary process that promotes genetic diversification and heterogeneity. The reverse is true of gene flow which, as the name suggests, is a homogenizing process whereby genes pass from a donor to a recipient population. This may occur in areas of population stasis where there are overlapping spheres of mate acquisition but it is more usual to consider gene flow in terms of an actual population migration, with the population acting as a vector for gene transmission.

Appendix Two

BONE GROWTH AND REMODELLING

Human skeletal structures are composed of two major tissue types - bone and cartilage - which differ markedly in their structure and function. Cartilage is an avascular, pliable, pressure tolerant tissue which provides flexible support in areas of direct compression. Cartilage may also partake in bone formation. Bone provides rigid support. It is vascular and forms in areas of high tensile stress, it is protected by a surrounding membrane, the periosteum, which ensures a supply of blood to the bone, and also partakes in bone growth. Mature bone is a structurally differentiated tissue which forms around a marrow cavity. The outside of a bone is surrounded by the periosteal membrane; a less well characterised membrane - the endosteal - separates the inside of a bone from the marrow cavity. Macroscopically bone can be described as either spongy (cancellous or trabecular) or compact. Spongy bone is always formed by the endosteum, it never forms on the outside of a bone and is always enclosed within a cortex of compact bone. Flat bones consist of two layers of bone, known as tables, sandwiching an inner compartment, called the diploe, which contains marrow and spongy bone. Bone can only grow appositionally, that is by marginal expansion, following either intramembraneous or endochondral ossification. It cannot uniformly expand.

Endochondral ossification occurs as chondrocytes within a cartilage anlage, or model, undergo a hypertrophy which is associated with the mineralisation of the cartilage matrix. The surrounding membrane adopts the functions of the periosteum and initiates vascularisation of the mineralised cartilage, whereupon undifferentiated connective tissue cells pass into the matrix and develop into bone forming osteoblasts. The osteoblasts form true bone while large polynuclear osteoclasts are active removing mineralised cartilage. Endochondral ossification is particularly associated with the human growth phase. During childhood, after partial ossification, cranial growth may continue to occur at cartilaginous synchondroses, the centrally located, basal, sphenooccipital synchondrosis being of particular importance. Such growth occurs as cartilage cells proliferate with subsequent mineralisation and bone deposition, bone itself does not physically expand.

Intramembraneous ossification occurs when undifferentiated connective tissue cells on the inner surface of the periosteum develop into osteoblasts which organise into sheets and lay down an intercellular matrix (osteoid), which consists primarily of collagen, on the surface of a pre-existing bone. This osteoid matrix is subsequently mineralised by hydroxy-apatite crystals to form new bone.

During growth a bone maintains its required shape and proportions by a process of remodelling (Enlow 1990). This is an intramembraneous process and entails the laying down of new bone on one surface being balanced by resorption on the opposite surface. The surfaces of growing bones are thus covered by a series of "depository" or "resorptive" growth fields. If a given periosteal surface area of a bone has a resorptive field then it will be balanced by an endosteal depository field, and vice versa. Rates of resorption and deposition are not balanced, however; during growth the rate of bone deposition exceeds that of resorption, thus allowing for both regional and overall enlargements of individual bones. Growth remodelling also allows bones to change location during growth, a process termed drift, or transformation. Similarly, structurally important features of a bone can maintain their position, or move, as required. Despite constant remodelling, as a bone grows, it retains a basically recognisable shape.

Intramembraneous growth and/or remodelling occur in response to forces acting upon the bone or its surrounding membrane. These forces may be passive in origin, arising out of surrounding tissue growth, or else result directly from the action of attached muscle. Two mechanisms of remodelling induction are currently known, one initiated within the periosteum and the other in the bone matrix itself.

Periosteal mediated remodelling occurs when the periosteum itself is stressed and the amount of blood arriving at the bone is thereby altered. Compression of the periosteal membrane occludes the vasculature and, therefore, reduces the blood flow into subjacent areas of bone tissue. This relative ischaemia inhibits osteoblast function, while at the same time encouraging osteoclasts to remove the affected bone and relieve the pressure. Conversely, in conditions of tension, blood vessels may be dilated, improving the blood supply and stimulating osteoblast activity and the deposition of new bone.

The second activating mechanism of remodelling is brought into play when the mineralised matrix of the bone itself is stressed. This occurs as mechanical loadings of the bone, caused by either contradictory growth vectors of adjacent tissues or else by muscle action, act to distort its normal shape. These distortions of the bone take the form of small, compressed, concave areas with corresponding tension stressed convexities. Responsive changes in the bioelectric charge of the distorted areas stimulate osteoblastic deposition in concavities and osteoclastic resorption in convexities. This bioelectric phenomenon is known as the piezo effect.

The mode of interaction between these two regulatory mechanisms of remodelling activity remains poorly characterised, particularly in the case of the muscle-bone interface. To some extent this is because muscle attachments to bone vary in type. Muscles may either attach directly to the calcified matrix of the bone by means of tendons or aponeuroses (sheets), or else terminate in the periosteum. It is not clear how these two types of muscle attachment influence remodelling activity although, intuitively, it would seem likely that periosteal attachments would promote a diffuse, membrane mediated, response while tendons might cause more localised remodelling by virtue of the piezo effect. The action of both mechanisms is ultimately expressed at the cellular level by modulation of levels of cytoplasmic calcium, which acts as a second messenger by either activating or suppressing the enzyme systems responsible for cell function.

Appendix Three

THE CHRONOLOGICAL AND CULTURAL RELATIONSHIPS OF BEAKER AND FOOD VESSEL POTTERY

The ceramic repertoire of early Bronze Age Britain is dominated by three ceramic types: Beakers, Food Vessels and Collared Urns. Traditionally, they were considered to constitute a diachronic sequence but more recently scholars have preferred social explanations of this ceramic trichotomy (Simpson 1968: 201-202, Burgess 1974: 176-178, Bradley 1984: 71-73). The different types of pottery are still considered to possess some degree of chronological order, with Beakers appearing first and Collared Urns persisting the longest, but it is thought that there was a long temporal overlap during which all types were in contemporary usage. Social considerations of status, fashion or whatever would have determined their selection for inclusion at burial. If this interpretation is correct, then it has ramifications for the craniometric study presented herein. The crania recovered with either Food Vessels or Beakers would belong to separate sectors of a contemporary population and any differences in cranial morphology might be the result of selective or exclusive breeding practices. Alternatively, if Beakers and Food Vessels can be used as chronological markers then any differences in cranial morphology would have to be interpreted within a longer term context of morphological change. It is argued below that the evidence for temporal overlap is rarely discussed and that a critical examination shows it to be quite tenuous, it is more probable that the use of Food Vessels did succeed that of Beakers and that it is correct to conceive of them as constitutive of a diachronic sequence. The evidence to be considered is of three types: stratigraphy, associations and C14 dates.

There is one case reported in the literature of a Food Vessel enjoying stratigraphical precedence over a Beaker. This was at Broad Down, Devon, where a cairn had apparently been built over a Food Vessel accompanied cremation, but with a later Beaker insertion (Fox 1948). However, this cairn was excavated by a certain Reverend R. Kirwan in the middle of the 19th century and whose technique consisted of driving a trench through the centre of a mound until an assumed primary burial was discovered. Furthermore, it is reported that he was often not present on site when discoveries were made by his workmen (Fox 1948: 3). In the absence of any corroborating comparanda this excavation cannot be held to have produced any reliable archaeological information.

It is frequently observed that Food Vessel burials are to be found in the upper parts of shaft graves that contain primary Beaker inhumations, and also fragmented Beaker pottery throughout the fill. This, it is suggested, is indicative of a close chronological relationship (Simpson 1968, Burgess 1980: 29); but it does not necessarily follow, it seems more likely that existing graves were dug out and reused. The fills of these graves are also found to contain broken and incomplete skeletons, probably the remains of earlier interments. There are, however, several instances reported of Beakers and Food Vessels being recovered from contemporary contexts. These include Fargo Plantation (Ashbee 1960: 138), Hawkhill (Simpson 1968: 201) and Edington Mill (Simpson 1968: 201). At Fargo Plantation, a flat grave was found to contain a single Beaker inhumation burial in association with three cremations, one of which had probably been accompanied by a Food Vessel; the site had been badly disturbed by rabbits, however, and the Food Vessel was fragmented and scattered, with only its base remaining close to the cremation (Stone 1938). The excavator believed that the inhumation burial, the Food Vessel cremation and one of the remaining cremations were contemporary as they were spaced apart on the bottom of the grave and covered by a compact layer of chalk. However, the skeleton was incomplete, and it was not centrally placed but was instead located in a corner of the grave. It seems likely that the Beaker inhumation may have been the original occupant of the grave, but had been subsequently exhumed and partially dismembered before being replaced in a position secondary to the now primary cremations. The Food Vessel at Edington Mill was recovered from a cist which was partially filled with soil, together with a few sherds of a Beaker (Craw 1913), the relationship of these sherds to the Food Vessel is questionable. The Food Vessel and the Beaker from Hawkhill came from separate cists (Tate 1851). It is significant that Clarke lists only one instance of a Beaker/Food Vessel association, at Brougham, but regards it as dubious (1970: 451).

There is, thus, little evidence to be recovered from a study of barrow stratigraphies that would point, unequivocally, to contemporary usage of both Beaker and Food Vessel pottery. Arguments derived from the evidence of shared associations are stronger perhaps, but still far from conclusive. It is true that Beaker and Food Vessel burials share some

Table A3. 1.   Food Vessel associated C14 dates.

Primary associations:

Dunfermline, Kinross.	Bone	SRR 292	3581±40BP
Trelystan I, Powys.	Charcoal	CAR 280	3645±70BP
	Charcoal	CAR 281	3695±70BP
Trelystan II, Powys.	Charcoal	CAR 283	3550±60BP
Strathallen B, Perth.	Bone	GU 1381	3490±65BP
Ardnave, Islay.	Charcoal	GU 1371	3610±85BP
	Charcoal	GU 1439	3680±65BP
	Bone	GU 1274	3325±80BP
	Charcoal	GU 1440	3687±60BP
	Charcoal	GU 1442	3655±60BP
Kneep, Lewis.	Charcoal	GU 1174	3410±55BP
Garton Slack 7, East Riding.	Charcoal	HAR 1236	3550±70BP
Harland Edge, Derby.	Charcoal	BM 178	3440±90BP
Radley, Oxford.	Bone	OxA 1884	3670±80BP

Secondary associations:

Trelystan II, Powys.	Charcoal layer cut by FV pit.	CAR 390	3550±65BP
Kentraw, Islay.	Bone fron inhumation underlying FV inhumation.	GU 2189	3510±50BP
Heslerton 1L, Yorkshire.	Charcoal underlying FV barrow.	HAR 6690	3840±40BP

artefact associations, but these are generally types with a broad chronological spread, v-bored conical buttons or double pointed awls, for example. Of the 4 bronze daggers associated with Food Vessels, two (Gerloff #260, Amble; Gerloff #288, Argyll) belong to Gerloff's rather heterogeneous "Flat Riveted Knife Dagger" classification, examples of which have been found in Beaker, Wessex I and Wessex II contexts. The dagger found with a Food Vessel cremation in a cist at Merthyr Mawr (Gerloff #48) is the archetype for another Gerloff classification which includes a dagger found with a Clarke S2 Beaker at Aldro 116. Gerloff suggested that members of her "Type Merthyr Mawr" category were closely related to those of her "Type Butterwick", examples of which have been found with Clarke S3 and S4 Beakers. The final dagger accompanied Food Vessel burial was the encisted cremation at Llandfyfnan. This dagger was included by Gerloff (#107) in her "Group Aylesford", also related to "Type Butterwick" although often with a pointille decorated blade reminiscent of Wessex II "Camerton-Snowshill" daggers.

There are a number of artefacts found in Food Vessel graves but not in those with Beakers. Single pointed awls with a flattened tang fall into this category as do bone, ring headed, pins. The classic Food Vessel association is, of course, the plano-convex flint knife which is never found with Beaker burials. Also distinctive of Food Vessel burials are the spacer-plate necklaces of jet, related to Wessex amber examples, and single-stranded jet bead necklaces. Although jet and amber beads are found in Beaker contexts, large quantities of perforated beads are not. Possible exceptions are at Dalgety (Watkins 1982), where a necklace of 210 shale disc beads and pieces of two broken jet pendants were discovered in a cist together with an inhumation and a Clarke S4 Beaker. This was similar to an assemblage of 188 jet disc beads with a triangular toggle discovered in association with a sub-Beaker Food Vessel (Clarke 1970 #1803).

Thus, although there are artefactual associations which are shared by both Food Vessel and Beaker burials, it is by Food Vessels and late Beakers, usually Clarke's S3 and S4. They do not share an integrated artefact "package". It would be expected for this to be the case in the chronological development of any society that did not experience a disjunctive culture change. Material culture assemblages are composed of a number of artefact types that may change or be substituted either independently, or else sometimes as a group, depending upon their functional or social interrelationships. Simply because the pottery used by a society changes in type it does not automatically follow that there will be associated changes in other areas of the material culture assemblages.

It remains to consider the C14 evidence for a Beaker/ Food Vessel overlap. On the face of it, the C14 dates currently available from Food Vessel and Beaker associated contexts appear to show a large degree of temporal overlap, but it is not altogether clear how credible this overlap is (Table A3.1, Figure A3.1). The Beaker culture is quite well dated, surviving for a period of approximately 800 years, from 2600 cal BC to 1800 cal BC. This chronological "bracket" was obtained after analysis of 35 samples of human bone and is probably the best estimate that present technology can offer (Kinnes et al 1991). The quality of Food Vessel related C14 dates compares unfavourably, however. The majority are from contexts antedating the Food Vessel, they are usually

Beaker and Food Vessel dates.

B = range of Beaker dates
FV-TPQ = individual Food Vessel T.P.Qs.
FV = individual Food Vessel dates

(For T.P.Qs only the lower end of the calibrated date range is shown. Calibrated dates obtained from uncalibrated date plus and minus 2 standard deviations).

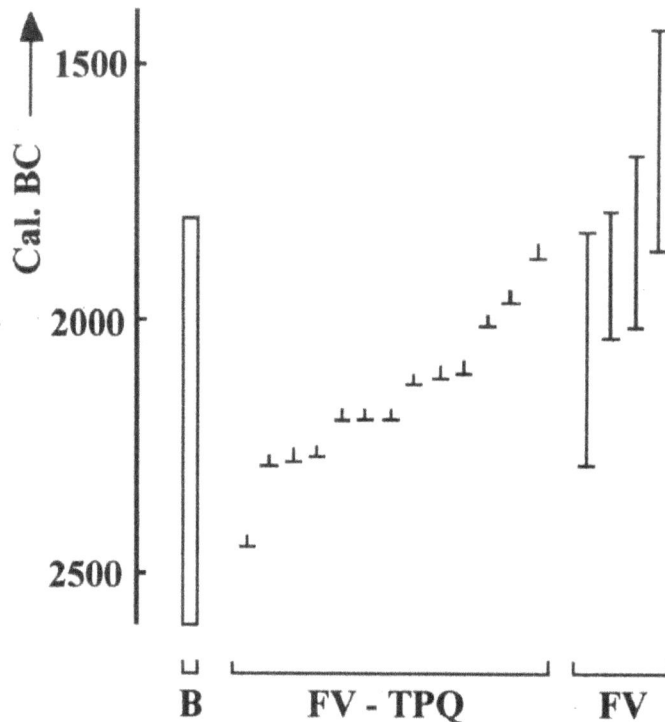

obtained from charcoal and, in effect, represent a series of terminus post quems. There are fewer of the more reliable bone-derived dates available, but those that are suggest a period of usage that extended over at least 500 years, from about 2050 calBC to 1600 calBC. This implies that Food Vessels and Beakers may have been in contemporary usage for a couple of centuries but there is a problem with this interpretation. It is questionable as to whether the precision currently available to C14 dating methodologies is sufficiently tight to permit sharp demarcation of chronologically successive cultural groups. Dates with a standard deviation of 60 C14 years provide 95% confidence limits that span 240 C14 years, the true timespan is even greater after calibration. Thus an apparent overlap of 200 years would in fact be expected, even if the cultural groups in question were chronologically distinct.

From the evidence adduced it might indeed be possible to argue for Food Vessel/Beaker contemporaneity, but the case is weak, a chronological succession of types provides a more parsimonious explanation and it is the one accepted here.

Appendix Four

CATALOGUE OF PREHISTORIC ENGLISH CRANIA

Each entry in this catalogue contains two sets of references. The initial reference set provides, where possible, the primary source of information for the archaeological context from which the cranium was recovered, followed by corpora references for associated artefacts. Crania of doubtful or uncertain provenance have not been included. The second set of references are to anatomical listings or studies. Where the cranium has been personally inspected the location and museum number are listed at the end of the entry. If published data were utilised instead of personal measurement the name of the anthropologist is provided within the second reference set. Each entry is followed by the chronological group to which it was assigned for purposes of the study.

All crania were sexed using anatomical features only, associated artefacts were ignored. It is possible that some young males were wrongly classified as females; cranium 019, an apparently female burial with bronze dagger and axe, seems particularly suspect.

Group Abbreviations

EN - Early Neolithic
LN - Late Neolithic
ON - Other Neolithic
BB - Bell Beaker
WG - Weapon Group
FV - Food Vessel
BA - Early Bronze Age
NG - Not grouped

Reference Abbreviations

Brewster 1980 - Brewster, T.C.M. 1980. *The Excavation of Garton and Wetwang Slacks*. London: R.C.H.M.

Brewster 1984 - Brewster, T.C.M. 1984. *The Excavation of Whitegrounds Barrow, Burythorpe*. Malton, Yorkshire: East Riding Archaeological Research Committee Publications.

CB - Davis, J.B., J.Thurnam. 1865. *Crania Brittanica*. London: Private Subscription.

CC - Pitt-Rivers, A.L.F. 1898. *Excavations at Cranborne Chase (Volumes I-IV)*. London: Private Printing.

Clarke - Clarke, D.L. 1970. *Beaker Pottery of Great Britain and Ireland*. Cambridge: Cambridge University Press.

Cunnington - Cunnington, M.E. 1929. *Woodhenge*. Devizes: Simpsons.

Garson - Garson, J.G. 1893. A Description of the Skeletons Found in Howe Hill Barrow. *Journal of the Anthropological Institute* 22: 8-20.

Gerloff - Gerloff, S. 1975. *The Early Bronze Age Daggers in Great Britain*. Munich: Prahistorische Bronzefunde V1/2.

Green - Green, H.S. 1980. *The Flint Arrowheads of the British Isles*. Oxford: British Archaeological Reports. British Series 75.

GRBB - Greenwell, W. 1877. *British Barrows*. London: Oxford University Press.

Grinsell - Grinsell, L. 1957. A List of Wiltshire Barrows, in R.B.Pugh (ed), *A History of Wiltshire, Volume 1*. London: Victoria History of the Counties of England.

JT - Thurnam, J.T. 1863-4. On the Principal Forms of Ancient British and Gaulish Skulls. *Memoirs of the Anthropological Society of London* 1: 120-168.

JTII - Thurnam, J.T. 1863-4. On the Principal Forms of Ancient British and Gaulish Skulls, Part 2. *Memoirs of the Anthropological Society of London* 1: 459-519.

JTIII - Thurnam, J.T. 1867. Further Researches and Observations on the Two Principal Forms of Ancient British Skulls. *Memoirs of the Anthropological Society of London* 3: 41-80.

Piggott - Piggott, S. 1962. *The West Kennet Long Barrow.* London: HMSO.

Roe - Roe, F.E.S. 1966. The Battle-Axe Series in Britain. *Proceedings of the Prehistoric Society* 32: 199-245.

Rolleston - Rolleston, G. 1877. Descriptions of Figures of Skulls and General Remarks upon the Series of Neolithic Crania, in W. Greenwell, *British Barrows.*

Schuster - Schuster, E.H.J. 1905-6. The Long Barrow and Round Barrow Skulls in the Collection of the Department of Comparative Anatomy, the Museum, Oxford. *Biometrika* IV: 351-62.

TYD - Bateman, T. 1861. *Ten Years' digging in Celtic and Saxon Grave Hills in the counties of Derby, Stafford and York from 1848 to 1858.* London.

Vestiges - Bateman, T. 1848. *Vestiges of the Antiquities of Derbyshire.* London.

Watts & Rahtz - Watts, C. & Rahtz, P. 1984. *Cowlam Wold Barrows.* York: Ebor Press.

Wright - Skulls from Round Barrows of East Yorkshire. *Journal of Anatomy and Physiology* 38: 119-132; 39: 417-449.

CATALOGUE OF PREHISTORIC ENGLISH CRANIA

Berkshire

001. RADLEY 3. Contracted male inhumation in grave under round barrow with bronze dagger. Oxoniensia 17 (1952) p24; Gerloff 63, Type Milston. Oxoniensia 13 (1948) p15. Cambridge Eu 1.4.5. Group: WG.

Cambridgeshire

002. BARNACK, GRAVE 28. Primary burial. Contracted male inhumation in grave under round barrow with W/MR Beaker, small tanged copper dagger, bone pendant and wristguard. Antiquaries Journal 57 (1977) p208. Wells, ibid, p219. Group: BB.

Derbyshire

003. ARBOR LOW. Contracted female inhumation in cist under round barrow with jet necklace. TYD p24, ln33. Bateman P103; CB pl35. Sheffield J93.942. Group: FV.

004. BAILEY HILL. Contracted female inhumation in grave under round barrow with Food Vessel and boars tusk. TYD p169, ln28. Bateman P168. Sheffield J93.946. Group: FV.

005. BALLIDON MOOR. Contracted male inhumation in cist under round barrow with flint ?arrowhead. TYD p58, ln34. Bateman P159; CB pl1. Sheffield J93.929. Group: BA.

006. BEE LOW. Contracted female inhumation in grave under round barrow with Beaker and serrated flint blade. TYD p72, ln19; Clarke 153, S2. Bateman P177. Sheffield J93.935. Group: BB.

007. BEE LOW. Disarticulated male skeleton in cist under round barrow, no associations. TYD p73, ln2. Bateman P178. Sheffield J93.944. Group: BA.

008. BLAKE LOW. Contracted female inhumation in grave under round barrow with Beaker. TYD p41, ln7; Clarke 135, N2. Bateman P112. Sheffield J93.941. Group: BB.

009. FIVE WELLS HILL, NEAR TADDINGTON. Male cranium from multiple inhumation in round chambered cairn. Vestiges p91. Bateman P89. Sheffield J93.937. Group: ON.

010. GOTAM, NEAR PARWICH. Contracted male inhumation in cist under round barrow with flint spearhead and bronze awl. Vestiges p105, ln5. Bateman P100. Sheffield J93.918. Group: BA.

011. GREEN LOW. Contracted male inhumation in cist under round barrow with Beaker, 3 flint barb and tanged arrowheads, flint dagger, 3 bone spatulae and bone awl. Vestiges p59, ln10; Clarke 115, S1; Green 131. Bateman P53; CB pl41. Sheffield J93.909. Group: BB.

012. LIFF'S LOW. Contracted male inhumation in cist under barrow with Seamer-type flint axe, antler hammerhead, flint arrowheads and round-bottomed ceramic vessel of uncertain type. Vestiges p42, ln13. Bateman P22. Sheffield J93.931. Group: LN.

013. MONSAL DALE. Disembodied female skull in grave under round barrow close to Beaker. TYD p76, ln1; Clarke 143, S2. Bateman P181. Sheffield J93.943. Group: BB.

014. MONSAL DALE. Contracted male inhumation in cist under round barrow with flint arrowhead. TYD p75, ln34. Bateman P183, CB pl60. Sheffield J93.911. Group: BA.

015. MONSAL DALE. Contracted male inhumation in grave under round barrow with "clay vase" and flint spearhead. TYD p78, ln12. Bateman P187. Sheffield J93.912. Group: BA.

016. MONSAL DALE. Contracted male inhumation in grave under round barrow, no associations. TYD p79, ln8. Bateman P190. Sheffield J93.908. Group: BA.

017. PARCELLY HAY. Sitting female inhumation in cist under cairn, no associations. TYD p22,ln28. Bateman P102. CB pl2. Sheffield J93.945. Group: BA.

018. SHUTTLESTONE, NEAR PARWICH. Contracted female inhumation in cist under round barrow with bronze axe, bronze dagger, jet bead and flint disc. TYD p34,ln25; Gerloff 54, Type Merthyr Mawr. Bateman P108. Sheffield J93.948. Group: WG.

019. SMERRILL MOOR. Contracted female inhumation in cist under round barrow with flint knife, adjacent to cist containing multiple disarticulated inhumation deposit. TYD p102, ln16. Bateman P231. Sheffield J93.923. Group: NG.

020. SMERRILL MOOR. Contracted male inhumation in round barrow mound, no associations. TYD p104, ln5. Bateman P234. Sheffield J93.940. Group: BA.

021. STAKOR HILL. Contracted female inhumation in grave under round barrow with Beaker. TYD p80, ln23; Clarke 122, FP. Bateman P192. Sheffield J93.922. Group: BB.

022. WAGGON LOW. Contracted male inhumation in grave under round barrow, no associations. TYD p86, ln10. Bateman P207. Sheffield J93.932. Group: BA.

Dorset

023. DORCHESTER. Museum documentation records that this male skeleton was found with a Beaker in its hands close to the Hospital gates, Dorchester. It is possibly Dorchester G5, recovered when lowering the floor of the Masonic Hall, with a Beaker in the arm of the skeleton. London SK26. Group: BB.

024. FRAMPTON G5. (LONG ASH LANE). Contracted female inhumation in grave under bowl barrow with single pointed bronze awl. Dorset Proceedings 80 (1959) p120. Cambridge Eu 1.4.23. Group: BA.

025. HANDLEY G1, (WOR BARROW). Multiple inhumation deposit in long barrow, male skull. CC IV p66, skeleton 3. Salisbury. Group: EN.

026. HANDLEY G1. (WOR BARROW). Multiple inhumation deposit in long barrow, male skull. CC IV p66, skeleton 4. Salisbury. Group: EN.

027. HANDLEY G1. (WOR BARROW). Multiple inhumation deposit in long barrow, male skull. CC IV p66, skeleton 5. Salisbury. Group: EN.

028. HANDLEY G1. (WOR BARROW). Contracted male inhumation in ditch deposits of long barrow with leaf shaped flint arrowhead in ribs. CC IV p63, skeleton 8; Green 201. Salisbury. Group: EN.

029. HANDLEY G1. (WOR BARROW). Contracted male inhumation in grave in long barrow mound with Beaker. CC IV p114; Clarke 191, FN. Salisbury. Group: BB.

030. HANDLEY, RUSHMORE BARROW 20. Contracted male inhumation in grave under round barrow with Beaker. CCII p5. Salisbury. Group: BB.

031. TARRANT LAUNCESTON G5. (CRICHEL DOWN 14). Contracted male inhumation in grave under bowl barrow with Beaker and flint flake. Archaeologia 90 (1944) p75; Clarke 201, W/MR. Proceedings of the Prehistoric Society (1940) p131. Cambridge Eu 1.4.57. Group: BB.

Gloucestershire

032. FROCESTER G1. (NYMPSFIELD). Multiple inhumation deposit in chambered tomb, male skull. JT p55. Cambridge. Eu 1.5.65. Group: EN.

033. RODMARTON G1. Multiple inhumation deposit in chambered tomb, female skull. JT p55. CB pl59, Schuster 39. London SK1823. Group: EN.

034. RODMARTON G1. Multiple inhumation deposit in chambered tomb, male skull. JT p55. Cambridge Eu 1.5.68. Group: EN.

035. SUDELEY G1. (BELAS KNAP). Multiple inhumation deposit in chambered tomb, male skull. Proceedings of the Society of Antiquaries, 3 (1866) p277, burial CIII. Cambridge. Eu 1.5.5. Group: EN.

036. SUDELEY G1. (BELAS KNAP). Multiple inhumation deposit in chambered tomb, male skull. Proceedings of the Society of Antiquaries, 3 (1866) p277, burial CV. Cambridge. Eu 1.5.6. Group: EN.

037. SUDELEY G1. (BELAS KNAP). Multiple inhumation deposit in chambered tomb, female skull. Proceedings of the Society of Antiquaries, 3 (1866) p277, burial CVI. Cambridge. Eu 1.5.7. Group: EN.

038. SUDELEY G1. (BELAS KNAP). Multiple inhumation deposit in chambered tomb, female skull. Proceedings of the Society of Antiquaries, 3 (1866) p277, burial DII. Cambridge Eu 1.5.3. Group: EN.

039. SUDELEY G1. (BELAS KNAP). Multiple inhumation deposit in chambered tomb, male skull. Proceedings of the Society of Antiquaries, 3 (1866) p277, burial DIV. Cambridge Eu 1.5.10. Group: EN.

040. SWELL G5. (UPPER SWELL 232). Multiple inhumation deposit in chambered tomb, female skull. GRBB p528, ln13. London SK1856. Group: EN.

041. SWELL G5. (UPPER SWELL 232). Contracted female inhumation in multiple inhumation deposit in chambered tomb. GRBB p529, ln5. London SK1857. Group: EN.

Kent

042. COLDRUM. Multiple inhumation deposit in chambered tomb, male skull. Journal of the Royal Anthropological Institute, 43 (1913) p78. Cambridge Eu 1.5.118. Group: EN.

Lincolnshire

043. GIANTS HILLS I. Multiple inhumation deposit in long barrow, female skull. Archaeologia, 85 (1936) p53. Cave, ibid, p90. Group: EN.

044. TALLINGTON. Contracted male inhumation under round barrow, no associations. Proceedings of the Prehistoric Society, (1976) p226, grave 2, secondary burial. Cambridge Eu 1.4.90. Group: BA.

Northamptonshire

045. ALDWINCLE. Disarticulated male inhumation in coffin under round barrow with Beaker, probably Clarke Type S3. Northamptonshire Archaeology, 11 (1976) p30. Cambridge. Group: BB.

Oxfordshire

046. ASCOTT-UNDER-WYCHWOOD. Multiple inhumation deposit in chambered tomb, female skull. Man, 12 (1977) p22-32. London. Group: EN.

047. ASCOTT-UNDER-WYCHWOOD. Multiple inhumation deposit in chambered tomb, male skull. Man, 12 (1977) p22-32. London. Group: EN.

048. CASSINGTON. Contracted female inhumation in flat grave, no associations. Antiquaries Journal, 14 (1934) p271, grave 2. London SK2028. Group: BA.

049. CASSINGTON. Contracted male inhumation in flat grave with Beaker. Antiquaries Journal, 14 (1934) p272, grave 6; Clarke 720F, ?S4. London SK2031. Group: WG.

050. CASSINGTON. Contracted male inhumation in grave under round barrow with flint flake. Oxoniensia, 11/12 (1946/7) p11. Cambridge Eu. 1.4.1. Group: BA.

051. EYNSHAM. Contracted male inhumation in flat grave with Beaker. Oxoniensia, 3 (1938) p21, burial 4; Clarke 743, S4. London SK2044. Group: WG.

052. EYNSHAM. Contracted male inhumation in single grave with Beaker. Oxoniensia, 3 (1938) p22, burial 14; Clarke 745, S4. London SK2049. Group: WG.

053. EYNSHAM. Contracted male inhumation in flat grave with Beaker and bronze dagger. Oxoniensia, 3 (1938) p22, burial 15; Clarke 746, FP; Gerloff 41, Type Butterwick. London SK2050. Group: WG.

Staffordshire

054. CASTERN. Contracted male inhumation in cist under round barrow with Beaker. Vestiges p87, ln 21; Clarke 835, S2. Bateman P84. Sheffield J93.915. Group: BB.

055. LONG LOW. Multiple inhumation deposit in cist in long cairn with two flint leaf arrowheads and a flint knife, male skull. TYD p146, ln21; Green 130. CB pl33; Bateman P145. Sheffield J93.930. Group: EN.

056. WETTON HILL. Contracted male inhumation in cist under round barrow with Food Vessel. TYD p139, ln23. CB pl12. Bateman P142. Sheffield J93.939. Group: FV.

Wiltshire

057. AMESBURY G51. Contracted male inhumation in round barrow mound with Beaker, bronze awl, antler slip, flint scraper and wooden objects. Wiltshire Archaeological Magazine, 70/71 (1978) p14, burial A; Clarke 1037 S2(E). Cambridge Eu 1.4.100. Group: BB.

058. AMESBURY G51. Contracted male inhumation in ditch under round mound with Beaker. Wiltshire Archaeological Magazine, 70/71 (1978) p16, burial B; Clarke 1036 W/MR. Cambridge EU 1.4.101. Group: BB.

059. AVEBURY G22. (WEST KENNET). Multiple inhumation deposit in chambered tomb, male skull. JT III p55, burial 1. Cambridge Eu 1.5.61. Group: EN.

060. AVEBURY G22. (WEST KENNET). Multiple inhumation deposit in chambered tomb, male skull. JT III p55, burial 2. Cambridge Eu 1.5.62. Group: EN.

061. AVEBURY G22. (WEST KENNET). Multiple inhumation deposit in chambered tomb, male skull. JT III p55, burial 13. Cambridge Eu 1.5.63. Group: EN.

062. AVEBURY G22. (WEST KENNET). Multiple inhumation deposit in chambered tomb, male skull. JT III p55, burial 4. CB pl50. Cambridge Eu 1.5.64. Group: EN.

063. AVEBURY G22. (WEST KENNET). Multiple inhumation deposit in north-east chamber of chambered tomb, female skull. Piggott (1962) p25 burial 1. Cambridge Eu 1.5.142. Group: EN.

064. AVEBURY G22. (WEST KENNET). Multiple inhumation deposit in south-west chamber of chambered tomb, female skull. Piggott (1962) p26 skull 1. Cambridge Eu 1.5.147. Group: EN.

065. AVEBURY G22. (WEST KENNET). Multiple inhumation deposit in south-west chamber of chambered tomb, female skull. Piggott (1962) p26 skull 3. Cambridge Eu 1.5.149. Group: EN.

066. AVEBURY G22. (WEST KENNET). Multiple inhumation deposit in north-west chamber of chambered tomb, male skull. Piggott (1962) p26, skull 1. Cambridge Eu 1.5.150. Group: EN.

067. BISHOPS CANNINGS G34. Contracted male inhumation in grave under round barrow, no associations. Wiltshire Archaeological Magazine, 6 (1860) p318. CB pl32. Cambridge Eu 1.4.32. Group: BA.

068. BRATTON G8A. Contracted male inhumation in cist under round barrow, no associations. Grinsell (1957) p161. Cambridge Eu 1.4.38. Group: BA.

069. CALNE/CHERHILL G5. (OLDBURY HILL). One of three skeletons in large shallow grave in long barrow, female. ? primary or secondary. Wiltshire Archaeological Magazine, 13 (1872) p104. JT II p473. Cambridge Eu 1.5.77. Group: NG.

070. CALNE/CHERHILL G5. (OLDBURY HILL). One of three skeletons in large shallow grave surrounded by blocks of sarsen stone, female. Wiltshire Archaeological Magazine, 13 (1872) p104. JT II p473. Devizes C8. Group: NG.

071. CHIPPENHAM G1. (LANHILL). Multiple inhumation deposit in chambered tomb, male skull. Proceedings of the Prehistoric Society, 4 (1938) p125, burial 1. Cambridge Eu 1.5.104. Group: EN.

072. CHIPPENHAM G1. (LANHILL). Multiple inhumation deposit in chambered tomb, female skull. Proceedings of the Prehistoric Society 4 (1938) p125, burial 2. Cambridge Eu 1.5.105. Group: EN.

073. CHIPPENHAM G1. (LANHILL). Multiple inhumation deposit in chambered tomb, female skull. Proceedings of the Prehistoric Society, 4 (1938) p125, burial 5. Cambridge Eu 1.5.107. Group: EN.

074. FIGHELDEAN G31. Single male inhumation under long barrow. JT III p55. Cambridge Eu 1.5.86. Group: EN.

075. FUSSELLS LODGE. Multiple inhumation deposit in long barrow, probably female skull. Archaeologia, 100 (1957) 1-80. London SK3312. Group: EN.

076. HEYTESBURY G1. (BOWLS BARROW). Multiple inhumation deposit in long barrow, male skull. JT II p473. Cambridge Eu 1.5.79. Group: EN.

077. HEYTESBURY G1. (BOWLS BARROW). Multiple inhumation deposit in long barrow, male skull. JT II p473. Cambridge Eu 1.5.80. Group: EN.

078. NETTLETON G1. (LUGBURY). Multiple inhumation deposit in chambered tomb, male skull. Grinsell 1957 p142. Cambridge Eu 1.5.52. Group: EN.

079. NETTLETON G1. (LUGBURY). Multiple inhumation deposit in chambered tomb, male skull. Grinsell 1957 p142. Cambridge Eu 1.5.53. Group: EN.

080. NETTLETON G1. (LUGBURY). Multiple inhumation deposit in chambered tomb, female skull. Grinsell 1957 p142. Cambridge Eu 1.5.59. Group: EN.

081. NORTON BAVANT G13. Multiple inhumation deposit in long barrow, female skull. JT III p55. Cambridge Eu 1.5.98. Group: EN.

082. NORTON BAVANT G13. Multiple inhumation deposit in long barrow, female skull. JT III p55. Cambridge Eu 1.5.99. Group: EN.

083. NORTON BAVANT G13. Multiple inhumation deposit in long barrow, male skull. JT III p55. Cambridge Eu 1.5.92. Group: EN.

084. NORTON BAVANT G13. Multiple inhumation deposit in long barrow, male skull. JT III p55. Cambridge Eu 1.5.93. Group: EN.

085. ROUNDWAY G8. Contracted male inhumation in grave under round barrow with Beaker, flint barbed and tanged arrowhead, tanged copper dagger, bracer and bronze pin. Wiltshire Archaeological Magazine, 3 (1857) p186; Clarke 1135, W/MR; Gerloff 1; Green 206. CB pl42. Devizes C14. Group: BB.

086. SHREWTON G5K. Contracted male inhumation in grave under bowl barrow with small tanged copper dagger and Beaker. Proceedings of the Prehistoric Society, 50 (1984) p275; Clarke 1140, N2; Gerloff 12. Wells, ibid, microfiche. Group: BB.

087. SHREWTON G24. Contracted male inhumation in grave under bowl barrow with late Southern beaker. Proceedings of the Prehistoric Society, 50 (1984) p285. Salisbury. Wells, ibid, microfiche. Group: WG.

088. STONEHENGE DITCH. Male inhumation in secondary ditch fill of henge monument with 2 hole slate bracer and 3 flint barbed and tanged arrowheads. Wiltshire Archaeological Magazine, 78 (1984) p13; Green 226/I. Salisbury. Group: BB.

089. UPAVON. Male inhumation with Beaker. Wiltshire Archaeological Magazine, 40 (1919) p6; Clarke 1150, W/MR. Devizes. Group: BB.

090. WEST OVERTON G1. Contracted male inhumation in grave under round barrow with bronze knife dagger and either a crutch headed pin or a bronze awl. (Uncertain associations, see entry in Guide Catalogue of Neolithic and Bronze Age Collections in Devizes Museum (1964) p52); Gerloff 271. CB pl11. Cambridge Eu 1.4.28. Group: BA.

091. WEST OVERTON G6b. Contracted male inhumation in grave under round barrow with Beaker, antler spatula, bronze awl, flint knife, flint flake and two slate objects. Proceedings of the Prehistoric Society, 32 (1966) p127; Clarke 1131, S2. London. Group: BB.

092. WINTERBOURNE MONKTON G2B. (CIST 300yds FROM MILL BARROW). Multiple inhumation deposit in large cist under a sarsen, male skull. Wiltshire Archaeological Magazine, 1 (1853) p303. Devizes. Group: NG.

093. WINTERBOURNE STOKE G1. Contracted male inhumation at base of long barrow with flint bludgeon, probably primary. JT I p141, burial A. Cambridge Eu 1.4.44. Group: EN.

094. WINTERBOURNE STOKE G1. Contracted male inhumation in long barrow mound with ?urn and flint knife, probably secondary. JT I p141, burial B. Cambridge Eu 1.4.43. Group: BA.

095. WINTERBOURNE STOKE G43. Contracted female inhumation in grave under round barrow, probably with Beaker. Wiltshire Archaeological Magazine, 67 (1972) p51. Dawes, ibid, p57. Group: BB.

096. WOODHENGE. Male inhumation holding axehammer with Beaker near skull. Cunnington. London SK49. Group: WG.

097. WOODHENGE. Male inhumation in grave with oxbones. Cunnington. London SK50. Group: BA.

Yorkshire

098. ACKLAM WOLD 124. Contracted male inhumation in grave under round barrow with flint dagger, flint knife, v-bored amber button, pyrites, bone pin, jet ring and Beaker. 40yrs p91, burial 4; Clarke 1210, S1. Wright 46. Hull 46. Group: BB.

099. ALDRO 52. Contracted female inhumation in grave under round barrow, no associations. 40yrs p62, burial 1. Hull 78. Group: BA.

100. ALDRO 54. Contracted male inhumation in grave under round barrow, no associations. 40yrs p64, burial 3. Wright 29. Hull 29. Group: BA.

101. ALDRO 113. Contracted female inhumation in grave under round barrow with 6 bone hairpins and 3 worked flints. 40yrs p76, centre burial. Wright 50. Hull 50. Group: BA.

102. BARROW NOOK 296. Contracted male inhumation in grave under round barrow, no associations. Yorkshire Archaeological Journal, 20 (1909) p491. Hull 108. Group: BA.

103. CALLIS WOLD 23. Contracted male inhumation in gravel under round barrow with Food Vessel and perforated stone battle-axe. 40yrs p154; Roe 250, IIIa. Wright 35. Hull 35. Group: FV.

104. CALLIS WOLD 275. Contracted male inhumation on old ground surface under round barrow. 40yrs p161, burial 3. Wright 44. Hull 44. Group: ON.

105. CALLIS WOLD 275. Contracted male inhumation on pavement under round barrow. 40 yrs p162, burial 9. Hull 92. Group: ON.

106. COWLAM WOLD 56. Contracted female inhumation in grave under round barrow with Food Vessel. Watts and Rahtz 1984. Dawes, ibid. Group: FV.

107. COWLAM WOLD 57. Contracted male inhumation on old ground surface under round barrow with antler macehead. GRBB p217, ln10, burial 4. Schuster 149. London SK1942. Group: LN.

108. COWLAM WOLD 57. Contracted female inhumation on old ground surface under round barrow with flint leaf arrowhead. GRBB p218, ln27, burial 6; Green 91. Schuster 150. London SK1943. Group: ON.

109. COWLAM WOLD 57. Multiple disarticulated inhumation deposit under round barrow, female skull associated with bone pin. GRBB p219, ln3, burial 7. Schuster 151. London SK1944. Group: ON.

110. DINNINGTON. Multiple inhumation deposit in long barrow, male skull. JT p132. Cambridge Eu 1.5.76. Group: EN.

111. DINNINGTON. Multiple inhumation deposit in long barrow, male skull. JT p132. London SK1807. Group: EN.

112. DINNINGTON. Multiple inhumation deposit in long barrow, male skull. JT p132. Schuster 21. London SK1813. Group: EN.

113. DINNINGTON. Multiple inhumation deposit in long barrow, male skull. JT p132. Schuster 22. London SK1814. Group: EN.

114. DINNINGTON. Multiple inhumation deposit in long barrow, male skull. JT p132. Schuster 25. London SK1816. Group: EN.

115. DINNINGTON. Multiple inhumation deposit in long barrow, male skull. JT p132. Schuster 29. London SK1820. Group: EN.

116. DINNINGTON. Multiple inhumation deposit in long barrow, female skull. JT p132. London SK1809. Group: EN.

117. DINNINGTON. Multiple inhumation deposit in long barrow, female skull. JT p132. Schuster 24. London SK1815. Group: EN.

118. DINNINGTON. Multiple inhumation deposit in long barrow, female skull. JT p132, p478. Schuster 26. London SK1817. Group: EN.

119. DINNINGTON. Multiple inhumation deposit in long barrow, female skull. JT p132, p478. Schuster 27. London SK1818. Group: EN.

120. DINNINGTON. Multiple inhumation deposit in long barrow, female skull. JT p132. Schuster 28. London SK1819. Group: EN.

121. DINNINGTON. Multiple inhumation deposit in long barrow, female skull. JT p132. Schuster 30. London SK1821. Group: EN.

122. DUGGLEBY HOWE 273. Contracted male inhumation in grave under round barrow with long bone pin, several transverse arrowheads and worked flints. 40yrs p27, burial C. Garson, ibid, C. Group: LN.

123. DUGGLEBY HOWE 273. Contracted male inhumation on old ground surface under round barrow with polished flint knife. 40yrs p28, burial D. Garson, ibid, D. Hull 70. Group: LN.

124. DUGGLEBY HOWE 273. Contracted male inhumation in grave under round barrow with antler macehead, flint axe and leaf-shaped flint arrowhead. 40yrs p28, burial G; Green 85. Garson, ibid, G. Hull 72. Group: LN.

125. DUGGLEBY HOWE 273. Contracted male inhumation in grave under a round barrow, no associations. 40yrs p28, burial I. Garson, ibid, I. Group: LN.

126. DUGGLEBY HOWE 273. Disembodied male skull in grave under round barrow. 40yrs p29, burial J. Garson, ibid, J. Hull 71. Group: LN.

127. DUGGLEBY HOWE 273. Contracted male inhumation in grave under round barrow with towthorpe bowl, 9 flint flakes and a core. 40 yrs p29, burial K. Garson, ibid, K. Hull 74. Group: LN.

128. DUGGLEBY HOWE 273. Contracted male inhumation in grave under round barrow, no associations. 40yrs p29, burial L. Garson, ibid, L. Hull 75. Group: LN.

129. EBBERSTON 221. Multiple inhumation/cremation deposit in long barrow, male skull. GRBB p486. Schuster 7. London SK1798. Group: EN.

130. EBBERSTON 221. Multiple inhumation/cremation deposit in long barrow, male skull. GRBB p486. Schuster 4. London SK1795. Group: EN.

131. FIMBER C33. Contracted female inhumation in grave under oval barrow with Food Vessel and 3 flint flakes. 40yrs p191, burial 2. Wright 45. Hull 45. Group: FV.

132. FOLKTON (ELF HOWE). Contracted male inhumation in grave under round barrow with collared vessel. GRBB p272, ln1; Longworth 1141. Schuster 173. London SK1966. Group: FV.

133. FOLKTON 70. Contracted female inhumation on old ground surface under round barrow with collared vessel. GRBB p273, ln14; Longworth 1137. Schuster 177. London SK1969. Group: FV.

134. FOLKTON 70. Contracted male inhumation in grave under round barrow with boars tusk pin and flint blade. GRBB p274 ln12. Schuster 178. London SK1970. Group: BA.

135. FOLKTON 71. Contracted female inhumation in grave under round barrow with Food Vessel, bronze awl, flint scraper and three bone beads. GRBB p275, ln8 from bottom. Rolleston p575; Schuster 180. London SK1972. Group: FV.

136. GANTON 21. Contracted male inhumation in grave under round barrow with Food Vessel. GRBB p163, ln25. Schuster 111. London SK1905. Group: FV.

137. GANTON 22. Contracted male inhumation in penannular ditch under round barrow, no associations. GRBB p166, ln7 from bottom. Schuster 114. London SK1908. Group: BA.

138. GANTON 22. Contracted female inhumation on old ground surface under round barrow, no associations. GRBB p166, ln2 from bottom. Schuster 115. London SK1909. Group: BA.

139. GANTON 27. Contracted female inhumation in round barrow mound with v-bored conical jet button. GRBB p174, ln32. Schuster 117. London SK1911. Group: BA.

140. GANTON 28. Contracted male inhumation in hollow under round barrow with ?plain vase. GRBB p176, ln7. Schuster 118. London SK1912. Group: BA.

141. GARROWBY WOLD 32. Contracted male inhumation in grave under round barrow with bronze dagger. 40yrs p146, burial 4; Gerloff 43, Type Butterwick. Hull 86. Group: WG.

142. GARROWBY WOLD 104. Contracted male inhumation in grave under round barrow with curved knife of black flint. 40yrs p134, burial 1. Wright 36. Hull 36. Group: BA.

143. GARROWBY WOLD 104. Contracted male inhumation in grave under round barrow with Beaker and piece of flint. 40yrs p135, burial2; Clarke 1293, S2. Wright 37. Hull 37. Group: BB.

144. GARROWBY WOLD 120. Contracted male inhumation in grave under round barrow, no associations. 40yrs p146, burial 1. Hull 87. Group: BA.

145. GARROWBY WOLD 120. Contracted male inhumation in mound of round barrow with Food Vessel. 40yrs p147, burial 4. Hull 88a. Group: FV.

146. GARTON SLACK, BREWSTER 29. Contracted male inhumation in flat grave, possibly ploughed out barrow, with N2 Beaker and flint flake. Brewster 1980 p573, BA burial 4. Hull. Group: BB.

147. GARTON SLACK 37. Contracted female inhumation on old ground surface under round barrow with bone pin. 40yrs p209, burial 3; Brewster 1980 p92. Wright 6. Hull 6. Group: BA.

148. GARTON SLACK 37. Contracted male inhumation in grave under round barrow with Beaker, flint dagger, perforated stone battle-axe and v-bored jet button. 40yrs p209, burial 6; Brewster 1980 p92; Clarke 1296, S1; Roe 261, Ia. Wright 1. Hull 1. Group: BB.

149. GARTON SLACK 37. Contracted female inhumation crouched on old ground surface under round barrow, no associations. 40yrs p210, burial 8; Brewster 1980 p92. Wright 2. Hull 2. Group: NG.

150. GARTON SLACK 37. Contracted female inhumation on old ground surface under round barrow, no associations. 40yrs p210, burial 9; Brewster 1980 p92. Wright 4. Hull 4. Group: NG.

151. GARTON SLACK 37. Contracted male inhumation on old ground surface under round barrow with gritstone pounder, lower jaw of ox or deer and flint flake. 40yrs p210, burial 12; Brewster 1980 p92. Wright 7. Hull 7. Group: NG.

152. GARTON SLACK 37. Contracted female inhumation on old ground surface under round barrow, no associations. 40 yrs p210, burial 10; Brewster 1980 p92. Wright 5. Hull 5. Group: NG.

153. GARTON SLACK 37. Contracted female inhumation on old ground surface under round barrow, no associations. 40yrs p210, burial 11; Brewster 1980 p92. Wright 3. Hull 3. Group: NG.

154. GARTON SLACK 37. Contracted male inhumation in grave under round barrow, no associations. 40yrs p211, burial 15; Brewster 1981 p92. Wright 8. Hull 8. Group: BA.

155. GARTON SLACK 40. Contracted male inhumation in grave under round barrow with Food Vessel, flint knife, two yellow quartz pebbles and a clay button. 40yrs p229, burial A. Wright 62. Hull 62. Group: FV.

156. GARTON SLACK 40. Disembodied male skull in grave under round barrow, no associations. 40yrs p230, at feet of burial B. Hull 99. Group: BA.

157. GARTON SLACK 75. Contracted female inhumation on old ground surface under round barrow with Food Vessel, bronze awl and plano-convex flint knife. 40 yrs p222, burial 1. Wright 25. Hull 25. Group: FV.

158. GARTON SLACK 75. Contracted female inhumation in grave under round barrow with Food vessel, jet disc necklace and bronze awl. 40yrs p222, burial 2. Wright 23. Hull 23. Group: FV.

159. GARTON SLACK 75. Contracted male inhumation in grave under round barrow with Beaker. 40yrs p223, burial 3; Clarke 1298, S1. Wright 24. Hull 24. Group: BB.

160. GARTON SLACK 81. Contracted female inhumation in grave under round barrow with v-bored, conical, jet button. 40yrs p240, burial 2. Hull. Group: BA.

161. GARTON SLACK 82. Contracted male inhumation in grave under round barrow with 2 flint flakes. 40yrs p233, burial F. Wright 39. Hull 39. Group: BA.

162. GARTON SLACK 82. Contracted male inhumation in grave under round barrow, no associations. 40yrs p234, burial H. Wright 41. Hull 41. Group: BA.

163. GARTON SLACK 82. Contracted female inhumation in grave under round barrow, no associations. 40yrs p234, burial I. Wright 38. Hull 38. Group: BA.

164. GARTON SLACK 82. Contracted male inhumation in grave under round barrow, no associations. 40yrs p234, burial J. Wright 40. Hull 40. Group: BA.

165. GARTON SLACK 107. Contracted male inhumation in grave under round barrow, no associations. 40yrs p230, burial A. Wright 21. Hull 21. Group: BA.

166. GARTON SLACK C40. Contracted male inhumation in grave under round barrow with Food Vessel and several splinters of flint. 40yrs p244, burial 1/a. Wright 30. Hull 30. Group: FV.

167. GARTON SLACK C40. Contracted male inhumation in grave under round barrow with Food Vessel. 40 yrs p244, burial B. Wright 26. Hull 26. Group: FV.

168. GARTON SLACK C41. Contracted female inhumation in grave under round barrow with handled Food Vessel and Accessory Vessel. 40yrs p259, burial 1. Wright 33. Hull 33. Group: FV.

169. GARTON SLACK C41. Contracted male inhumation in grave under round barrow with pig bones. 40yrs p259, burial 2. Wright 34. Hull 34. Group: BA.

170. GARTON SLACK C52. Contracted female inhumation in grave under round barrow with bronze awl and two splinters of flint. 40yrs p217, burial 1. Wright 49. Hull 49. Group: BA.

171. GARTON SLACK C52. Contracted male inhumation in grave under round barrow, no associations. 40 yrs p217, burial 2. Hull 97. Group: BA.

172. GARTON SLACK C52. Contracted male inhumation in grave under round barrow with jet button, flint dagger and knife. 40yrs p217, burial 5. Wright 20. Hull 20. Group: BA.

173. GARTON SLACK C55. Contracted male inhumation in grave under round barrow with two splinters of flint. 40yrs p219, burial J/1. Wright 11. Hull 11. Group: BA.

174. GARTON SLACK 155. Contracted male inhumation in grave under round barrow, no associations. 40yrs p219, burial 2. Wright 10. Hull 10. Group: BA.

175. GARTON SLACK 156. Contracted female inhumation in grave under round barrow with bronze awl and two splinters of flint. 40yrs p220, burial 1. Wright 15/47. Hull. Group: BA.

176. GARTON SLACK 157. Contracted female inhumation in grave under round barrow, no associations. 40yrs p259, burial 1. Wright 16. Hull 16. Group: BA.

177. GARTON SLACK 162. Contracted male inhumation in grave under round barrow, no associations. 40yrs p213, burial 2. Wright 54. Hull 54. Group: BA.

178. GARTON SLACK 162. Contracted male inhumation in grave under round barrow, no associations. 40yrs p213, burial 5. Wright 52. Hull 52. Group: BA.

179. GARTON SLACK 162. Contracted male inhumation in grave under round barrow with plano-convex flint knife. 40yrs p213, burial 6. Wright 55. Hull 55. Group: FV.

180. GARTON SLACK 162. Contracted male inhumation in grave under round barrow, no associations. 40yrs p213, burial 7. Hull. Group: BA.

181. GARTON SLACK 163. Contracted male inhumation in grave under round barrow with Beaker and flint knife. 40yrs p214, burial 1, grave B; Clarke 1304, N3. Wright 12. Hull 12. Group: BB.

182. GARTON SLACK 163. Contracted male inhumation in grave under round barrow with Beaker, bone pin, polished flint axe, flint knife and three flint flakes. 40yrs p215, burial 2; Clarke 1305, N3. Wright 14. Hull 14. Group: BB.

183. GARTON SLACK 163. Contracted male inhumation in grave under round barrow with Beaker, bronze pricker and seven flint flakes. 40 yrs p215, burial 3; Clarke 1306, N3. Hull 96. Group: BB.

184. GARTON SLACK 163. Contracted female inhumation in grave under round barrow, no associations. 40yrs p215, burial 4. Wright 13. Hull 13. Group: BA.

185. GARTON SLACK 167. Contracted female inhumation in grave under round barrow, no associations. 40yrs p243, burial 5. Wright 58. Hull 58. Group: BA.

186. GARTON SLACK 171. Contracted female inhumation under round barrow, no associations. 40yrs p225, ?burial. Wright 61. Hull 61. Group: BA.

187. GARTON SLACK 171. Contracted female inhumation under round barrow, no associations. 40yrs p225, ?burial. Wright 60. Hull 60. Group: BA.

188. GARTON SLACK 171. Contracted male inhumation under round barrow, no associations. 40yrs p225, ?burial. Wright 59. Hull 59. Group: BA.

189. GOODMANHAM 99. Contracted male inhumation in grave under round barrow, no associations. GRBB p308, ln21. Schuster 190. London SK1984. Group: BA.

190. GOODMANHAM 103. Contracted male inhumation in grave under round barrow with Food Vessel. GRBB p313, ln19. Schuster 193. London SK1987. Group: FV.

191. GOODMANHAM 111. Contracted female inhumation in grave under round barrow, no associations. GRBB p319, ln17. Schuster 199. London SK1993. Group: BA.

192. GOODMANHAM 111. Contracted female inhumation on old ground surface under round barrow with flint block at face. GRBB p320, ln12. Schuster 201. London SK1995. Group: BA.

193. GOODMANHAM 112. Contracted female inhumation in grave under round barrow with single pointed bronze awl. GRBB p321, ln14. Schuster 202. London SK1996. Group: FV.

194. GOODMANHAM 113. Disturbed female inhumation in grave under round barrow, no associations. GRBB p323, ln4. London SK2000. Group: BA.

195. GOODMANHAM 117. Contracted male inhumation in grave under round barrow, no associations. GRBB p327, ln15. Schuster 212. London SK2005. Group: BA.

196. GOODMANHAM 120. Contracted male inhumation in grave under round barrow, no associations. GRBB p329, ln20. London SK2007. Group: BA.

197. GREENGATE HILL, PICKERING. Contracted male inhumation in grave under round barrow, no associations. CB, text accompanying CB plates 2,3. London SK58. Group: BA.

198. GREENGATE HILL, PICKERING. Contracted male inhumation in grave under round barrow, no associations. CB, text accompanying CB plates 2,3. London SK59. Group: BA.

199. HANGING GRIMSTON 27. Contracted male inhumation in grave under round barrow with Food Vessel. 40yrs p110. Hull 79. Group: FV.

200. HANGING GRIMSTON 56. Contracted female inhumation in grave under round barrow with Beaker. 40yrs p99, burial 3. Wright 42. Hull 42. Group: BB.

201. HEDON HOWE 281. Disturbed female inhumation in cist. 40yrs p348, grave 3, body 2. Hull 106. Group: ON.

202. HEDON HOWE 281. Crouched male inhumation in cist under round barrow. 40yrs p349, burial 5. Wright 56. Hull 56. Group: ON.

203. HELPERTHORPE 41. Contracted male inhumation in grave under round barrow with flint knife and two antler tines. GRBB p191, last line. Rolleston p617; Schuster 125. London SK1919. Group: BA.

204. HELPERTHORPE 49. Contracted male inhumation on old ground surface under round barrow with bronze dagger. GRBB p207, ln7; Gerloff 79, Type Masterton. Schuster 141. London SK1934. Group: WG.

205. HESLERTON 5. Contracted male inhumation in grave under oval barrow with Food Vessel. GRBB p142, ln6. Rolleston p579; Schuster 96. London SK1891. Group: FV.

206. HUGGATE AND WARTER WOLD 264. Sitting male inhumation in grave under round barrow, no associations. 40yrs p319. Hull. Group: BA.

207. LANGTON 2. Contracted male inhumation on ground surface under round barrow with flint flake. GRBB p136, last line. Rolleston p603; Schuster 93. London SK1887. Group: BA.

208. LANGTON 2. Contracted female inhumation in round barrow mound with three bronze awls (one single pointed), jet disc bead, shell and bone beads and boars tusk implement. GRBB p137, last line. Schuster 94. London SK1888. Group: FV.

209. LIFF HILL 294. Contracted male inhumation in grave under round barrow with bronze rivetted knife dagger, flint knife and several splinters of flint. 40yrs p203, burial 1. Hull 93. Group: WG.

210. LIFF HILL 294. Contracted female inhumation in round barrow mound with flint knife and scraper. 40yrs p204, burial 2. Hull 94. Group: BA.

211. LIFF HILL 294. Contracted female inhumation in grave under round barrow with Food Vessel. 40yrs p204, burial 3. Wright 51. Hull 51. Group: FV.

212. LONDESBOROUGH 123. Contracted male inhumation in grave under round barrow, no associations. GRBB p332, ln4. Schuster 218. London SK2011. Group: BA.

213. MILL HILL, BROUGH. Male inhumation found in gravel pit with bronze dagger and pin. Antiquary, 38 (1902) p80; Gerloff 125, Armorico-British B, Type Cressington. Hull 111. Group: FV.

214. PAINSTHORPE WOLD 98. Contracted female inhumation in grave under round barrow, no associations. 40 yrs p131, burial A. Hull 82. Group: BA.

215. PAINSTHORPE WOLD 98. Contracted male inhumation in grave under round barrow with Food Vessel. 40yrs p131, burial B. Wright 28. Hull 28. Group: FV.

216. PAINSTHORPE WOLD 98. Contracted male inhumation in grave under round barrow with Food Vessel and worked flint point. 40yrs p132, burial C. Wright 27. Hull 27. Group: FV.

217. PAINSTHORPE WOLD 118. Contracted male inhumation in grave under round barrow with jet link. 40yrs p127, burial M. Wright 57. Hull 57. Group: LN.

218. RUDSTON 61. Contracted female inhumation in grave under round barrow with Beaker and antler pick. GRBB p231, ln1; Clarke 1366, N2. Schuster 156. London SK 1950. Group: BB.

219. RUDSTON 63. Contracted male inhumation in round barrow mound, no associations. GRBB p248, ln12. London SK1955. Group: BA.

220. RUDSTON 63. Contracted male inhumation in round barrow mound with Food Vessel and flint barbed and tanged arrowhead. GRBB p248, line 3 from bottom; Green 323. Rolleston p591. Schuster 165. London SK1958. Group: FV.

221. RUDSTON 63. Contracted male inhumation on old ground surface under round barrow, no associations. GRBB p250, ln19. Schuster 166. London SK1959. Group: BA.

222. RUDSTON 68. Contracted male inhumation in grave under round barrow with bronze knife, perforated stone battle-axe and flint point. GRBB p265, ln24. Roe 274,IIc. London SK1962. Group: WG.

223. RUDSTON 224. Multiple inhumation/cremation deposit in long barrow, male skull. GRBB p497, p501 ln1. London SK1802. Group: EN.

224. RUDSTON 224. Multiple inhumation/cremation deposit in long barrow, male skull. GRBB p501, ln6. Rolleston p613; Schuster 19. London SK1803. Group: EN.

225. SHERBURN 7. Contracted female inhumation on old ground surface under round barrow. GRBB p146, ln35. Rolleston p609; Schuster 99. London SK1894. Group: ON.

226. SHERBURN 13. Contracted female inhumation in grave under round barrow with Food Vessel and flint plano-convex knife. GRBB p152, ln23. Schuster 104. London SK1899. Group: FV.

227. SHERBURN 13. Contracted male inhumation in grave under round barrow with Food Vessel. GRBB p154, ln1. Schuster 105. London SK1900. Group: FV.

228. STAXTON 5. Burial 5, contracted male inhumation on subsoil, no covering mound, flint block on chest. Yorkshire Archaeological Journal 40 (1959) 129-145, p133. Denston, ibid, p139. Group: BA.

229. TOWTHORPE 7. Contracted male inhumation on old ground surface under round barrow, no associations. 40yrs p22. Hull 68. Group: BA.

230. TOWTHORPE 21. Contracted female inhumation in grave under round barrow with Beaker. 40yrs p12, bottom of grave; Clarke 1400, S2. Hull 65. Group: BB.

231. TOWTHORPE 43. Contracted male inhumation under round barrow with Food Vessel. 40yrs p14, burial 1. Hull 66a. Group: FV.

232. TOWTHORPE 106. Contracted male inhumation in grave under round barrow, no associations. 40yrs p13, burial A. Hull. Group: BA.

233. WEAVERTHORPE 42. Disembodied female skull on old ground surface under round barrow with quartzite hammerstone. GRBB p193, ln9. London SK1920. Group: BA.

234. WEAVERTHORPE 42. Contracted male inhumation on old ground surface under round barrow with Beaker. GRBB p193, ln14; Clarke 1403, N3. Schuster 127. London SK1921. Group: BB.

235. WEAVERTHORPE 43. Contracted male inhumation in round barrow mound, no associations. GRBB p195, ln18. London SK1926. Group: BA.

236. WEAVERTHORPE 43. Contracted male inhumation in grave under round barrow with flint knife and flake. GRBB p195, ln33. Schuster 133. London SK1927. Group: BA.

237. WEAVERTHORPE 44. Contracted male inhumation in round barrow mound with flint plano-convex knife. GRBB p198, ln11. Rolleston p619. Schuster 134. London SK1928. Group: FV.

238. WEAVERTHORPE 46. Contracted male inhumation on old ground surface under round barrow with flint flake. GRBB p200, ln19. Rolleston p571, Schuster 135. London SK1929. Group: BA.

239. WEAVERTHORPE 46. Contracted female inhumation in mound of round barrow with hammerstone. GRBB p200, ln11 from bottom. Schuster 136. London SK1930. Group: BA.

240. WESTOW 223. Secondary female burial contracted in cist in long barrow mound. GRBB p492, ln8. Schuster 13. London SK1801. Group: BA.

241. WHARRAM PERCY 65. Contracted male inhumation in grave under round barrow with a circular piece of worked flint. 40yrs p48, burial 1. Wright 32. Hull 32. Group: BA.

242. WHARRAM PERCY 66. Upper half of female body in round barrow mound with plano-convex flint knife. 40yrs p49, burial 2. Hull 77. Group: FV.

243. WHITEGROUNDS. Multiple inhumation deposit under round barrow, female skull. Brewster 1984 p8, skeleton 1. Dawes, ibid, p25. Group: ON.

244. WHITEGROUNDS. Multiple inhumation deposit under round barrow, female skull. Brewster 1984 p8, skeleton 2. Dawes, ibid, p25. Group: ON.

245. WHITEGROUNDS. Contracted male inhumation in grave under round barrow with jet slider and Seamer-type flint axe. Brewster 1984 p10. Dawes, ibid, p25. Group: LN.

246. WHITEGROUNDS. Multiple inhumation deposit under round barrow, male skull. Brewster 1984 p10. Dawes, ibid, p25. Group: ON.

247. WILLERBY 33. Contracted female inhumation in grave under round barrow, no associations. GRBB p183, ln7. Schuster 121. London SK1915. Group: BA.

248. WOLD NEWTON 284. Contracted female inhumation on old ground surface under round barrow. 40yrs p350, burial 2. Wright 17. Hull 17. Group: ON.

249. WOLD NEWTON 284. Contracted male inhumation in round barrow mound with leaf shaped flint arrowhead. 40yrs p351, burial 7; Green 325. Wright 18. Hull 18. Group: ON.

Appendix Five.   Craniometric Data.   Measurements in mm.

ID	SEX	GOL	XCB	WCB	ASB	BBH	FRK	PAK	OCK	FRC	PAC	OCC	NAH	BNL	BAL	OH	OB	NLH	NLB	PAL	PAB	GRP	C.I.
1	M	186	144	100			135	113	120	119	104	104										WG	77.4
2	M	191	151	104									74			34	43	52	27	53	42	BB	79.1
3	F	180	140	95	109	137	125	126	110	109	114	91	64	103	97	32	39	47	23	43	43	FV	77.8
4	F	170	134	92	107	134	119	112	115	106	100	98	63	101	96	35	39	49	26	44	36	FV	78.8
5	M	188	140	99	113	149	135	127	114	116	114	96	65	112	99	30	42	52	26	43	44	BA	74.5
6	F	186	137	94			124	127	114	110	113	96	64			32	37	49	23	44	44	BB	73.7
7	M	176	151																			BA	85.8
8	F	174	141	91			119	128	108	100	113	88	63			33	39	48	23			BB	81.0
9	M	198	134	106	107		132	142	123	117	126	100	68			32	42	52	23			ON	67.7
10	M	180	140	100	108	147	132	116	118	114	104	96	76	108	92	34	41	57	26	46	44	BA	77.8
11	M	191	155	105	116	149	130	135	124	116	121	100	71	109	90	34	40	55	24	42	39	BB	81.2
12	M	190	142				130	150		112	131		70			34	39	55	24	51	39	LN	74.7
13	F	184	142																			BB	77.2
14	M	192	150	103	115	137	149	144	122	122	129	99	59	97	92	29	39	48	22	43	41	BA	78.1
15	M	173	152	97	119	133	123	122	103	110	106	89	62	103	96			46		47	44	BA	87.9
16	M	185	150	105	104	142	128	129	111	108	117	85	72	108	93	34	39	56	25	42	44	BA	81.1
17	F	188	147	104	114	136	131	130	119	113	117	94	67	107	104	32	42	52	24	49	44	BA	78.2
18	F	181	147																			WG	81.2
19	F	163	138	92	111	137	126	127	102	106	111	82	58	95	94	33	37	45	22	46	36	NG	84.7
20	M	181	149	104	112	138	133	134	114	110	119	93	63	102	95	34	37	51	24	44	42	BA	82.3
21	F	171	143	94	113	125	121	115	119	102	104	89	51	92	85	27	38			38	37	BB	83.6
22	M	189	140	100	112	149	130	131	122	112	116	99		111	94							BA	74.1
23	M	175	141	97	113	129	129	130	115	111	115	87	63	94	92	32	40	51	23	43	43	BB	80.6
24	F	178	135	99	109	139	124	118	115	110	107	97	67	108	103	32	40	49	25	46	36	BA	75.8
25	M	206	139	101	115	126	135	134	134	115	120	101	71	108	107	33	42	52	24	46	41	EN	67.5
26	M	190	133	95	110	131	121	136	121	110	120	100	71	102	95	34	40	54	22	42	38	EN	70.0
27	M	193	139																			EN	72.0
28	M	198	136	104	111		145	154	116	124	136	98				33	37	52	23			EN	68.7
29	M	173	140	99	110	121	110	125	106	96	114	88	63	97	88							BB	80.9
30	M	173	146	97	112	131	129	114	110	110	104	87	75	101	101	33	41	50	22	53	44	BB	84.4
31	M	188	145	102	114	145	137	134	115	121	118	96	73	106	94	34	43	53	26	46	39	BB	77.1
32	M	197	147	98	119	140	145	135	128	125	121	103	70	106	99	34	41	53	25	44	38	EN	74.6
33	F	187	140	93		132	128	135	125	112	120	101	60	99	95	30	38	44	22	44	38	EN	74.9
34	M	205	144	95	121	143	137	134	145	118	123	116	70	105	98	32	43	51	23	46	43	EN	70.2
35	M	200	139	102	116	139	130	130		114	121			106								EN	69.5
36	M	196	142																			EN	72.4
37	F	186	127																			EN	68.3
38	F	185	132	94			126	119	125	110	111	99										EN	71.4
39	M	190	142	99	118		129	127	129	115	115	104										EN	74.7
40	F	172	129	87			125	127	109	106	116	89										EN	75.0
41	F	182	134	101	101	127	123	130	110	107	113	91	69	97	98	31	39	51	22	48	37	EN	73.6
42	M	197	135																			EN	68.5
43	F	183	132																			EN	72.1
44	M	186	141	99	114	135	129	118	121	110	107	96	71	106	103	29	40	51	26	47	40	BA	75.8
45	M	179	147	97	119	138	126	121	111	112	112	93	74	106	102	28	42	53	23	48	42	BB	82.1
46	F	186	139	100	108	128	127	126	120	109	115	96										EN	74.7
47	M	186	132	97	112	138	130	134	118	112	120	99	64	104	97	31	38	49	21	43	35	EN	71.0
48	F	188	139	103			136	139	119	115	124	95										BA	73.9
49	M	175	151	99			132	124	112	116	110	94								45	40	WG	86.3
50	M	182	142	94	112	138	126	121	124	110	109	101		105	88							BA	78.0
51	M	183	137	101	105		132	120	112	114	108	92								44	34	WG	74.9
52	M	185	144	100			126	142	115	106	125	98								46	43	WG	77.8
53	M	196	144	93			125	130	126	113	119	101								45	38	WG	73.5
54	M	191	159	100	126		139	133	121	119	121	101	71			34	42	51	25	48	42	BB	83.2
55	M	201	133	99	115	142	143	135	135	124	125	111	71	106	100	36	41	52	22	44	40	EN	66.2
56	M	184	155	101	108	132	135	120	125	110	108	98	72	103	98	32	42	54	28	45	43	FV	84.2
57	M	191	150	93	120		145	120		117	111		61					53	28	45	42	BB	78.5
58	M	184	152	108	119		142	125		128	112		72					54	30	47	43	BB	82.6
59	M	201	149	96	124	142	150	144	121	126	131	96	72	111	104	34	39	53	20	44	37	EN	74.1
60	M	203	141																			EN	69.5
61	M	200	140	99	116	133	121	145	115	109	128	95		113						53	46	EN	70.0
62	M	199	131	102	112	146	134	141	120	118	126	99	65	113	107	29	40	46	23	45	38	EN	65.8
63	F	189	129	94			130	124		115	116		65			33	43	48	23			EN	68.3
64	F	188	130																			EN	69.1
65	F	194	142	98	115	130	127	131	124	111	117	96	70	101	100	32	41	49	22	44	43	EN	73.2

Appendix Five. Craniometric Data. Measurements in mm.

ID	SEX	GOL	XCB	WCB	ASB	BBH	FRK	PAK	OCK	FRC	PAC	OCC	NAH	BNL	BAL	OH	OB	NLH	NLB	PAL	PAB	GRP	C.L
66	M	199	145	101	110	156	134	124	151	121	116	121	75	109	99	35	39	52	23	46	39	EN	72.9
67	M	194	144	98	116	133	131	132	126	112	118	102	77	103	99	37	40	59	24	46	36	BA	74.2
68	M	191	134	102	111	145	130	118	124	116	108	99	73	122	115	37	40	56	23	45	44	BA	70.2
69	F	197	132	93			135	134	118	116	118	97										NG	67.0
70	F	185	142	99	114		126	124	122	108	112	99										NG	76.8
71	M	190	135	94	109	140	137	134	120	119	122	100	69	103	99	33	41	53	26	44	37	EN	71.1
72	F	190	135	92	109		125	135	124	110	123	98	58			29	42	46	24			EN	71.1
73	F	176	135																			EN	76.7
74	M	205	137																			EN	66.8
75	F	189	136	97	113	131	125	133	119	111	118	97										EN	72.0
76	M	195	137	99	115	140	132	135	125	115	124	101	67	105	95	31	39	54	20	42	38	EN	70.3
77	M	198	129	95	109		126	142	125	112	125	102										EN	65.2
78	M	197	135	102			132	136	126	115	123	100										EN	68.5
79	M	195	133																			EN	68.2
80	F	194	135	96			132	132	129	115	119	103										EN	69.6
81	F	206	131																			EN	63.6
82	F	187	137	98	115		131	132		114	118											EN	73.3
83	M	196	144	99	117	137	134	145	127	115	130	97		104								EN	73.5
84	M	199	142																			EN	71.4
85	M	189	154	103	115	143	142	129	120	122	119	94	73	108	94	35	44	56	27	39	40	BB	81.5
86	M	191	151	96	115	147	123	128	132	114	120	103	71	106	96	32	47	46	26	49	37	BB	79.1
87	M	168	145	99			124	122	118	108	102	89	69			33	43	53	27		41	WG	86.3
88	M	185	146	103	118	150	140	131	111	118	117	91	73	115	111	30	37	55	26	51	46	BB	78.9
89	M	178	150	95	116		125	123	117	108	110	95	67			35	40	50	22			BB	84.3
90	M	200	143	103	120		138	127	129	122	115	104	78			40	44	56	26			BA	71.5
91	M	183	154	102	112		133	119	117	113	108	97										BB	84.2
92	M	202	149	100			134	140		114	126		74			34	43	52	25	45	38	NG	73.8
93	M	181	147	97	108		134	125	121	115	113	101	64			34	43	50	22	44	38	EN	81.2
94	M	173	154	103	112	139	138	125	104	114	111	87	76	105	97	36	40	57	23	41	40	BA	89.0
95	F	180	149	100	112	133	127	133	104	111	111	91										BB	82.8

ID	SEX	GOL	XCB	WCB	ASB	BBH	FRK	PAK	OCK	FRC	PAC	OCC	NAH	BNL	BAL	OH	OB	NLH	NLB	PAL	PAB	GRP	C.L
96	M	182	149																			WG	81.9
97	M	196	135	97	110	137	130	137	112	113	122	91	74	111	102	36	41	51	21	46	35	BA	68.9
98	M	195	154	111	123	138	145	127	129	119	114	101	68	102	100	33	41	52	26	49	34	BB	79.0
99	F	168	150	96	112	131	131	111	104	112	99	92		99								BA	89.3
100	M	180	130				128	132														BA	72.2
101	F	179	144	104	111	132	120	125	120	103	110	98	63	102	98	28	37	46	23			BA	80.4
102	M	193	142	101	114	145	147	127	119	123	113	96	71	106	102	32	41	53	24	46	44	BA	73.6
103	M	182	155	99			133	127														FV	85.2
104	M	197	141	100	114	137	127	141	119	112	125	100	75	106	96	34	42	58	23	52	52	ON	71.6
105	M	206	138	93			151	142	126	121	130	100										ON	67.0
106	F	184	139	97	116	136	116	123	120	104	110	99		111	98	31	39			44	33	FV	75.5
107	M	188	148	98	113	133	129	136	117	113	123	92		105		33	40					LN	78.7
108	F	179	136	96	100	127	119	135	117	103	116	92		96								ON	76.0
109	F	191	132	95	105		128	126	126	111	116	101										ON	69.1
110	M	202	140	96	120	143	138	125	146	119	116	113	69	102	96	32	38	52	20	45	38	EN	69.3
111	M	200	137	89			139	129	134	123	115	112										EN	68.5
112	M	196	140	101	114	143	133	129	137	114	121	109	66	106	98	34	39	52	22	45	39	EN	71.4
113	M	189	136	96	115	133	121	140	132	106	127	108	63	97	88	31	39	49	22	41	41	EN	72.0
114	M	185	140	100	112	138	130	150	112	113	130	94	68	103	97	33	41	54	25	47	40	EN	75.7
115	M	196	132	94			127	142	115	112	127	98										EN	67.3
116	F	189	135	88			139	121	139	112	112	112										EN	71.4
117	F	187	138	92	116	140	124	135	129	110	125	107		101		31	38	51	24	38	34	EN	73.8
118	F	181	136	90	109	140	126	142	120	110	125	100	58	98	88	30	38	48	22	43	40	EN	75.1
119	F	177	132	84		140	128	136	118	110	119	99	63	97	88			48	21	39	36	EN	74.6
120	F			90		142							65	98		32	37	51	22	48	37	EN	
121	F	181	135	86	112		128	128	121	110	116	96										EN	74.6
122	M	200	133	100			145	140	113				70									LN	66.5
123	M	201	133	88		132	134	143	130	119	127	104										LN	66.2
124	M	204	142	106	117	140	130	145	124	113	129	100	75									LN	69.6
125	M	194	132	94			132	127					73									LN	68.0
126	M	185	139	101																		LN	75.1
127	M	196	132																			LN	67.3
128	M	190	152	101		140	143	146	114													LN	80.0
129	M	193	130	91			136	137	120	115	126	97										EN	67.4
130	M	187	131	99	108		141	139	111	108	122	91										EN	70.1

ID	SEX	GOL	XCB	WCB	ASB	BBH	FRK	PAK	OCK	FRC	PAC	OCC	NAH	BNL	BAL	OH	OB	NLH	NLB	PAL	PAB	GRP	C.I.
131	F	172	139	100		139	122	126	115	109	112	98	66	95	90	34	39	51	24	42	41	FV	80.8
132	M	174	147	97	112	138	124	125	123	110	112	104		100								FV	84.5
133	F	184	139	95			134	121	121	114	109	99										FV	75.5
134	M	184	148	99	115	147	135	130	115	119	118	95	69	108	101	31	41	54	23	45	37	BA	80.4
135	F	175	143	100	110	141	132	128	105	117	112	94	66	100	99	33	41	43	23	42	41	FV	81.7
136	M	200	134	97	110	149	138	134	128	123	122	102	70	105						48	41	FV	67.0
137	M	184	136	101	110		123	132	110	108	118	88										BA	73.9
138	F	188	139	100			122	138	114	108	121	89										BA	73.9
139	F	182	148	93	104	135	135	128	113	116	115	90		108								BA	81.3
140	M	203	141	106			130	133	122	112	120	103								52	38	BA	69.5
141	M	199	137	105	108		135	135	125	116	122	102										WG	68.8
142	M	194	147	101		142	143	130	129				75	104	98			53	25			BA	75.8
143	M	200	157	110	123		141	132	124	119	119	96	73					55	28			BB	78.5
144	M	188	142	105	118	136	120	119	130	106	111	106	73	112	117	34	40	55	24	47	43	BA	75.5
145	M	195	142	106	109	139	124	136	122	111	121	101	71	105	100	32	38	53	24	47	39	FV	72.8
146	M	182	144	98	114	131	129	130	113	112	118	96		95								BB	79.1
147	F	193	141	102			121	121	125													BA	73.1
148	M	192	132	91			134	132	115				64			35	41	49				BB	68.8
149	F	186	134	107																		NG	72.0
150	F	180	132	96			126	142	109	106	123	86										NG	73.3
151	M	184	138	95			133	135		114	113	100										NG	75.0
152	F	173	128	95			120	135														NG	74.0
153	F	188	135				139	131	113	115	118	94										NG	71.8
154	M	187	149	103	106	138	138	142	113	116	125	91	67			31		50	26			BA	79.7
155	M	183	142	87	114		129	118	132	112	104	102										FV	77.6
156	M	188	142	96	107		135	122	122	117	111	96								44	35	BA	75.5
157	F	181	143	97	107	120	124	115	122	109	104	100	56			31		43	19	45	35	FV	79.0
158	F	178	138	95		132	122	121	115	108	107	96	61	103	98	31	40	48	25	48	45	FV	77.5
159	M	185	145	103		139	121	132	113	105	119	90	68	114	108	32	41	49	23	43	41	BB	78.4
160	F	182	135	100	108	133	130	123	106	113	112	90	62	97	84	32	38	50	25	40	43	BA	74.2

ID	SEX	GOL	XCB	WCB	ASB	BBH	FRK	PAK	OCK	FRC	PAC	OCC	NAH	BNL	BAL	OH	OB	NLH	NLB	PAL	PAB	GRP	C.I.
161	M	181	148	100	114		134	127	99	117	114	81	62									BA	81.8
162	M	191	147	103	110	139	147	125	112	127	112	92	78	100	93	39	41	55	26	45	34	BA	77.0
163	F	182	145	88	106	130	121	112	127	105	102	100	57	96	88	32	38	47	23	39	41	BA	79.7
164	M	185	145	103	101		130	142	102	116	121	87	59			32	41	49	25	46	41	BA	78.4
165	M	196	155	109	119	135	135	130	131	114	116	106	68	103	99	32	40	56	29	45	36	BA	79.1
166	M	194	140	101			134	131	125	116	116	94	68							46		FV	72.2
167	M	180	157	102		135	128	134	115				64	101	95			50	28			FV	87.2
168	F	177	143	93		134	145	125	109				62	95	92			51	25			FV	80.8
169	M	185	146	98			132	129	119	117	113	99	78	114	92	39	43	57	24	43	40	BA	78.9
170	F	166	136	97	94	130	124	110	110	106	103	89	64	98	92	32	36	48	24	44	40	BA	81.9
171	M	196	141														32	45	51	25			BA	71.9
172	M	185	140	104			131	126	118				68					48	26			BA	75.7
173	M	176	146	102	125		134	122	114	116	109	95	67			34	37	46	24	49	37	BA	83.0
174	M	182	152	106	105	142	132	127	117	114	113	97	70	105	98	31	45	56	26	51	41	BA	83.5
175	F	169	138	94	111	136	132	118	107				68	93	88	34	38	50	26			BA	81.7
176	F	179	140	98		130							61	101	91			47				BA	78.2
177	M	173	153	103	114	136	122	116	113	105	104	96	56	102	97	37	39	48	24			BA	88.4
178	M	188	142	93	108		133	129	109	111	115	89	58			32	42	49	27			BA	75.5
179	M	168	146																				FV	86.9
180	M	189	137	100	119	137	129	139	112	109	120	93		105						50	40	BA	72.5
181	M	194	145	104	121	150	138	129	122				70	118	107	34	39	56	23			BB	74.7
182	M	173	159	97	124	131	128	122	111	111	117	91	71	100	92	35	41	52	21	49	42	BB	91.9
183	M	178	148	87	119	139	134	120	109	110	108	92		104								BB	83.1
184	F	181	132	93			115	130														BA	72.9
185	F	177	131	85	107	126	116	115	109	105	105	93	63	104	102	32	35	49	24	37	39	BA	74.0
186	F	186	147	101		125	120	130	113													BA	79.0
187	F	169	134	87		138	120	114	109					101	99			49	25			BA	79.3
188	M	190	149	102	117	153	136	127	116	121	117	102	71	116	99			49	23	45	36	BA	78.4
189	M	192	147	100	115	141	136	130	118	120	117	97	72	107	94	32	43			46	41	BA	76.6
190	M	189	137	101	109	153	124	130	116	110	115	99	66	120	107	33	41	50	27	43	42	FV	72.5
191	F	167	142	92			131	112	118	111	100	97										BA	85.0
192	F	179	142	94			130	108	135	110	99	108										BA	79.3
193	F	174				137	124	115	114	110	105	97	64	103	91	33	41	50	25	41	42	FV	0.0
194	F	182	149	93			141	123	126	115	109	101										BA	81.9
195	M	180	140	100	107		121	120	119	103	110	97	64			34	38	50		43	39	BA	77.8
196	M	186	154	102	121		138	124	115	119	114	96								45	39	BA	82.8

Appendix Five.   Craniometric Data.   Measurements in mm.

ID	SEX	GOL	XCB	WCB	ASB	BBH	FRK	PAK	OCK	FRC	PAC	OCC	NAH	BNL	BAL	OH	OB	NLH	NLB	PAL	PAB	GRP	C.I.
197	M	180	142	96	110	134	127	136	112	110	118	84	64	104	99	32	39	48	23	47	43	BA	78.9
198	M	191	144	104	112		138	131	123	116	117	98										BA	75.4
199	M	197	144	99		148	135	138	120	122	123	96		111								FV	73.1
200	F	176	138	96		135	130	131	102				63	97	88			48	23			BB	78.4
201	F	187	130	97	102		122	129	122	107	118	102	60			33	43	50	19			ON	69.5
202	M	194	138	98	111	142	139	139	131	121	124	105	67	103	100	31	36	52	24	48	39	ON	71.1
203	M	198	139	101			124	133	125	113	122	106	73					48	24	47	42	BA	70.2
204	M	196	148	100			132	136	120	119	124	96										WG	75.5
205	M	180	144	100	98	136	124	115	134	108	104	104	66	101	96	27	38	50	26	47	42	FV	80.0
206	M	181	150	97	111	140	127	122	118	107	109	101	68	105	99	30	37	53	25	49	43	BA	82.9
207	M	201	132	97	115	137	128	129	132	112	118	102	77	112	103	34	43	56	26	44	38	BA	65.7
208	F	184	133	97	107	137	122	129	121	107	115	101	69	103	99	34	39	45	24	49	38	FV	72.3
209	M	188	139	97	118		126	134	121	110	118	100	64			32	41	53	22			WG	73.9
210	F	175	141		104	127	130	125	110	111	110	91	64	108		33	40	53	29		39	BA	80.6
211	F	176	143	93	104		131	125	120	111	113	94	68			33	38	52	27			FV	81.3
212	M	181	149	101	121	139	131	131	114	113	115	90	69	101	92	33	37	50	24	44	36	BA	82.3
213	M	181	138	99	109	134	125	130	110	110	115	92	66	99	92	29	39	49	26	47	43	FV	76.2
214	F	182	137	98	107	149	127	128	105	114	112	92	57	119	110	30	38	43	23	45	35	BA	75.3
215	M	194	139	95			125						75									FV	71.6
216	M	175	139	98	110	140	120	120	108	108	104	94	71	109	101	35	40	55	22	43	41	FV	79.4
217	M	194	134	101			133	134	121				71					52	26			LN	69.1
218	F	180	146	103	111	134	126	119	117	110	108	93	67	116	106	36	43	51	24	44	43	BB	81.1
219	M	190	147	97			130	135	125	109	119	101										BA	77.4
220	M	191	148	99	123	129	135	112	119	115	102	97	68	103	95	33	47	53	24	43	37	FV	77.5
221	M	179	148	96			129	131		111	117											BA	82.7
222	M	215	160	108			136	140	135	122	126	110										WG	74.4
223	M	208	137	103	113		134	129	138	116	120	107										EN	65.9
224	M	198	137	101	101		132	138	135	118	123	106	75			38	40	52	23	49	40	EN	69.2
225	F	182	124	87	102	133	128	121	122	107	111	97	70	97	83	34	39	53	25	41	37	ON	68.1
226	F	163	144	93			119	124	108	106	110	88	68			35	38	50	22	40	39	FV	88.3
227	M	187	137	97	112		126	125	119	107	110	96	66			31	41	48	24		41	FV	73.3
228	M	192	146	99	119	135	129	131	124	115	120	105	74	100	92	36	44	55	21	45	36	BA	76.0
229	M	192	131	89	101		129	123	108	115	112	89										BA	68.2
230	F	183	129	98			128	130	104	114	116	87	65			35	41	49			38	BB	70.5
231	M	178	143	97	113		123	109	127	110	100	107	76			33	42	52	25	45	39	FV	80.3
232	M	187	138	96	107	129	126	120	114	112	110	93	62	101	95	32	37	50	26	41	39	BA	73.8
233	F	194	133	97			124	138	132	110	125	107										BA	68.6
234	M	183	159	100	127	132	127	140	117	110	121	93	75	99	88	31	39	58	26	43	47	BB	86.9
235	M	191	154	101			139	132	129	121	116	99										BA	80.6
236	M	192	153	101		120	139	138	112	118	122	90		99								BA	79.7
237	M	199	135	97			138	135	122	121	119	98										FV	67.8
238	M	183	139	101	114		125	123	125	112	113	106	70			31	39	46	24			BA	76.0
239	F	169	140	101	106	128	120	126	99	103	109	83		93								BA	82.8
240	F	172	140	101			118	120		104	105											BA	81.4
241	M	193	151	103	122		140	120	125	121	108	103	70			36	42	52	27	45	37	BA	78.2
242	F	182	147	104	107	132	125	134	116	109	119	95	59	95	88	32	37	46	20	42	46	FV	80.8
243	F	189	124	87		125		127	108		111	86										ON	65.6
244	F	185	114	94	103	120	127	135		110	111		65	95	105							ON	61.6
245	M	193	138	96	112	136	126	123	119	112	110	98	70	112	98	32	46		28			LN	71.5
246	M	194	139		128	131			137			105		100								ON	71.6
247	F	176	141	100	114	127	123	132	113	106	112	87		92								BA	80.1
248	F	187	131	95		133	130	135	120	112	121	98	66	95	90	34	36	52	24	53	40	ON	70.1
249	M	206	135	100	113		130	126	122	117	118	99										ON	65.5

BIBLIOGRAPHY

ADAMS, W.Y. 1968. Invasion, Diffusion, Evolution. *Antiquity* 42: 194-215.

ADAMS, W.Y., D.P. VAN GERVEN & R.S. LEVY. 1978. The retreat from migrationism. *Annual Review of Anthropology* 7: 483-532.

ABERCROMBY, J. 1902. The oldest Bronze Age ceramic type in Britain, its close analogies on the Rhine, its probable origin in central Europe. *Journal of the Royal Anthropological Institute* 32: 373-397.

AMMERMAN, A. 1989. On the Neolithic transition in Europe: a comment on Zvelebil and Zvelebil. *Antiquity* 63: 162-5.

AMMERMAN, A.J. & L.L. CAVALLI-SFORZA. 1979. The wave of advance model for the spread of agriculture in Europe, in C. Renfrew & K.L. Cooke (eds.), *Transformations, Mathematical Approaches to Culture Change*. New York: Academic Press.

ANTHONY, D.W. 1990. Migration in archaeology: the baby and the bathwater. *American Anthropologist* 92: 895-914.

ARNOLD, D.E. 1985. *Ceramic Theory and Cultural Process*. Cambridge: Cambridge University Press.

ASHBEE, P. 1960. *The Bronze Age Round Barrow in Britain*. London: Phoenix House.

ASHBEE, P. 1978a. *The Ancient British*. Norwich: Geo Books.

ASHBEE, P. 1978b. Amesbury Barrow 51: Excavations 1960. *Wiltshire Archaeological Magazine* 70/71: 1-61.

ASHBEE, P. 1984. *The Earthen Long Barrow in Britain*. Norwich: Geo Books.

ASMUS, G. 1973. Mesolithische Menschenfunde aus Mittel-Nord- und Osteuropa, in I. Schwidetsky (ed.), *Die Anfange des Neolithikums vom orient bis Nordeuropa*. Cologne.

BAMFORD, H. 1982. *Beaker Domestic Sites in the Fen Edge and East Anglia*. Norfolk: East Anglian Archaeology 16.

BARFIELD, L. 1987. The Italian dimension of the Beaker problem, in W. Waldren & R. Kennard (eds.), *Bell Beakers of the Western Mediterranean*. Oxford: British Archaeological Reports. International series 331.

BARTH, F. 1969. Introduction, in F. Barth (ed.), *Ethnic Groups and Boundaries*. Boston: Little, Brown and Company.

BATEMAN, T. 1852. Upon a few of the barrows opened at various times in the more hilly districts near Bakewell. *Journal of the British Archaeological Association* 7: 210-220.

BAUM, J.D. & D. SEARLS. 1971. Head shape and size of pre-term, low birthweight, infants. *Developmental Medicine Child Neurology* 13: 576-581.

BEALS, K.L. 1972. Head form and climatic stress. *American Journal of Physical Anthropology* 37: 85-92.

BEALS, K.L., C.L. SMITH & S.M. DODD. 1983. Climate and the evolution of brachycephalisation. *American Journal of Physical Anthropology* 62: 425-437.

BEALS, K.L., C.L. SMITH & S.M. DODD. 1984. Brain size, cranial morphology, climate and time machines. *Current Anthropology* 25: 301-330.

BEECHER, R.M. & R.S. CORRUCCINI. 1981. Effects of dietary consistency on craniofacial and occlusal development in the rat. *The Angle Orthodontist* 51: 61-69.

BENEDICT, R. 1935. *Patterns of Culture*. Boston: Houghton Mifflin.

BERNHARD, W., A. HANCKE, G. BRAUER & V.P. CHOPRA. 1980. Quantitative genetical analysis of morphological characters of the human head and face. *Journal of Human Evolution* 9: 621-626.

BOARDMAN J. 1980. *The Greeks Overseas*. London: Thames and Hudson.

BOAS, F. 1910-1913. Changes in bodily form of descendants of immigrants, in F. Boas, 1940, *Race, Language and Culture*. New York: Free Press.

BOGUCKI, P. 1988. *Forest Farmers and Stockherders*. Cambridge: Cambridge University Press.

BOHANNON, P. 1955. Some principles of exchange and investment among the Tiv. *American Anthropologist* 57: 60-70.

BOURDIEU, P. 1990. *The Logic of Practice*. Cambridge: Polity Press.

BOGUE, A.G. 1976. Comment, in Easterlin 1976.

BRACE, C.L. & A. MONTAGU. 1978. *Human Evolution*. New York: Macmillan.

BRACE, C.L., K.R. ROSENBERG & K.D. HUNT. 1987. Gradual change in human tooth size in the late Pleistocene and post-Pleistocene. *Evolution* 41: 705-720.

BRADLEY, R. 1984. *The Social Foundations of Prehistoric Britain*. London: Longman.

BRADLEY, R. 1988. Status, wealth and the chronological ordering of cemeteries. *Proceedings of the Prehistoric Society* 54: 327-329.

BRASH, J.C., D. LAYARD & M. YOUNG. 1935. The Anglo-Saxon skulls from Bidford on Avon, Warwickshire and Burwell, Cambridgeshire. *Biometrika* 27: 373-407.

BRAUN, D.P. 1991. Why decorate a pot? Midwestern household pottery 200BC - AD600. *Journal of Anthropological Archaeology* 10: 360-397.

BREWSTER, T.C.M. 1973. Two Bronze Age barrows in the North Riding of Yorkshire. *Yorkshire Archaeological Journal* 45: 55-95.

BREWSTER, T.C.M. 1980. *The Excavation of Garton and Wetwang Slacks*. London: R.C.H.M.

BREWSTER, T.C.M. 1984. *The Excavation of Whitegrounds Barrow, Burythorpe*. Malton, Yorkshire: East Riding Archaeological Research Committee Publications.

BRINDLEY, J.C. 1984. Petrological examination of Beaker pottery from the Boyne Valley sites, in G. Eogan, *Excavations at Knowth 1*. Dublin: Royal Irish Academy.

BROTHWELL, D.R. 1960. The Bronze Age people of Yorkshire: a general survey. *Advancement of Science* 16: 311-322.

BROTHWELL, D.R. & W. KRZANOWSKI. 1974. Evidence of biological differences between early British populations from Neolithic to Medieval times, as revealed by eleven commonly available cranial vault measurements. *Journal of Archaeological Science* 1: 249-260.

BROTHWELL, D.R. 1981. *Digging up Bones*. Oxford: British Museum/Oxford University Press.

BRYCE T.H. 1902. Comment, in J. Abercromby, page 396.

BURGESS, C. 1974. The Bronze Age, in C. Renfrew (ed.), *British Prehistory*. London: Duckworth.

BURGESS, C. 1980. *The Age of Stonehenge*. London: Dent.

BURGESS, C. 1976. An Early Bronze Age settlement at Kilellan Farm, Islay, Argyll, in C. Burgess & R. Miket (eds.), *Settlement and Economy in the 3rd and 2nd Millenia BC*. Oxford: British Archaeological Reports. British series 33.

BURGESS, C. & S.J. SHENNAN. 1976. The Beaker phenomenon: some suggestions, in C. Burgess & R. Miket (eds.), *Settlement and Economy in the 3rd and 2nd millenia BC*. Oxford: British Archaeological Reports. British series 33.

BURL, A. 1987. *Stonehenge People*. London: Dent.

CALCAGNO, J.M. 1986. Dental reduction in post-Pleistocene Nubia. *American Journal of Physical Anthropology* 70: 349-363.

CARLSON, D.S. & D.P. VAN GERVEN. 1977. Masticatory function and post-Pleistocene evolution in Nubia. *American Journal of Anthropology* 46: 495-506.

CASE, H. 1969. Neolithic explanations. *Antiquity* 43: 176-186.

CASE, H. 1977. The Beaker culture in Britain and Ireland, in R. Mercer (ed.), *Beakers in Britain and Europe*. Oxford: British Archaeological Reports. International series 26.

CASE, H. 1987. Postscript, in W. Waldren & R. Kennard (eds.), *Bell Beakers of the Western Mediterranean*. Oxford: British Archaeological Reports. International series 331.

CHAMPION, T. Mass migration in later prehistoric Europe, in P. Sörbom (ed.), *Transport Technology and Social Change*, Stockholm: Tekniska Museet.

CHAMPION, T., GAMBLE, C., SHENNAN S. & A. WHITTLE. 1984. *Prehistoric Europe*. London: Academic Press.

CHESNAIS, J-C. 1992. *The Demographic Tradition*. Oxford: Clarendon Press.

CHILDE, V.G. 1929. *The Danube in Prehistory*. Oxford: Clarendon Press.

CHILDE, V.G. 1933. Races, peoples and cultures in prehistoric Europe. *History* 18: 193-203.

CHILDE, V.G. 1935. Changing methods and aims in prehistory. *Proceedings of the Prehistoric Society* 1: 1-15.

CHILDE, V.G. 1939. *The Dawn of European Civilisation*, 3rd edition. London: Kegan Paul.

CHILDE, V.G. 1947. *Prehistoric Communities of the British Isles*. London: Chambers.

CHILDE, V.G. 1956. *Piecing Together the Past*. London: Routledge Kegan Paul.

CHILDE, V.G. 1958. Valediction. *Bulletin of the Institute of Archaeology* 1: 1-8.

CHILDE, V.G. 1963. *Social Evolution*. London: C.A. Watts.

CHILDE, V.G. 1969. *Prehistoric Migrations*. Lieden.

CLARK, J.G.D. 1952. *Prehistoric Europe: the Economic Basis*. London: Methuen.

CLARK, J.G.D. 1966. The invasion hypothesis in British prehistory. *Antiquity* 40: 172-189.

CLARKE, D.L. 1968. *Analytical Archaeology*. London: Methuen.

CLARKE, D.L. 1970. *Beaker Pottery of Great Britain and Ireland*. Cambridge: Cambridge University Press.

CLARKE, D.L. 1972. Models and paradigms in contemporary archaeology, in D.L. Clarke (ed.), *Models in Archaeology*. London: Methuen.

CLARKE, D.L. 1976. The Beaker network - social and economic models, in J.N. Lanting & J.D. van der Waals (eds.), *Glockenbeckersymposion Oberried 1974*. Bussum/Harlem.

CLARKE, D.V., T.G. COWIE & A. FOXON (eds.). 1985. *Symbols of Power*. Edinburgh: HMSO.

CLEARY, R. 1983. The ceramic assemblage, in C. O'Kelly (ed.), *Newgrange: The Late Neolithic/Beaker Period Settlement*. Oxford: British Archaeological Reports. International series 190.

COLDSTREAM, J.N. 1977. *Geometric Greece*. London: Ernest Benn.

COOMBS, D. 1976. Beakers from Callis Wold, Barrow 275, Humberside, in C. Burgess & R. Miket (eds.), *Settlement and Economy in the Third and Second Millenium BC*. Oxford: British Archaeological Reports. British series 33.

COON, C. 1939. *The Races of Europe*. New York: McMillan.

CORNELL, S. 1988. The transformation of tribe: organization and self-concept in Native American ethnicity. *Ethnic and Racial Studies* 11: 27-45.

CORRUCCINI, R.S. 1987. Shape in morphometrics: comparative analyses. *American Journal of Physical Anthropology* 73: 289-303.

COURBIN, P. 1982. *Qu'est-ce l'archeologie?* Paris: Payot.

CRAW, J. 1913. Cist at Edington Mill, Chirnside. *Proceedings of the Society of Antiquaries of Scotland* 48: 316-333.

CRAWFORD, O.G.S. 1925. *Long Barrows of the Cotswolds*. Gloucester: John Bellows.

CROGNIER, E. 1981. Climate and anthropometric variations in Europe and the Mediterranean area. *Annals of Human Biology* 8: 99-107.

DANIEL, G. & C. RENFREW. 1988. *The Idea of Prehistory*. Edinburgh: Edinburgh University Press.

DAVIES, D.M. 1972. Influence of Teeth, Diet and Habits on the Human Face. London: William Heinemann.

DAVIS, J.B. 1862. Distortions in the crania of ancient Britons. *Natural History Review*: 290-297.

DAVIS, J.B. & J. THURNAM. 1865. *Crania Brittanica*. London: Private Subscription.

DAWES, J.D. & J.R. MAGILTON. 1980. *The Cemetery of St. Helen-on-the-Walls, Aldwark*. York: York Archaeological Trust.

DENT, J. 1979. Bronze Age burials from Wetwang Slack. *Yorkshire Archaeological Journal* 51: 23-30.

DENT, J. 1983. A summary of the excavations carried out in Garton Slack and Wetwang Slack 1964-1980. *East Riding Archaeologist* 7: 1-13.

DIETLER, M. 1990. Driven by drink: the role of drinking in the political economy and the case of early Iron Age France. *Journal of Anthropological Archaeology* 9: 352-406.

DOUGLAS, M. 1967. Primitive Rationing, in R. Firth (ed.), *Themes in Economic Anthropology*. London: ASA Monographs 6, Tavistock.

DREWETT, P. 1977. The excavation of a Neolithic causewayed enclosure on Offham Hill, east Sussex. *Proceedings of the Prehistoric Society* 43: 201-242.

EASTERLIN, R.A. 1976. Factors in the decline of farm family fertility in the United States. *Journal of Economic History* 36: 45-75.

EHRET, C. 1988. Language change and the material correlates of language and ethnic shift. *Antiquity* 62: 564-574.

EHRICH, R.W. & C.S. COON. 1948. Occipital flattening among the Dinarics. *American Journal of Physical Anthropology* VI: 181-186.

EKHOLM, K. 1977. External exchange and the transformation of Central African social systems, in J. Friedman & M.J.Rowlands (eds.), *The Evolution of Social Systems*. London: Duckworth.

ELSTER, J. 1986. *An Introduction to Karl Marx*. Cambridge: Cambridge University Press.

ENLOW, D.H. 1990. *Facial Growth*. Philadelphia: W.B. Saunders.

EVANS, J.G. 1975. *The Environment of Early Man in the British Isles*. London: Elek.

EVANS, J.G. 1981. The environmental background to British prehistory ,in J.V. Megaw & D.D.A. Simpson (eds.), *Introduction to British Prehistory*. Leicester: Leicester University Press.

EVANS, J.G. 1990. Notes on some late Neolithic and Bronze Age events in long barrow ditches in southern and eastern England. *Proceedings of the Prehistoric Society* 56: 111-116.

FEREDAY, J. 1956. Statistics and the study of Prehistoric races. *Incorporated Statistician* 7: 23-40.

FOX, A. 1948. The Broad Down necropolis and the Wessex culture in Devon. *Proceedings of the Devon Archaeological Society* 4: 1-19.

FRANCISCUS, R.G. & J.L. LONG. 1991. Variation in human nasal height and breadth. *American Journal of Physical Anthropology* 85: 419-427.

FRAYER, D.W. 1977. Metric dental change in the European Upper Palaeolithic and Mesolithic. *American Journal of Physical Anthropology* 46: 109-120.

FRIEDMAN, J. & M.J. ROWLANDS. 1977. Notes towards an epigenetic model of the evolution of "civilisation", in J. Friedman & M.J. Rowlands (eds.), *The Evolution of Social Systems*. London: Duckworth.

GARSON, J.G. 1893. A Description of the Skeletons Found in Howe Hill Barrow. *Journal of the Anthropological Institute* 22: 8-20.

GERLOFF, S. 1975. *The Early Bronze Age Daggers in Great Britain*. Munich: Prahistorische Bronzefunde V1/2.

GIBSON, A. 1982. *Beaker Domestic Sites*. Oxford: British Archaeological Reports. British series 107.

GOLDSCHNEIDER, C. 1984. *Rural Migration in Developing Areas*. Boulder City: Westview Press.

GOODMAN, C.N. & G.M. MORANT. 1940. Human remains of the Iron Age and other periods from Maiden Castle, Dorset. *Biometrika* 31: 295-312.

GOODY, J. 1977. *Production and Reproduction: a Comparative Study of the Domestic Domain*. Cambridge: Cambridge University Press.

GREEN, H.S. 1980. *The Flint Arrowheads of the British Isles*. Oxford: British Archaeological Reports. British Series 75.

GREENFIELD, E. 1960. The excavation of barrow 4 at Swarkestone, Derbyshire. *Derbyshire Archaeological Journal* 80: 1-48.

GREENWELL, W. 1877. *British Barrows*. London: Oxford University Press.

GREENWELL, W. 1890. Recent researches in barrows. *Archaeologia* 52: 1-72.

GRIGSON, C. 1982. Porridge and pannage: pig husbandry in Neolithic England, in M. Bell & S. Limbrey (eds.), *Archaeological Aspects of Woodland Ecology*. Oxford: British Archaeological Reports. International series 146.

GUGLIELMINO-MATESSI, C.R., P. GLUCKMAN & L.L. CAVALLI-SFORZA. 1979. Climate and the evolution of skull metrics in man. *Americal Journal of Physical Anthropology* 50: 549-564.

HARRIS, D. 1990. Editorial. *Cornish Archaeology* 29: 1.

HARRISON, R. 1980. *The Beaker Folk*. London: Thames and Hudson.

HEATHCOTE, G.M. 1986. *Exploratory Human Craniometry of Recent Eskaleutian Regional Groups from the Western Arctic and Subarctic of North America*. Oxford: British Archaeological Reports. International series 301.

HEDGES, J.W. 1983. *Isbister*. Oxford: British Archaeological Reports. British series 115.

HELMS, M. 1988. *Ulysses' Sail*. Princeton, New Jersey: Princeton University Press.

HERTZBERG, H.W. 1971. *The Search for an American Indian Identity*. Syracuse: Syracuse University Press.

HIERNAUX, J. 1977. Long term biological effects of human migration from the African savanna into the equatorial forest, in G.A. Harrison (ed.), *Population Structure and Human Variation*. Cambridge: Cambridge University Press.

HODDER, I. 1982. *Symbols in Action*. Cambridge: Cambridge University Press.

HODDER, I. 1986. *Reading the Past*. Cambridge: Cambridge University Press.

HOOKE, B.G. 1926. A third study of the English skull with special reference to the Farringdon Street crania. *Biometrika* 18: 1-55.

HOWELL, J. 1983. The late Neolithic of the Paris Basin, in C.Scarre (ed.), *Ancient France*. Edinburgh: Edinburgh University Press.

HOWELLS, W.W. 1973. *Cranial Variation in Man*. Peabody Museum Papers 67. Cambridge MA: Peabody Museum.

HOWELLS, W.W. 1988. Physical anthropology of the prehistoric Japanese, in R.J. Pearson, G.L. Barnes & K.L. Hutterer (eds.), *Windows on the Japanese Past*. Ann Arbor: University of Michigan Press.

HYLANDER, W.L. 1977. The adaptive significance of Eskimo craniofacial morphology, in A.A. Dahlberg & T.M. Graber (eds.), *Orofacial Growth and Development*. The Hague: Mouton.

JOHNSTON, L.E. 1979. The functional matrix hypothesis: reflections in a jaundiced eye, in J.A. McNamara (ed.), *Factors Affecting the Growth of the Midface*. University of Michigan Press.

JOHNSTONE, P. *Seacraft of Prehistory*. London: Routledge Kegan and Paul.

JONES, M. 1980. Carbonised cereals from Grooved Ware contexts. *Proceedings of the Prehistoric Society* 46: 61-63.

JORGENSEN, J.B. 1973. Anthropologie des Skandinavischen Neolithikums, in I. Schwidetsky (ed.), *Die Anfange des Neolithikums vom Orient bis Nordeuropa*. Cologne.

KINNES, I. 1979. *Round Barrows and Ring Ditches in the British Neolithic*. London: British Museum.

KINNES, I., A. GIBSON, R. BOAST, J. AMBERS, M. LEESE & S. BOWMAN. 1991. Radiocarbon Dating and British Beakers. *Scottish Archaeological Review* 8: 35-68.

KOBYLIANSKY, E. 1983. Changes in cephalic morphology of Israelis due to migration. *Journal of Human Evolution* 12: 779-786.

KOPYTOFF, I. 1987. The internal African frontier, in I. Kopytoff (ed.), *The African Frontier*. Bloomington: Indiana University Press.

KUHN, T.S. 1970. *The Structure of Scientific Revolutions*. Chicago: University of Chicago Press.

LAMB, H.H. 1988. *Weather, Climate and Human Affairs*. London: Routledge.

LANTING, J.N. & J.D. VAN DER WAALS. 1976. Beaker culture relations in the lower Rhine basin, in J.N. Lanting & J.D. van der Waals (eds.), *Glockenbechersymposion Oberried 1974*. Bussum/Harlem.

LATHAM, R.A. & J.H. SCOTT. 1970. A newly postulated factor in the early growth of the human middle face and the theory of multiple assurance. *Archives of Oral Biology* 15: 1097-1100.

LEE, E.S. 1966. A Theory of Migration. *Demography* 3: 47-57.

LEMONNIER, P. 1986. The study of material culture today: towards an anthropology of technical systems. *Journal of Anthropological Archaeology* 5: 147-186.

LEWIN, R. 1989. *Human Evolution*. Boston: Blackwell.

LEWIS, G.J. 1982. *Human Migration*. London: Croom Helm.

LEWTHWAITE, J.G. 1987. The Braudelian beaker: a chalcolithic conjoncture in western Mediterranean prehistory, in W. Waldren & R. Kennard (eds.), *Bell Beakers of the Western Mediterranean*. Oxford: British Archaeological Reports. International series 331.

LITTLE, K.L. 1943. A study of a series of human skulls from Castle Hill, Scarborough. *Biometrika* 33: 25-35.

LIVI-BACCI, M. 1992. *A Concise History of World Population*. Oxford: Blackwell.

LONGWORTH, I. 1984. *Collared Urns of the Bronze Age in Great Britain and Ireland*. Cambridge: Cambridge University Press.

McDONELL, W.R. 1904. A study of the variation and correlation of the human skull, with special reference to English crania. *Biometrika* 3: 191-244.

McDONELL, W.R. 1906/7. A second study of the English skull, with special reference to Moorfields crania. *Biometrika* 5: 86-104.

MABOGUNJE, A.K. 1970. A systems approach to a theory of rural-urban migration. *Geographical Analysis* 2: 1-18.

MANBY, T.G. 1958. A neolithic site at Craike Hill, Garton Slack, East Riding of Yorkshire. *Antiquaries Journal* 38: 223-236.

MANBY, T.G. 1970. Long barrows of northern England: structural and dating evidence. *Scottish Archaeological Forum* 2: 1-27.

MANBY, T.G. 1980a. Excavation of barrows at Grindale and Boynton, East Yorkshire, in 1972. *Yorkshire Archaeological Journal* 52: 19-47.

MANBY, T.G. 1988. The Neolithic period in Eastern Yorkshire, in T.G. Manby (ed.), *Archaeology in East Yorkshire*. Sheffield: Sheffield University Press.

MAZEIR, R.E. 1984. Rural out-migration and labor allocation in Mali, in C.G. Goldschneider (ed.), *Rural Migration in Developing Nations*. Boulder Colorado: Westview Press.

MEGAW J.V.S. & D.D.A. SIMPSON. 1981. *Introduction to British Prehistory*. Leicester: Leicester University Press.

MERCER, R.J. 1977. Beaker studies in Britain and Europe, in R.J. Mercer (ed.), *Beaker Studies in Britain and Europe*. Oxford: British Archaeological Reports. International series 26.

MERCER, R.J. 1980. *Hambledon Hill - a Neolithic Landscape*. Edinburgh: Edinburgh University Press.

MERCER, R.J. 1985. Second millenium BC settlement in northern Scotland, in D. Spratt & C. Burgess (eds.), *Upland Settlement in Britain*. Oxford: British Archaeological Reports. British series 143.

MILES, A.E.W. 1989. *Early Christian Chapel and Burial Ground on the Isle of Ensay, Outer Hebrides, Scotland*. Oxford: British Archaeological Reports. British series 212.

MILLER, D. 1985. *Artefacts as Categories*. Cambridge: Cambridge University Press.

MORANT G.M. 1926. A first study of the craniology of England and Scotland from Neolithic to early Historic times. *Biometrika* 18: 56-98.

MORTIMER, J.R. 1905. *Forty Years' Researches in British and Saxon Burial Mounds of East Yorkshire*. London: A. Brown & Sons.

MOSS, M.L. 1969. The differential roles of periosteal and capsular functional matrices in oro-facial growth. *Transactions of the European Orthodontic Society* 45: 193-206.

NEUSTUPNY, E. 1984. The Bell Beaker culture in east-central Europe, in J.Guilaine (ed.), *L'Age du Cuivre Européen*. Paris: CNRS.

ORME, B. 1981. *Anthropology for Archaeologists*. London: Duckworth.

PAGANINI-HILL, A, A.O. MARTIN & M.A. SPENCE. 1981. The S-Leut anthropometric traits: genetic analysis. *American Journal of Physical Anthropology* 55: 55-67.

PARRY, M.L. 1985. Upland settlement and climatic change: the Medieval evidence, in D. Spratt & C. Burgess (eds.), *Upland Settlement in Britain*. Oxford: British Archaeological Reports. British series 143.

PEARSON, K. & L.H. TIPPETT. 1924. On stability of the cephalic indices within the race. *Biometrika* 16: 118-138.

PEARSON, M.P. 1990. The production and distribution of Bronze Age pottery in south-western Britain. *Cornish Archaeology* 29: 5-27.

PETERSON, F. 1969. Early Bronze Age timber graves and coffin burials on the Yorkshire Wolds. *Yorkshire Archaeological Journal* 42: 262-267.

PETERSON, F. 1972. Traditions of multiple burial in later Neolithic and early Bronze Age England. *Archaeological Journal* 129: 22-55.

PIGGOTT, S. 1963. Abercromby and after - the Beaker cultures of Britain re-examined, in I. Foster & A. Alcock (eds.), *Culture and Environment*. London: Routledge Kegan and Paul.

PIGGOTT, S. 1965. *Ancient Europe*. Edinburgh: Edinburgh University Press.

PIERPOINT, S. 1980. *Social Patterns in Yorkshire Prehistory*. Oxford: British Archaeological Reports. British series 74.

POUNDS, N.J.G. 1990. *An Historical Geography of Europe*. Cambridge: Cambridge University Press.

POWELSLAND, D. 1986. Excavations at Heslerton, North Yorkshire, 1978-1982. *Archaeological Journal* 143: 53-173.

PUCCIARELLI, H.M. 1980. The effects of race, sex and nutrition on craniofacial differentiation in rats. *American Journal of Physical Anthropology* 53: 359-368.

PUCCIARELLI, H.M. & E.E. OYHENART. 1987. Effects of maternal food restriction during lactation on craniofacial growth in weanling rats. *American Journal of Physical Anthropology* 72: 67-75.

RAVENSTEIN, E. 1885. The laws of migration. *Journal of the Royal Statistical Society* 48: 167-227.

REID, R.W. & G.M. MORANT. 1928. A study of the Scottish short cist crania. *Biometrika* 20b: 379-388.

RENFREW, C. 1973. *Before Civilisation*. London: Jonathan Cape.

RENFREW, C. 1977. Space, time and polity, in J. Friedman & M.J. Rowlands (eds.), *The Evolution of Social Systems*. London: Duckworth.

RENFREW, C. 1982. Socio-economic change in ranked societies, in C. Renfrew & S. Shennan (eds.), *Ranking, Resource and Exchange*. Cambridge: Cambridge University Press.

RENFREW, C. 1985. Varna and the emergence of wealth in prehistoric Europe, in A. Appadurai (ed.), *The Social Life of Things*. Cambridge: Cambridge University Press.

RENFREW, C. 1987. *Archaeology and Language*. London: Jonathan Cape.

REX, J. 1986. *Race and Ethnicity*. Milton Keynes: Open University Press.

RICE, P. 1987. *Pottery Analysis*. Chicago: University of Chicago Press.

RICHARDS, C. & THOMAS, J. 1984. Ritual activity and structured deposition in later Neolithic Wessex, in R.J. Bradley & J. Gardner (eds.), *Neolithic Studies*. Oxford: British Archaeological Reports. British series 133.

RICHARDS, J. 1984. The development of the Neolithic landscape in the ennvirons of Stonehenge, in R.J Bradley & J. Gardner (eds.), *Neolithic Studies*. Oxford: British Archaeological Reports. British series 133.

RITCHIE, G. & H. WELFARE. 1983. Excavations at Ardnave, Islay. *Proceedings of the Society of Antiquaries of Scotland* 113: 302-366.

RIQUET, R. 1973. Anthropologie du Neolithique de la France et des Provinces Limitrophes, in I. Schwidetsky (ed.), *Die Anfange des Neolithikums vom Orient bis Nordeuropa*. Cologne.

ROE, F.E.S. 1966. The battle-axe series in Britain *Proceedings of the Prehistoric Society* 32: 199-245.

ROLLESTON, G. 1877. Descriptions of Figures of Skulls and General Remarks upon the Series of Neolithic Crania, in W. Greenwell, *British Barrows*.

RUFF, C.B. 1991. Climate and body shape in hominid evolution. *Journal of Human Evolution* 21: 81-105.

SACKETT, J.R. 1986. Isochrestism and style: a clarification. *Journal of Anthropological Archaeology* 5: 266-277.

SACKETT, J.R. 1990. Style and ethnicity in archaeology: the case for isochrestism, in M.Conkey & C.Hastorf (eds.), *The Uses of Style in Archaeology*. Cambridge: Cambridge University Press.

SAHLINS, M. 1974. *Stone Age Economics*. London: Routledge.

SANKAS, S. 1930. Relation of cranial module to capacity. *American Journal of Physical Anthropology* 14: 305-316.

SAXE, A. 1970. *The Social Dimensions of Mortuary Practices*. Ann Arbor: University Microfilms.

SCHUSTER, E.H.J. 1905-6. The Long Barrow and Round Barrow Skulls in the Collection of the Department of Comparative Anatomy, the Museum, Oxford. *Biometrika* IV: 351-62.

SCOTT, G.M. 1990. A resynthesis of the primordial and circumstantial approaches to ethnic solidarity: towards an explanatory model. *Ethnic and Racial Studies* 13: 147-169.

SHANKS, M. & C. TILLEY. 1987. *Re-constructing Archaeology*. Cambridge: Cambridge University Press.

SHANKS, M. & C. TILLEY. 1989. Archaeology into the 1990s. *Norwegian Archaeological Review* 22: 1-54.

SHENNAN, S.J. 1976. Bell Beakers and their context in central Europe, in J.N. Lanting & J.D. van der Waals (eds.), *Glockenbeckersymposion Oberried 1974*. Bussum/Harlem.

SHENNAN, S.J. 1977. The appearance of the Bell Beaker assemblage in central Europe, in R. Mercer (ed.), *Beakers in Britain and Europe*. Oxford: British Archaeological Reports. International series 26.

SHENNAN, S.J. 1982. Exchange and ranking: the role of amber in the earlier Bronze Age of Europe, in C. Renfrew & S. Shennan (eds.), *Ranking, Resource and Exchange*. Cambridge: Cambridge University Press.

SHENNAN, S.J. 1986. Interaction and change in 3rd millenium BC western and central Europe, in C. Renfre & J. Cherry (eds.), *Peer Polity Interaction and Social Change*. Cambridge: Cambridge University Press.

SHENNAN, S.J. 1989. Archaeological approaches to the cultural identity, in S.J. Shennan (ed.), *Archaeological Approaches to the Cultural Identity*. London: Unwin Hyman.

SHERRATT, A. 1981. Plough and pastoralism: aspects of the secondary products revolution, in I. Hodder, G. Isaac & N.Hammond (eds.), *Patterns of the Past*. Cambridge: Cambridge University Press.

SHERRATT, A. 1987. Cups that cheered, in W.Waldren & R. Kennard (eds.), *Bell Beakers of the Western Mediterranean*. Oxford: British Archaeological Reports. International series 331.

SHEPHERD, I.A.G. 1985. Jet and amber, in D.V. Clarke, T.G. Cowie & A. Foxon (eds.), *Symbols of Power*. Edinburgh: HMSO.

SIMPSON, D.D.A. 1968. Food Vessels: associations and chronology, in J.M. Coles (ed.), *Studies in Ancient Europe*. Leicester: Leicester University Press.

SIMPSON, W.G. 1976. Barrow cemetery of the second millenium BC at Tallington, Lincolnshire. *Proceedings of the Prehistoric Society* 42: 215-239.

SMITH, A.D. 1986. *The Ethnic Origins of Nations*. Oxford: Basil Blackwell.

SMITH, A.G. 1981. The Neolithic, in I. Simmons & M. Tooley (eds.), *The Environment in British Prehistory*. London: Duckworth.

SMITH, I.F. 1974. The Neolithic, in C. Renfrew (ed.), *British Prehistory - a new outline*. London: Duckworth.

SOKAL, R.R., H.T. UYTTERSCHAUT, F.W. ROSING & I. SCHWIDETSKY. 1987. A classification of European Skulls from three time periods. *American Journal of Physical Anthropology* 74: 1-20.

STEAD, I. 1959. The excavation of Beaker burials at Staxton, East Riding, 1957. *Yorkshire Archaeological Journal* 40: 129-144.

STEARNS, S.C. 1982. The role of development in the evolution of life-histories, in J.T. Bonner (ed.), *Evolution and Development*. Berlin: Springer-Verlag.

STEPAN, N. 1982. The Idea of Race in Science. Basingstoke: Macmillan.

STEPONAITIS, V. 1984. Comment made in discussion of P. Rice, Change and conservatism in pottery producing systems, in S.E. van der Leeuw & A. Pritchard (eds.), *The Many Dimensions of Pottery*. Amsterdam: University of Amsterdam.

STERNER, J. 1989. Who is signalling whom? Ceramic style, ethnicity and taphonomy among the Sirak Bulahay. *Antiquity* 63: 451-459.

STONE, J.F. 1938. An early Bronze Age grave in Fargo Plantation near Stonehenge. *Wiltshire Archaeological Magazine* 48: 357-370.

SUSANNE, C. 1975. Genetic and environmental influences on morphological characteristics. *Annals of Human Biology* 2: 279-287.

TATE, G. 1851. On cist-vaens and sepulchral urns in a tumulus or barrow near Lesbury, Northumberland. *Proceedings of the Berwickshire Naturalists Club* 3: 63-67.

TAYLOR, J.J. 1983. Problems and parallels: wealthy graves in early Bronze age society in Wessex and Brittany. Paris: CNRS.

THOMAS, J. 1987. Relations of production and social change in the Neolithic of north-west Europe. *Man* 22: 405-430.

THOMAS, J. 1991. *Rethinking the Neolithic*. Cambridge: Cambridge University Press.

THOMAS, K.D. 1982. Neolithic enclosures and woodland habitats on the south Downs in Sussex, England, in M. Bell & S. Limbrey (eds.), *Archaeological Aspects of Woodland Ecology*. Oxford: British Archaeological Reports. International series 146.

THOMPSON, A. & L. BUXTON. 1923. Mans nasal index in relation to certain climatic conditions. *Journal of the Royal Anthropological Institute* 59: 92-122.

THORPE, I.J. & C.C. RICHARDS. 1984. The decline of ritual authority and the introduction of Beakers into Britain, in R.J. Bradley & J. Gardiner (eds.), *Neolithic Studies*. Oxford: British Archaeological Reports. British series 133.

THURNAM, J.T. 1863. On the Principal Forms of Ancient British and Gaulish Skulls. *Memoirs of the Anthropological Society of London* 1: 120-168.

THURNAM, J.T. 1864. On the Principal Forms of Ancient British and Gaulish Skulls, Part 2. *Memoirs of the Anthropological Society of London* 1: 459-519.

THURNAM, J.T. 1867. Further Researches and Observations on the Two Principal Forms of Ancient British Skulls. *Memoirs of the Anthropological Society of London* 3: 41-80.

TILLEY, C. 1989. Interpreting material culture, in I. Hodder (ed.), *The Meaning of Things*. London: Unwin Hyman.

TINSLEY, H.M. 1981. The Bronze Age, in I. Simmons & M. Tooley (eds.), *The Environment in British Prehistory*. London: Duckworth.

TRIGGER, B. 1989. *A History of Archaeological Thought*. Cambridge: Cambridge University Press.

TUCKWELL, A. 1975. Patterns of burial orientation in the round barrows of East Yorkshire. *Bulletin of the Institute of Archaeology* 12: 95-123.

TURNER, W. 1917. A contribution to the craniology of the of the people of Scotland, part II. *Transactions of the Royal Society of Edinburgh* 51: 171-255.

UBELAKER, D.H. 1989. *Human Skeletal Remains*. Washington: Taraxacum.

VAN DER WAALS, J.D. 1984. Bell Beakers in continental north-west Europe, in J. Guilaine (ed.), *L'Age du Cuivre Européen*. Paris: CNRS.

WAUGH, L.M. 1937. Influence of diet on the jaws and face of the American Eskimo. *Journal of the American Dental Association* 24: 1640-1647.

WATKINS, T. 1982. The excavation of an early Bronze Age cemetery at Dalgety, Fife. *Proceedings of the Society of Antiquaries of Scotland* 112: 48-141.

WEIDENREICH, F. 1945. The brachycephalisation of recent mankind. *Southwestern Journal of Anthropology* 1: 1-54.

WEINER, J. 1954. Nose shape and climate. *American Journal of Physical Anthropology* 12: 1-4.

WHITTLE, A. 1981. Later neolithic society in Britain: a realignment, in C. Ruggles & A. Whittle (eds.), *Astronomy and Society during the Period 4000 - 1500* BC. Oxford: British Archaeological Reports. British series 88.

WHITTLE, A. 1985. *Neolithic Europe, a Survey*. Cambridge: Cambridge University Press.

WILSON, D. 1851. *The Archaeology and Prehistoric Annals of Scotland*. Edinburgh: Sutherland and Knox.

WILSON, D. 1863. *The Prehistoric Annals of Scotland*. London: Macmillan.

WOLF, E.R. 1982. *Europe and the People without History*. Berkeley: University of California Press.

WOLPOFF, M.H. 1968. Climatic influence on the skeletal nasal aperture. *American Journal of Physical Anthropology* 29: 405-423.

WOLPOFF, M.H. 1980. *Palaeoanthropology*. New York: Macmillan.

WRIGHT, W. 1903. Skulls from the Danes' graves, Driffield. *Journal of the Royal Anthropological Institute* 33: 66-73.

WRIGHT, W. 1904. Skulls from the round barrows of eastern Yorkshire. *Journal of Anatomy and Physiology* 38: 119-32.

WRIGHT, W. 1905. Skulls from the Round Barrows of eastern Yorkshire (contd.). *Journal of Anatomy and Physiology* 39: 417-449.

YANIN, V.L. 1990. The archaeology of Novgorod. Reprinted in 1994, *Ancient Cities*, Scientific American special issue: 120-127.

ZELINSKY, W. 1971. The hypothesis of the mobility transition. *Geographical Review*: 61: 219-249. ??

www.ingramcontent.com/pod-product-compliance
Lightning Source LLC
Chambersburg PA
CBHW061005030426
42334CB00033B/3373